Into Abyssinia
THE ODYSSEY OF A FAMILY

CARL E. HANSEN

WESTBOW
PRESS®
A DIVISION OF THOMAS NELSON
& ZONDERVAN

WestBow Press books may be ordered through booksellers or by contacting:

WestBow Press
A Division of Thomas Nelson & Zondervan
1663 Liberty Drive
Bloomington, IN 47403
www.westbowpress.com
844-714-3454

Cover designed by Destiny Joy Gomez-Kreider of "Destiny Designs," a granddaughter of the author, using a photo of daughter, Karen, age six, standing beside the Toyota Landcruiser on the "Bedeno road."

ISBN: 978-1-6642-9068-6 (sc)
ISBN: 978-1-6642-9070-9 (hc)
ISBN: 978-1-6642-9069-3 (e)

Library of Congress Control Number: 2023901631

Print information available on the last page.

WestBow Press rev. date: 03/25/2023

"Ethiopia will stretch out her hands to God."
– Psalms 68:31 Jerusalem Bible

CONTENTS

DEDICATION

To my beloved wife and constant companion, Vera Dorothy (King) Hansen, who faithfully shared the challenges, failures, and triumphs of our odyssey over the past fifty-eight years.

In reflecting back, I am amazed at her courage and the self-giving support she gave through those difficult years. Coming into Abyssinia as inexperienced "missionary associates" straight from college, we were absolutely "green," without any cultural or language orientation. Vera especially, being very pregnant in the midst of unpacking and setting up housekeeping and giving birth to our second daughter only two weeks after our arrival, did not complain or draw back. In the busy routine of homemaking with a growing family in a totally new environment, she bravely adjusted to the unfamiliar culture with its expectations and taboos and economic restrictions. Lesser women, suffering post-partum depression, would have taken the first flight available heading "home"!

Vera's virtues of strength and courage and self-giving devotion were put to the test later as we entered our "Bedeno years." For three years we lived in the remote eastern province of Harar, directing a rural development project among the peasant population of then feudal Ethiopia. While I engaged in a lot of interesting and exciting activities which included frequent travel that often kept me away from home for periods varying from a few days up to two weeks, Vera was "stuck at home" with our four small children.

There she endured an indescribable loneliness, cut off from contact with people familiar with her own culture, struggling with an enormous language barrier, and geographically isolated by the only semi-accessible "Bedeno road." Alone, she bore responsibility for our small children without reliable security and without convenience of accessible phone or postal service. (There were no cell phones, email, nor internet communications in those days.)

Countless long dark nights she lay awake alone, vainly listening for the distant sound of an engine on the deserted, silent, empty Bedeno road, sleep-depriving questions rotating in her anxious mind, wondering where her husband and father of her four little ones might be. Perhaps tonight he might come? Perhaps there was a breakdown, or a delay, or, God forbid, an accident? There was no way of knowing.

Then, as the seeming-eternal darkness finally gave way to the dawning of a new day, as she prepared breakfast for her little ones, the persistent lingering questions continued rotating, tormenting her sleep-deprived mind: "Perhaps today?"

In reflecting back, to put it mildly, the most amazing thing is the realization that Vera has stuck with me all these years and is still with me today!

Thank you, Vera, for your steadfast love and devotion and faith! May God reward you! And may your children rise up and call you "blessed" (cf. Proverbs 31:28)!

ACKNOWLEDGEMENTS

First of all, I must give credit to God who shaped me from my mother's womb, called me, and preserved me through the many experiences and circumstances of life, forgave me for my many blunders, both intentional and unintentional. He has granted me good health and long years in which to reflect on and put into writing some of those experiences. I have always felt invulnerable, safe, somehow protected, especially in those tense situations when it would have been understandable had I felt fear.

Next to God, I owe a debt of gratitude to my mother, Elizabeth Winifred (Friesen) Hansen, whose prayers for our safety and success were obviously heard. She wisely kept our letters all those years while we were "away" doing the things recorded in this book. Then, at the proper time, she returned the stash of correspondence which became the basis upon which this book took shape.

Also, I was encouraged by my dear wife, Vera, who sacrificed so much in living out the stories in this book. Then later, she continued with a lesser sacrifice, enduring many quiet evenings as I returned to my keyboard, leaving her alone in the empty living room.

Further, I must express gratitude to my daughter, Karen Hansen, for contributing her skills as a middle school English teacher in reading my manuscript and editing and correcting my careless spelling and grammar. She gave many days of her time in this labor of love while recuperating from a broken foot she suffered while exploring the ancient rock hewn churches in Lalibela, Ethiopia.

Finally, I am deeply grateful for the comradery and cooperation of my granddaughter, Destiny Joy Gomez-Kreider of "Destiny Designs" in designing the cover of this my third book as she has done so well in my first two books, *Pilgrims Searching for a Home* and *Shaping of a Servant*.

ACRONYMS

AMBS	Associated Mennonite Biblical Seminary
EPID	Extension Project Implementation Division
EMBMC	Eastern Mennonite Board of Missions and Charities
EMM	Eastern Mennonite Missions
MAF	Missionary Aviation Fellowship
MCC	Mennonite Central Committee
MEDA	Mennonite Economic Development Associates
MKC	Meserete Kristos Church
SIDA	Swedish International Development Assistance
SIM	Society of International Missions, formerly known as "Sudan Interior Mission"
SMO	Swiss Mennonite Organization

PREFACE

In deciding on a title for this book I have chosen to use the ancient name *"Abyssinia"* rather than *"Ethiopia"* for a reason. Earliest references in the biblical Old Testament times spoke of the land south of Egypt as *"Kush."* That broad term included the land south of the first cataract on the Nile, including Nubia, a power between 540 B.C. and 339 A.D. and the land east all the way to the Red Sea.

The New Testament spoke of the "Ethiopian eunuch." In Greek, the term *"Aithiopia"* is used broadly to include the land of those with dark complexions, "burnt faces," in other words, all the lands of sub-Saharan Africa. The "eunuch" mentioned in Acts 8:26–40 was the chief treasurer of Candace, the "queen of Ethiopia." It is likely Candace ruled from her capital, Meroe, in what is now Sudan.

The term *"Abyssinia"* derives from the more ethnically specific *"Habesha peoples,"* those now known as "Tigrean," "Amhara," and "Gurage," who spoke semitic languages, mostly Tewahedo Orthodox Christians occupying the northern highlands west of the Red Sea across from Yemen.

The earliest known use of this term, *"'abassha"* is found on a Sabean inscription of the second or third century. Arab Muslims used this term to refer to their Christian neighbors. Europeans followed, referring to those people as *"Habesha"* in the 16th century. The English were referring to this land as "Abyssinia" since 1620. The map of Africa drawn up by the European powers in their Berlin Conference in 1885 named this territory under the rule of Emperor Menelik II as "Abyssinia."

However, the term *"habesha"* was understood as a restrictive name excluding Muslims, Oromos, and all of the other seventy-eight ethnic groups making up the empire ruled by the habesha emperors of the "Solomonic dynasty." Emperor Menelik and later, Haile Selassie, in the interest of unifying their huge diverse empire, preferred to call their empire by the much more inclusive name, "Ethiopia." Yet, the habesha were still the ruling class, their Amharic was the official language, and Orthodox Tewahedo Christianity remained the state religion. In reality, the empire was still *"Abyssinia."*

At the time we came fifty-five years ago, the Empire was in a state of transition. Officially, it was becoming "Ethiopia," a modern inclusive nation, but, practically, it was still a feudal "Abyssinia." We entered "into Abyssinia" at the beginning of our brief stay. During our stay of eight years, we witnessed the end of the Solomonic dynasty and the death throes of feudal Abyssinia. We exited during the very painful and troubled birthing of what was hoped to become a modern "Ethiopia."

I wish to remind my readers that the Ethiopia I describe in this book is the Ethiopia as we experienced it more than half a century ago. It is certainly not the same Ethiopia one would experience today. At that time the population was around twenty-eight million, mostly illiterate peasants. Today the population numbers over one hundred and fifteen million and is growing by about five million each year.

Since that time the country of Ethiopia has undergone amazing changes, first by the revolution which jolted the people awake out of their centuries long feudal nightmare. Then, with the introduction of democratic political reforms, modern education, and access to the global world of information through the modern media and transportation, the culture including its religion, and the economy was further transformed.

Today emerging cities, connected with better highways and communication systems, and offering better health care, educational opportunities, and employment, are absorbing millions of dissatisfied rural citizens who migrate to large urban areas seeking a better life. Truly Ethiopia is emerging as a new twenty-first century nation along with its problems and challenges. But that is beyond the scope of this book.

CHAPTER 1

Ten Thousand Miles and Three Thousand Years in Three Days

Ten Thousand Miles

We hugged Dad and Mom and younger siblings goodbye for the last time and disappeared from their sight through the airport entrance. We would not see them again for three years—or perhaps, ever! Being a bit late, we were hurriedly escorted to the waiting Air Canada DC-8, where we showed our boarding passes again and entered. We stowed our hand luggage overhead and took our seats. Then I looked out the little, round window searching for the familiar face of a family member to wave to, but there was none. As far as our loved ones were concerned, we were gone.

We buckled our seat belts and surveyed our new surroundings.

My spouse, Vera, our two-and-one-half year-old daughter, Cindy, and I had never been on an airplane before, not even a little one.

Ever since I was a little boy, airplanes have held a special fascination for me. I longed for a chance to get up close to an airplane, to admire it, to touch it, to look inside, to even ride in it. I dreamed that someday I would learn to fly one of those marvelous machines.

Now, more than twenty years later, here I was at last, seated in this huge modern flying machine. It was a moment to cherish, not without a bit of apprehension. The engines were already running.

Soon the flight attendant was demonstrating all the safety features of the plane and instructing us in all the procedures we should undertake should an emergency occur. We paid close attention. The very mention of a possible emergency brought a certain uneasiness to our minds, visions of fiery crashes and heroic escapes that we read about in *Reader's Digest*. Anyone who might have cared to notice would have immediately detected that we were green in this business—new and uninitiated as world travelers.

As we reached the head of the runway and turned, the flight attendant completed her demonstration and prepared for takeoff. Now the huge engines screamed, and the plane lurched forward.

We found ourselves being pulled back deep into our seats by the force, a sensation just as thrilling, but more powerful than, what I used to feel in Dad's '53 Super 88 Oldsmobile when we teenagers tried to break the acceleration record from zero to sixty at the Duchess corner.

Now we were hurtling down the runway at more than two hundred miles per hour. Suddenly, the rumbling tires made a few final skips and jumps and fell silent. We were airborne. What a thrill!

The pilot turned the nose up, and it almost seemed like we were stalling as the mighty engines struggled to lift the hundreds of tons of mass out of the grasp of gravity. The buildings, highways, and cars quickly grew smaller and smaller as the plane turned to the east and the city of Calgary was left behind. For us, it was more than just a city that was left behind. It was a family, a home, a country, a culture, twenty-six years of history, a way of life!

This was the historic moment, the "great divide" when the past becomes but prologue to the future. We were on our way at last, opening a new chapter in the story of our lives. What exciting adventures lie ahead? What hardships and suffering? What successes or failures? A tremendous thrill of anticipation and excitement whelmed up within me.

We were now flying over the ranches and grain fields of southern Alberta. We watched the farms get smaller and smaller until the people, the cows, and the cars disappeared and only the bare outline of the fields could be seen like a giant endless patchwork quilt, something like the ones the ladies at church make for the poor. White wisps of cloud whizzed by far below us. The sky was deep blue and the sun exceedingly bright. The flight attendants brought a nice hot meal, and we turned our attention to that.

By the time we finished eating, the "patchwork quilt" of neat little farms was behind us. Smoke from a dozen forest fires could be seen scattered among the thousands of sparkling lakes reflecting the evening sunshine across northern Ontario. Looking out the window soon became old and pointless as we entered the high humidity zone of the east. Now was a suitable time to relax, reflect, and just enjoy the ride.

The date was September 27, 1967, a day for which we had prepared a long time and awaited with eager anticipation. It was amazing how the disjointed pieces of our lives were falling into place in a pattern that pleased us and gave us confidence that the One we believed in and trusted was actually leading us in this great odyssey called "life."

After five years of grueling studies in preparation for "a life of Christian service" in our denomination's college in Harrisonburg, Virginia, I had sensed deep down inside that it was time to move out from academia into that "life of service," whatever it might be. As always, God led us one step at a time. The next step was never revealed until after we, in obedience, took the step at hand.

Back when I was a young grade-nine dropout and would-be farmer, the divine directive had been clear and simple: "Go back and finish high school!" With that accomplished, the next order was, "Go to Eastern Mennonite College and prepare yourself for Christian ministry!"

It was at that college where Vera and I met, got wedded, and started a family. This time the order was again clear: "Enough of school for now!" These were not loud voice messages we heard from above the clouds, but deep impressions of the Spirit on our consciousness that we just knew were of God and that brought deep peace when we responded in obedience.

When we responded, the pieces always fell into place in a remarkable way. No sooner had we decided to quit seminary than a mission board recruiter found us and offered us an opportunity to serve in a "Mission Associates" capacity for a three-year term as a teacher couple in Ethiopia. Once again, we sensed that God was in favor. We did not know much about Ethiopia, hardly even knew where it was, yet we left school and our first love nest in June, sold or packed away our few possessions, and prepared ourselves for this new challenge.

All went well with the moving, the preparations, the orientation at the mission headquarters in Salunga, Pennsylvania, the commissioning service, and the trip back to say farewell to my folks and family in

Alberta. All was falling together except one thing: the visa was not coming through from Ethiopia!

Waiting in Alberta, we were a whole month late, and Vera was now eight months pregnant with our second child. Were we not to go to Ethiopia after all? Had we heard wrongly? Should I have been looking for a job to support my growing family?

My dad thought so. It was okay for a single man to go to the remotest "ends of the earth" and struggle and suffer and even die there. But why should a married man with a growing number of children subject them and their mother to the dangers and unknown hardships of living in remotest Africa? Was I really acting responsibly? Did I know what I was really getting them into? These were unsettling questions, yet we felt we could trust God. He would be with us on this pilgrimage. We were at peace.

Then Grandmother Justina Friesen died. It was not a surprise. She had been fighting a losing battle with cancer for at least eight months. I was in the cemetery helping dig her grave when the message came that our visa was granted, and tickets would be sent as soon as we set the departure date. We decided to leave on the day immediately following the funeral. God's timing!

It was just yesterday we had buried Grandma. It amazed us again how thoughtful God was to delay our departure so that we could have those special last days with her and then join with the whole family in celebrating her life and departure. All fourteen of her children were able to attend. What a bonus to be with all my aunts, uncles, and cousins at this sacred moment! It truly marked the end of an era.

Now, we were on our way to Ethiopia, a far-off, mystical land that held her ancient secrets—secrets waiting to mingle with and shape the secrets of our destiny. For us, this was a pivotal point in time, a watershed event. What challenging adventures lie on the far side?

We knew that Grandma approved of our going. She knew, better than we, that God would be with us. Had she not also, at our age, bid a tearful and final "goodbye" to parents and family and home in Russia, and together with her husband and three babies set out as pilgrims in search of a new home in Canada, a country she did not know? Through all the pain of separation and the hardships they faced in carving out a home and building a new life in a strange land with its foreign customs and difficult language, her sustaining strength had always been her deep confidence in the faithful God who had led them in their departure and undergirded them through all their trials and sufferings.

Grandma's life was an adventure that included hardship and suffering, but she was also victoriously happy and enjoyed life to the fullest. She loved her God, her family, her church, her neighbors, and her adopted country. She loved life intensely and claimed a big stake in eternal life. The competition was tough, the obstacles humongous, but she had finished the race. She was a winner!

Now she had gone to claim her prize, and the torch had passed to us to keep the faith. The God who sustained her was able and would also sustain us. We had nothing to worry about. We were young, and life was good, a sacred gift from God to be received with gratitude and to be cherished. Life was an adventure, an odyssey that beckoned us to pursue with enthusiasm and abandonment. If life was more kind to us and generous, then it also gave us greater responsibility to share its goodness with those who were less fortunate. The secret of finding and living life to the fullest is in dying to selfishness, in giving, in passing on its goodness to others!

Now we were embarking on our life's greatest adventure; we were on our way to Ethiopia. At age twenty-six, we were both young and inexperienced. Apart from summer employment, I had never held a real job. We had never traveled in foreign countries, and we had never lived among a people of another language and culture. This was going to be something very new for both of us. Apprehension mingled with our excitement. We did not know Ethiopia, and we did not know the Ethiopian people, but we hoped somehow, we would be able to share our lives with them. In turn, our lives would be enriched by them. Additionally, there was the comfort of God's promise, "I am with you always, even to the ends of the earth!"

Flying against the time zones, this was the shortest night of our lives. By the time we finished eating our second supper, the eastern sky was beginning to light up with a faint reddish glow. I could not sleep, not because of the second supper, but because I was excited.

Looking out the window at 36,000 feet and watching the new dawn from above the clouds was a worship experience for me. I felt so close to the Creator up there and watched him paint his ever-changing masterpieces. It was inexpressibly gorgeous.

As it got lighter, we could see the snow-covered mountains of Greenland, the ice flows off its shores, then Iceland where my uncle, Christian Hansen, had lived and worked on a farm for a year back in the late forties. Soon we were gliding over Ireland. In the early morning, it looked like the greenest patchwork quilt we ever saw. Now I understood why it was known as "The Emerald Isle."

Friendly flight attendants served us breakfast on the plane before we landed at Heathrow International Airport near London, England. We would be having a day and a half layover here, so we would be escorted to a hotel at airline expense.

Yes, our luggage had miraculously arrived with us. We checked it out and took it with us through customs, got our passports stamped, and were transported to the Skylark Hotel near the airport.

I wanted to make the most of my first stop and my first day as a truly international traveler. I wanted to catch a bus, go downtown, and see London's famous landmarks such as Buckingham Palace, Westminster Abbey, and the London Tower. However, Vera was tired and wanted to rest in the soft bed first, so we laid down and tried to sleep.

Vera slept a bit, but I was too excited. I got up and went outside to look around. England was different from Canada. They drove on the "wrong" side of the road, and the traffic signs were different.

I went back upstairs to see if Vera was ready for a bus adventure. She was not. She said she did not feel well and did not want to go anywhere. This was quite a blow to me, as I did not want to go alone.

Then I remembered that she was at least eight months pregnant, and that airlines, as a rule, would not take expectant mothers on the plane at all if they were over seven months along. By God's grace, no one thought to ask her, so here we were in London, halfway to Ethiopia. I decided we better not push our "luck" too far. If she was not feeling well, I had better stay with her, so we spent the day and night at the hotel. We had our first bout with "jet lag." We slept many hours that day, then were wide awake most of the night. By the next day when it was time to go, we were sleepy again.

That afternoon we took all our luggage back to the check-in counter. They weighed it and found it to be forty pounds over the allowed limit. So, they charged us eighty-five dollars. We argued that at Calgary they accepted it, though they knew it was a "few" pounds overweight.

The haughty Englishman just coldly responded, informing me that this was London, not Calgary, and that they were working according to the rules. If we wanted it to go, we must pay. If we did not want to pay, then we must remove some of our articles and leave them behind. His directive was clear and simple.

Fortunately, we had one hundred dollars with us, so we left eighty-five in London and traveled the next 5,351 miles with fifteen Canadian dollars in reserve, "just in case of an emergency." Years later I wondered what we would have done if Vera had gone into labor in that hotel? We had no bank account and never heard of credit cards. We were young, ignorant, naive, and full of faith, and as things worked out, we saved ourselves needless worry by being so!

Years later, we learned that we could have checked our heavy luggage straight through to Addis Ababa instead of to London, and we would have saved all the unnecessary lugging to the bus and to the hotel and back to the airport as well as those eighty-five dollars. Such is the high cost of ignorance and inexperience.

After waiting in Frankfurt, Germany, for a few hours, we boarded an Ethiopian Airline's Boeing 707, which at that time was the state of the art in flying machines and certainly Ethiopia's pride and joy. It was night again when we made brief touchdowns at Athens and Beirut.

From there the plane headed south across Egypt. Cindy was enjoying jet travel immensely. She especially liked the thrilling feelings that went with changing altitude and acceleration. For months thereafter she would be talking about and playing "airplane rides."

Too excited, I did not sleep at all that night. When dawn broke, we were following the Nile River valley, a narrow ribbon of green winding through a light brown sea of sand that stretched from east to west as far as the eye could see. We were leaving upper Egypt and passing over lower Sudan. The sunrise over the eastern desert was breath-taking. This was our first glimpse of Africa. What a vast open empty country. If there were five hundred million people living in Africa, there certainly was no sign of them anywhere near here!

Shortly we would be landing in Ethiopia. Many questions flooded my mind. What kind of country would it be? What were Ethiopian people like? Would they be friendly or hostile? In what kind of conditions did they live? What kind of house would we be living in?

At first, I assumed that all Africans lived in grass-roofed mud houses and that we would do the same, but then Gerald Stoner had sent a letter of welcome from Nazareth informing us that we would be living in "a new brick house." What kind of brick house? We did not know. What would the Bible Academy be like? How would the staff treat us? What would the students be like? We were now very eager to find out.

We would be beginning a missionary career. I had read the biographies of great missionaries, those towering watershed heroes such as St. Patrick, David Livingstone, or William Carey. I had met and heard missionaries tell their stories, show their pictures, display their artifacts, and make their appeals. Since I was a small boy, I had always idealized them and saw them as great heroes and people of enormous spiritual magnitude. There was no way I could ever join their company among the pinnacles, but at least it would be a great honor if I could work in their shadows. I was just a green kid out of college. I felt so inexperienced and spiritually immature. Perhaps I could start out and be a fairly good schoolteacher, but could I ever become a "real missionary"? The prospect seemed an overwhelming challenge!

On African Soil

We first touched down on Ethiopian soil at Asmara. We were allowed to disembark for one hour to breath the fresh early morning African air, but we were not allowed into the airport terminal. We were to go through immigration and customs at Addis Ababa.

Asmara was the second largest city in Ethiopia at that time. It was amazingly cool. Was not Africa supposed to be hot? We were to discover that most of Ethiopia has a fairly high altitude and enjoys a moderate climate with comfortable temperatures.

By 9:30 o'clock Sunday morning, we were landing and disembarking at the Bole International Airport in Addis Ababa. The airport building was impressive for its neat modern lines and its modest dimensions appropriate to a recently "emerging" nation. It was an attractive, almost new two-story concrete and glass construction. There was a spectator's deck on the upper floor where people could wave off or welcome their friends.

Several of the Addis missionaries were there on that deck to welcome us. These included the mission director, Paul Gingrich, the business and office managers, Dan and Mary Ellen Ness, and Gerald and Elaine Stoner, a teacher and nurse from Nazareth. They helped us get through the legal hassles with reasonable speed. The Ethiopian officials were very polite and understood our English.

Then Gerald and Elaine escorted us to a little yellow Opel station wagon, their mission vehicle. As tour guides, they pointed out and explained the highlights of this impressive young capital city as we drove along. The Bole Airport Boulevard, a new four-kilometer stretch of four-lane divided highway, was lined with beautiful flowering shrubs and trees in the median, flanked by sidewalks and electric light posts. On both sides of this highway were open fields with the beginnings of new housing developments and business establishments and hotels, a few newly completed and the rest in various stages of construction. For new visitors like us, this was a very impressive introduction to modern Ethiopia. The road fed into Meskel Square ("Cross Square").

As we continued straight ahead around the traffic circle that used to be there, we saw the Jubilee Palace, the royal residence of His Imperial Majesty, Haile Selassie I, on the left. Directly across from it on the right was the very impressive OAU building, the very modern new $4,000,000 headquarters for the Organization for African Unity which Haile Selassie had provided as a gift to Africa. Next to it was the massive twelve story Hilton Hotel that was still under construction. Other government buildings and hotels adorned this outstanding avenue. A very appropriate entre to this royal city. From this vantage point, a visitor could agree that the name, "Addis Ababa" (translated "New Flower") was very fitting.

Teacher and nurse, Gerald & Elaine Stoner
with their firstborn, Ann Marie - 1967

Finally, we turned down a short narrow alley and came to a halt before a gate covered with corrugated iron sheets painted a sickly pale green. Gerald beeped the horn, and soon a man in a cheap tattered uniform came and opened the gate and welcomed us into the Mennonite Guest House. Gerald introduced us to him as he closed the gate and came up to help us with our luggage. As he welcomed us in his mother tongue, we were tongue-tied as we found no intelligible way to respond to his strange smooth flow of syllables.

This was my first jolt of "culture-shock." Something strange happens inside when for the first time as an adult, one's verbal ability is instantaneously reduced to the equivalence of a helpless baby. How much we depend on words! When one's flow of understanding is suddenly and completely blocked by total incomprehension for the first time, one is not prepared to make improvisations, to explore and use the options. One learns that later.

At the time, one goes into a momentary state of shock and seeks to get away as quickly as is politely possible. One looks to avoid further embarrassing encounters by staying inside or by hanging closely to one's own kind of people and avoiding exposure to the strange kind of people.

The Mennonite Guest House was an older rented building that had eight bedrooms for the guests. Good western-style meals were served in the dining room. The manner in which meals were served brought a few surprises for us. For example, the host kept a little bell by her plate. She used this to summon the waiter for any need. This went against the grain of my egalitarian rural Mennonite upbringing. Do we call human beings with bells or whistles like dogs?

Years later, I realized, of course we do. What else are we doing with church bells, school bells, telephone bells, doorbells, service bells, fire alarms, and factory whistles?

This guest house was a low one-story structure of pale-yellow stuccoed walls and an old roof of corrugated iron painted red. It stood in a large yard that was beautified with flowers and tropical trees and shrubs. The yard was surrounded by an eight-foot-high fence and the corrugated iron gate that a watchman guarded day and night. A tiny "guardhouse" nearby provided shelter from the rain but little else in the way of human comforts.

Miss Sarah Rush, an elderly, portly veteran American missionary nurse, was a gracious hostess. She could give a visitor helpful information and advice about what to see and how to go about seeing it. She had old friends all over the empire including members of the royal family. In her earlier years, she pioneered with the Mission in medical work. In her later years, she went to Israel and was helping in some work there when she died suddenly. She was buried there in Israel, a very fitting conclusion to her kind of life.

Later in the day, we were taken to a Sudan Interior Mission church service where my former teacher and renowned East African missionary, Dr. Don Jacobs, was preaching. He was interrupted by a drunken heckler. Our first taste of "persecution" of our unpopular foreign religion in the staunchly traditional Orthodox nation.

Back Three Thousand Years

Excitement oozed out of our pores as we loaded our luggage into the Mission's little yellow Opal station wagon the next morning. With Gerald driving and Elaine pointing out the sights, we set off for Nazareth. We could explore Addis Ababa in more detail later. Today, on this special Monday, we would finally get to see our new house and the school where we would be living and working for the next three years.

The road from the highlands of Addis Ababa at 8,000 feet winds downward to Nazareth in the Great Rift Valley at 5,000 feet. It runs in a south-easterly direction for one hundred kilometers, following the railroad. First it passes through the outskirts of industrial Addis with its rusty *"korkoro ketemas"* ("tin towns") and mixture of old and new factories and places of business.

This narrow potholed road was the main thoroughfare for a vast assortment of buses, lorries, taxis, private cars, bicycles, pedestrians, cattle, sheep, goats, and donkeys, each intent on going their own way. The drivers maneuvered their vehicles, swerved in and out, dodging the potholes and bicycles as well as people and animals, all the while blasting their horns whenever they noticed anything ahead that might possibly frustrate or inconvenience them. We had never heard so much horn blowing in our entire lives.

Eventually, we made it to the open countryside, only to be slowed down again as we passed through the congested little industrial suburbs of Akaki and Kaliti.

From there the road led us through a country landscape that could, for one who has never visited Palestine, almost pass for Bible lands in Bible times. Even the names of the principal towns such as "Debre Zeit" ("Mount of Oil" i.e., Olives) and "Nazaret" had a Biblical flavor. The irregular little fields were a giant patchwork of many shades of green and gold and brown. The tin-roofed houses of the towns gave way to the mud and thatched huts of the peasants.

Like the irregular fields, the homesteads were widely scattered in a seemingly random fashion. They were usually surrounded by a rough fence of sticks or thorn branches, a planting of cacti, or some other hedge material. Often there were a few randomly planted eucalyptus trees growing in the yards.

Besides the main thatched hut, each homestead had several small structures nearby such as a separate kitchen, maybe a cow shed, and one or two *"gotteras."* The kitchen was a simple structure where the wat was cooked and the enjera baked over an open fire. As such its walls were always permanently coated with the accumulated smoke residue of a thousand fires over the years.

The *gotteras* were large woven wicker basket-like structures used for storing grain. They were covered with a thatched roof and sealed inside with a thin layer of cow dung to keep the grain from leaking out. These were built high on stilts to discourage small animals from digging into them.

Peasants were beginning to harvest their crops. In some of the fields, we could see small groups of people, maybe family members or neighbors, working together. Each worker stooped forward and grasped a handful of grain with one hand and cut it off at the base with a sickle in the other, placed the cut grain on a pile on the ground until a bundle could be tied together. These bundles would be gathered later and stacked in a suitable place to dry until threshing time. Not a tractor nor a swather nor a combine could be seen anywhere. The scene could have been a re-enactment of how harvesting was done 3,000 years ago in the biblical days of Ruth and Boaz.

Now Gerald pointed out that occasional single standing Acacia trees were widely scattered throughout the fields. These were twisted trunks of trees from which most of the limbs had been cut. This spoke loudly of the shortage of fuel and building and fencing materials.

One would not want to cut down the whole tree, for that would eliminate the supply entirely, but one needs the material so badly that he keeps harvesting the branches before they can reach a significant length.

Of course, in a feudal society, one would not think of planting many trees, for the landlord will claim the trees and may even evict the peasant from his land for being too progressive, the unforgivable sin of seeming to assume that one will have permanent access to "his" land.

The view was captivating, but the driver dared not look to enjoy it. The road was narrower now and still generously sprinkled with deep potholes and lined with eroded and broken edges that made it necessary to swerve towards the middle of the road at any moment. Cattle and donkeys and people on foot were still the principal users.

The large, massive oncoming lorries did not budge an inch from the center of the road. It was up to the small guy to find a safe place for passage as they met. Slow moving lorries could only be passed with great caution at significant risk, often by driving with one wheel on the rough eroded shoulder of the opposite lane.

About halfway to Nazareth, we drove through the town of Debre Zeit, locally known by its Oromo name as "Bishoftu." It is built in the vicinity of seven extinct volcanoes. Some of these have very deep crater lakes. This small but growing modern town was home for the Ethiopian Air Force, and we could see a row of jet fighter planes standing close to the end of a runway. The emperor had a palace in the vicinity. There was also a junior college at that time run by the Evangelical Church Mekane Yesus and the Norwegian Lutheran Mission. The Ministry of Agriculture ran an Agricultural Research Station on the edge of town.

The next town along the way was Mojo, a small crossroads town where one meets the then newly paved road that leads to Shashemene, the Rift Valley lakes, and all points south to the Kenya boarder at Moyale. It is the main overland connection to Nairobi, Kenya. Later, we would take this road to Lake Langano.

The countryside between Mojo and Nazareth has long stretches of rough, dry, rocky, scrubby eroded wasteland. Here we saw a lot of goat and sheep herders with their flocks grazing on the small shrubs and sparse grass among the rocks and deeply eroded gullies. Sellers sat or lay in the sparse shade of a gnarled acacia tree or under a few upright sticks with a tattered cloth canopy stretched across while guarding their piles of grey sacks of charcoal or piles of acacia firewood which they hoped to sell to passing motorists.

We came to a sharp turn in the road and suddenly, there spread out before us was the fabulous panorama of the Great Rift Valley. We stopped and got out of the car to take it all in.

Immediately before us lay the sizable town of Nazareth. Across the valley about fifty or sixty kilometers to the southeast were the mountains and fertile highlands of Arussi Province. To the south stretching as far as eye could see were the vast green sugarcane estates of Wonji and Shoa.

Koka Dam, to the southwest collects and holds the waters that drain from the highlands around Addis Ababa. Besides generating electricity, this dam controls the waters that flow into the Awash River which, in turn, supplies the irrigation schemes which make the sugar estates possible.

This river has carved out a valley that slopes eastward where it waters another sugar estate at Metahara and various fruit and cotton plantations before it is eventually lost in the great salt plains of the Danakil Desert.

Pointing down from the escarpment, Gerald showed us where

the Bible Academy was located, about two kilometers south to our right on the road that connects Nazareth with Wonji. Immediately between where we stood, and the Academy was an army barracks and training ground.

Other private dwellings bordered both sides of the road. Most of them had tin roofs and showed other signs of modernity. Visions of living in a village of grass-roofed mud houses faded.

Now we were desperate to cross the last two kilometers to reach the "promised land," our new home. We squeezed back into the little yellow Opal and quickly made our descent.

CHAPTER 2

A Home in Abyssinia

The Mission

M ennonite involvement in Ethiopia began in 1945 Orie Miller approached the Ethiopian Government to explore ways they could assist in recovery from the devastating war with Italy.

A welcome response resulted in the Mennonite Relief and Service Committee (MRC) of MCC and the Mennonite Board of Missions sending a shipment of relief supplies including food and clothing, along with signing a contract with the Ethiopian government to begin a medical work.

The Mennonites provided staff and administration, and the Ethiopian government made available a cotton factory complete with buildings, machinery, a manager's house, and a large, fenced compound in Nazareth to be used for the medical work. This factory had been built by the Italians during their brief occupation but had never been used.

The facility was renovated into a hospital and outpatient clinic that served the medical needs of a vast area south and east of Addis Ababa through the Awash Valley for many years until other clinics, pharmacies, and hospitals could be set up. It was named "Haile Mariam Mammo Memorial Hospital" (HMMMH) in honor of Lej Haile Mariam Mammo, a youthful "patriot" who distinguished himself for dedication and bravery in the resistance against fascist aggression until he paid the supreme sacrifice in battle in 1938. Today it is called "Adama Hospital Medical College" and serves as the major teaching and referral hospital in the region.

The Eastern Mennonite Board of Missions and Charities (EMBMC) of Salunga, Pennsylvania, joined the work in 1948 and took over in

1950 when Mennonite Relief Committee phased out its involvement. The terms of agreement by which EMBMC was allowed to enter Ethiopia stipulated that they should engage in medical and educational work to better the well-being of the people and that they could evangelize Muslims or pagans, but they must not make converts among members of the Orthodox Tewahedo community. Nazareth was considered a "closed" area to proselytism or evangelism.

In 1952, the Nazareth Dresser Bible School was established to train forty competent medical assistants ("dressers") for the hospital. The program was highly successful because it met a great need for honest, reliable trained medical personnel to staff the many hospitals and clinics and pharmacies that were springing up everywhere. Hundreds of graduates were serving with honor throughout the Empire by the time we arrived in Ethiopia.

The Mennonites had been working there for twenty-one years already. The work had expanded to include a second hospital at Deder and several clinics including one at Bedeno, all in Harar Province.

A School for the Blind had been successfully started in Addis Ababa and had already been turned over to the government. The Menno Bookstore was well established and was the largest Christian bookstore in the nation with branches in Nazareth, Dire Dawa, and Asmara, and was serving the churches and the whole community efficiently.

A string of elementary schools and clinics stretched across the eastern hinterlands of Harar Province surrounding the communities of Deder and Bedeno, serving an area where there had never been a school nor a clinic before. The Nazareth Bible Academy was already eight years old and represented the Mission's commitment to developing better leadership through higher education.

The Mission had its head office in Addis Ababa and was running a guest house. It was also cooperating with the General Conference Baptists through Globe Publishing in developing Christian literature in Amharic. The Mennonites were working with four other missions (Presbyterians, Lutherans, General Conference Baptists, and Southern Baptists) to run the Good Shepherd School for several hundred missionary children from grades one to twelve.

The Church

Around this immense amount of institutional development and service, a small church was developing. In 1967, there were about six hundred names on its membership list. These few people making up five congregations were already organized as the autonomous "Meserete Kristos Church" (literally "Foundation Christ Church") often known by its initials as "MKC." It had its own constitution and executive committee that was responsible to a general assembly of delegates from the congregations that met semi-annually.

This church was refused registration as a religious society by the Imperial Government, so was compelled to work in the legal shadow of the Mennonite Mission in Ethiopia for many years. The Mennonite Mission, being a foreign entity, was not allowed to own real estate. This was a significant problem for the new Church. Since the Orthodox community did not allow non-Orthodox a place in their cemeteries, where could these new believers bury their dead? How could the Church develop institutions without owning land? Most properties could be rented, but renting is not a good long-term solution. Besides, there were few meeting houses to be rented.

When the Bible Academy was built, three church elders had their names put on the title deed, so, in a legal sense, the school was built on private land. This did not appear to be very satisfactory either, but under the circumstances, what else could be done?

A Superlative House

Our new house was quite a surprise to us. It certainly was not what one would call a "grass hut"! It was a two-story orange-red brick duplex with identical apartments upstairs and downstairs. Gerald and Elaine Stoner with their one-year-old daughter, Ann, would be our closest neighbors occupying the upstairs apartment while we would occupy the one downstairs.

This duplex was a recently built modern house with electricity and running water, hot and cold, with proper sanitation facilities. There were four large bedrooms, a big living room, dining room, and kitchen. All the rooms had ten-foot ceilings and pale green and grey-colored cement tile floors. The walls were all made of brick and were plastered on the inside. Even the ceiling was concrete so that every word one said echoed as if it was said inside an empty concrete cistern. It had steel doors, and all the windows had a lattice work of iron bars for security reasons.

Kitchen cupboards and bedroom closets were not yet installed. There was an electrical servant-bell system with a button to press in each room to summon the servant from the kitchen whenever needed. We did not have the heart nor the conscience nor did we see the need to use it, but Cindy found it a very entertaining plaything.

Our "grass hut" turned out to be a modern duplex, our home on the ground floor with the Stoner family and later Herb and Sharon Kraybill living on the upper floor.

We were quite overwhelmed with our magnificent house. We three poor missionaries, having come with our four barrels and six suitcases prepared to live humbly and sacrificially, felt like we could get lost in its cavernous halls. I had never lived in such a spacious modern dwelling in my whole life! Actually, by modern western standards, it was very modest, plain, and simple, but for us at that stage in our lives, it was a superlative surprise.

Since the house was brand new, Stoners were still landscaping and planting shrubs and flowers in the yard. The yard was surrounded with a brick fence and steel gate that was a good seven feet high for security purposes. Built against the compound wall at the back of the house, there were three rooms plus a squat "Asian type" toilet room, all intended as living quarters for the workers.

Stoners introduced us to their house help, Belihu, a single mother who lived in one of those rooms with her four-year old daughter, Italemau. Since Gerald worked as a teacher at the Academy, and Elaine worked at our mission hospital in Nazareth, they found Belihu indispensable to keep their house in order and to care for little Ann.

In the afternoon, Ato Illihu ("Ato" means "Mr.") came around to assume his duties as "zebunya" or watchman. He watered the flowers, weeded them, washed the car, ran errands for us, opened and closed the gate for us whenever we needed to take the car in or out, and watched the compound for possible intruders until ten o'clock at night when he went home to sleep with his large family of ten children in their two-roomed house.

After ten o'clock, the compound was left unguarded, based upon an unproved assumption that would-be thieves also went to bed by ten o'clock. Later it was proved that there were a few exceptions to this rule.

Our house and the Bible Academy were on the east side of the Nazareth-Wonji road. There were two small plots or fields and a brick-walled garage and welding shop between us and the school. The garage was owned and ran by some older Italians. South of us were open fields. Across the road was one small hut and several fields. Immediately to the south of that was an Italian-owned and operated brick factory which hired hundreds of laborers.

The road itself was not something easily forgotten. It was a busy, dusty, gravel road, built and maintained by the Dutch company that developed and operated the Wonji and Shoa sugar estates twelve kms to the south. It served as the only link between the two sugar factories and the railroad station in Nazareth and the nascent highway system and the emerging market for sugar and candy.

The road was well-traveled by horse-drawn carts, horse-drawn chariot-like taxis known as "garies," donkeys, great herds of slow-moving skinny zebu cattle with their long horns, goats, and sheep with their herd boys, pedestrians, water-carrying or firewood-laden women, and many others.

Among this diverse and exotic stream of traffic lumbered huge WWII Italian or German trucks laden with sugar, long three or four-wagon sugar trains pulled with noisy high-speed tractors, as well as buses, smaller trucks, and cars which, all together, kept a steady stream of dust rising. The prevailing winds blew this dust across the fields and yards and into the houses where it settled into every crack, coating all the floors and furniture with a generous layer every day.

Periodically the company "paved" the road with molasses to settle the dust a bit. It did! However, this sweet-smelling road also attracted zillions of flies and ants that added another dimension to the mass of traveling creatures.

Due to the peculiar structure of the soil there, each passing heavy vehicle sent earth tremors that shook our concrete and brick fortress-house, rattling the dishes in the cupboards. I often wondered how the tremors would rate on the Richter Scale.

The Nazareth Bible Academy

After moving our suitcases into the house and meeting Belihu and inspecting the house and yard, it was time to take a tour of the school.

The Nazareth Bible Academy had its origins in the vision of missionaries and Ethiopian Christians who saw the need of higher education for Christian young people.

It first opened its doors on September 29, 1959, in the town of Nazareth. It began in humble circumstances in rented quarters under the direction of two teachers, Mr. Chester L. Wenger, and Ato Daniel Lemma, with three girls and thirteen boys enrolling. It was more like a large family than a secondary school. Students took their meals at Haile Mariam Mammo Memorial Hospital. There was no library or science laboratory, amenities so essential to a good high school. Yet the students did very well academically. The school was sponsored by the Eastern Mennonite Board of Missions and Charities.

With the help of church elders, the Mission had bought twenty-two acres of open semi-arid land four kilometers southwest of Nazareth along the Wonji road. The plot lay on a gentle slope just east of a high volcanic rock ridge the shadow of which made the setting of the evening sun considerably premature. Campus buildings had been erected. The Bible Academy moved into its permanent campus at the

21

beginning of its second year. Enrollment that year was twelve girls and thirty-one boys.

By the time we arrived, the Academy had been in operation for eight years. It was a small, fully accredited four-year co-educational boarding secondary school. It was run under the supervision of a Board of Education appointed by the Meserete Kristos Church in cooperation with the Mennonite Mission in Ethiopia. It had one hundred and nine boarding students in grades nine through twelve, and nine teachers.

At that time the campus consisted of four classrooms for the four grades, boarding facilities for sixty-nine boys and forty girls, a kitchen and dining hall, a chapel, a workshop, and four faculty residences. Trees had been planted, and now they were beginning to afford a little shade for the students from the hot equatorial sun.

The Wonji-Nazareth road divided the campus into two about-equal parts. The buildings were on the east side of the road, and the football field and one teacher's residence were on the west side. Our two-story duplex residence was off campus.

The twenty-two-acre Nazareth Bible Academy campus, 1971

The Nazareth Bible Academy Entrance

Ato Shemsudin Abdo was the director of the school. There were four full-time expatriate staff members besides me: Gerald Stoner, Calvin Shenk, Marie Shenk, and Esther Becker, and two part-time teachers: Nevin and Blanch Horst. Alemu Checole was the only other full-time Ethiopian teacher at that time. A drill sergeant from the army camp helped part-time with athletics. There was also a part-time Amharic teacher.

That evening, the staff put on a guinea fowl barbecue to welcome us. Calvin Shenk, among other things, was famous for his hunting hobby. He kept his freezer full of wild guinea fowl and wild pig or warthog.

Then on Friday, there was a get-acquainted social at the school for students and staff.

A new school year was just beginning. Since we were a month late in arriving, we were informed that we would be given a week to get settled and to set up housekeeping.

The house had been furnished before we arrived, though the sparse mission furniture hardly did justice to the spacious living room. It always echoed to any noise like an empty cistern.

We turned one of the four bedrooms into our office, and since it was also big, and since my busy schedule kept me there most of the time, it was, in essence, our real "living room." We moved in a couch, and in the evenings, after putting the children to bed, Vera would leave the emptiness and loneliness of the spacious living room for the coziness and companionship found in my office.

Those first few days, the missionary community rallied around us with hospitality, inviting us to their homes for meals. That gave us time to get our house in order.

The four barrels of our household goods that we had shipped from Virginia arrived ten days before we did. They were waiting to be cleared through customs as soon as we presented our passports. Since the Suez Canal had been closed that June by the "Six-day War," our shipment had cleared the Cape of Good Hope in three months' time. We were grateful.

When unpacking, Cindy was delighted to see her toys again, and when her highchair was assembled, she climbed up in it and sat there for the longest time. Some tangible links to her past gave her an added sense of security.

Nazareth

Later we were taken on a tour of the town of Nazareth. We began with the Haile Mariam Mammo Memorial Hospital located in the eastern part of the town, about five kilometers from our house.

The hospital consisted of several large dull red brick buildings that had originally been built by the Italians as a cotton factory.

The factory had been extensively renovated and now, twenty-one years later, was serving the community in significant ways. It was the main medical center serving a vast area between Addis and Asebe Teferi in the east and Shashemene in the south. Its staff gave supervision to many clinics and pharmacies in that area.

It also ran the Dresser Bible School which gave medical training to about forty dressers. Two missionary doctors, their wives, and three expatriate nurses gave training, supervision, and leadership to a developing national staff.

At that time, Rohrer Eshelman was the doctor in charge. His wife, Mabel, besides raising their four children, helped as a nurse. Dr. and Mrs. Roy and Esther Wert were, like us, new recruits adjusting to missionary life in Ethiopia. They, like us, had one daughter, Glenda.

We had a lot in common. Other nurses were Grace Keeport, Amy Pieffer, and Elaine Stoner.

The hospital chapel served a double purpose as a chapel and as the worship center in Nazareth for the fledgling church. At this point in time, the Meserete Kristos Church was not registered as a legal entity, and any non-Orthodox church activity was apt to stir animosity and opposition from either the government or the Orthodox community. The nascent Church was conceived and birthed in the protective womb of the hospital, and as a child in the security of its parent's lap, it still felt safer in the shade of the hospital walls.

The town of Nazareth itself was showing some signs of prosperity and growth. Older missionaries could remember when the mission car was about the only car in town in the late 1940s. Now the main streets were wide paved boulevards with a median strip planted with beautiful flowering shrubs. There were many cars and trucks, although traffic was quite disorganized and treacherous with pedestrians and animals taking priority regardless of traffic regulations.

New shops and industries and better living quarters were being built of brick and stone. Mud huts and grass roofs were gone from the center of town. Even in the back streets, corrugated iron roofs replaced grass on most of the mud houses.

The Marketplace

We were introduced to the marketplace in Nazareth where we would do much of our shopping for fruit and vegetables and basic supplies.

The marketplace was a dirty, noisy, smelly congestion of shops, stalls, and people-packed space. Open sewers held what stinking grey fluids failed to sink into the porous sandy soil. Dust and flies seemed to be everywhere. The stench of rotting garbage and overripe fruit and vegetables and onions mingled with the strong smell of a sweating humanity obviously not used to frequent bathing or the use of deodorants. The sweat-soaked and muddy-dusty color of the tattered clothing of most of the people confirmed the source of the smells as well as their poverty.

Goats and donkeys and cattle mingled with the people adding their noises to the din of voices.

Hordes of dirty ragged little children followed us through the market shouting, "*Ferinj! Ferinj!*" and watched intently each move we made as if we were a rare species of god or mammal, and then commented excitedly among themselves and giggled about whatever struck them as "odd" in our appearance or behavior. We learned that "*ferinj*" is a generic term taken from "French" or perhaps "foreigner" but applied to all white people.

Traders spread their produce and wares out on the ground or displayed them in the crowded little stalls. They all called out to us in unintelligible Amharic or broken English as we passed by. We could grasp a few words which sounded like "Welcome!" "Come this way!" and "I give cheap price!" We had to learn not to be shocked by the highness of the "cheap price" first mentioned. They expected us to bargain until we agreed on a reduced price of 65% or often 50% and sometimes even 25% of the first mentioned "cheap price."

Beggars added their voices to the din. Specimens of every category of desperate and broken humanity seemed to be present: the stooped and shriveled skeletons of the aged pitifully pleading in the names of the various saints for a piece of bread, blind people with their walking sticks, or sighted assistants chanting their memorized lines of importunity, the cripples shuffling along on homemade "crutches" or skidding around on all fours on worn pieces of inner tube managing to maneuver their outstretched empty cups in front of the approaching "*ferinjoch,*" pleading for compassion "*Silla Mariam!*" or "*Silla Gabriel!*" (For the sake of St. Mary or St. Gabriel), or even "*Silla Yesus!*"

The lame sat alongside the shops near open doorways displaying to maximum advantage their gruesome "elephantiasis" leg or foot swollen to double or triple its normal size and covered with huge raw running ulcers on which the pesky flies freely fed. They did not move around but sat there in the most pathetic posture possible and called out loudly for mercy as we passed by.

As newcomers to this kind of scene, our missionary hearts moved us with compassion, and we soon emptied our pockets of the change, but the more we gave, the more they came. It quickly became obvious that our resources were not going to meet the need. How we regretted we could not say, like Jesus, "Be healed!" or "Rise up and walk!"

We were impressed with the flies which were in abundance everywhere. They were not like the flies we were used to. These were such small, high speed, clingy pests that always managed to escape every attempt to swat them and came right back to the same sensitive spot on one's nose or lip to pester some more. They especially clung around the unwashed eyes and noses and mouths of the children attracted by the body fluids available there. The children had long ago given up their vain attempts at chasing them away.

Buyers and sellers raised their voices dramatically in highly animated arguments as they bartered cash for goods. To us who could not understand the words nor the customs, it seemed like the argument would rise in intensity until they appeared to be trading in insults.

When the argument seemed to reach its hottest and we feared they were about to become violent, suddenly someone would give in, and the buyer would calmly count out his money and take the goods. They would both smile, shake hands, exchange some pleasantries such as "You are now my *'dumbunia!'* (special customer). Come back again and I will always give you a special low price!"

We were pleasantly surprised how friendly the people were towards foreigners. They were very curious about us oddities. They seemed to have largely forgiven the Italians for the suffering they inflicted upon them in their five-year struggle to colonize them. Unlike other African countries, they had no other colonial memories to cause them to use foreigners as scapegoats for their problems and frustrations. The Orthodox Church was officially antagonistic towards us foreign missionaries, but otherwise we got the feeling of being welcomed.

Taxis

A *"gari"* was a light two wheeled "chariot" pulled by one horse that served as a taxi. It had a seat built for two that often carried four or five. You could flag it down as it went by, and upon the payment of a *"sumuny"* or about twelve cents, the driver would slide over to the edge and let you climb up beside him and would take you as far as you wished to go in Nazareth.

It was incredibly cheap transportation and amazingly fast too. It was fun to go by *"gari,"* enjoying the sun and the fresh wind and all the secret back alleys and shortcuts that a car could never find, and at the slow easy pace, one could leave all the driving worries to the driver and get a much better view of the scenery.

There were quite a few *garies* in Nazareth. There was no society for the prevention of cruelty to animals, and some of these owners abused their horses terribly. They worked them from sunup to sundown, gave them very little food, and when there was no grass, which was nine months of the year, they had very little to graze on at night, and if they grazed there was little time to sleep. Like the prisoners of Auschwitz, these horses were nothing but skin and bones. Often there were hideous open sores where the ill-fitting harness rubbed the skin from the bones. Then in their greed to squeeze out of their bones the last cent of profit, the drivers whipped the poor wretches mercilessly.

Occasionally the poor horse would just drop in its harness and die on the spot. When that happened, the driver would pull off the harness and leave the corpse where it fell. In one or two nights, the hungry hyenas would have devoured every bone and square inch of scabby flea-infested horse hide, hair, and all.

Our Ethiopian Baby

As I was easing into my job as teacher, Vera was putting our home in order and getting a nest ready for the soon expected baby. I built a changing table in the "baby room" out of wooden packing crates with shelves beneath for diapers and clothes and painted it a canary yellow. Vera made curtains for the windows and matching curtains for the shelves. We felt proud of our preparations.

We weren't as early in getting ready as we expected, for exactly two weeks after arriving in Ethiopia, about 2:00 a.m. on Saturday morning of October 14th, 1967, Vera awakened me reporting that she was feeling some cramps. We got ready, and around 4:30, Gerald Stoner took us to the hospital in Nazareth.

I was allowed to stay in the delivery room with Vera for the long painful ordeal, holding her hand, and comforting her. Since I was standing idle and getting in the way, Dr. Eshelman recruited me to be the chief anesthetist! I poured on the ether whenever he ordered it! Can you imagine that happening in a Sentara hospital in the USA?

Sometime in the middle of the delivery, the doctor became aware that the baby was coming out breech, that is, buttocks first. This made him a bit nervous because of the extra danger of strangulation when the head is last to come out. The doctor managed to work the feet out first.

He made an episiotomy cut, and at exactly 12:57 p.m., a beautiful, red-skinned dark-haired girl lay in the hands of the attending nurse. She weighed six pounds and eleven ounces and was nineteen-and one-half inches tall. She was normal and healthy in every way and at once began sucking her thumb. We were happy, and Cindy was immensely proud to have a sister.

The next morning at school, the grade nine girls came up to console me, "Mr. Hansen, we are sorry for you that you did not get a son!" Obviously, the women's lib movement hadn't made its influence felt in that part of the world yet!

We thought our new daughter deserved a pretty Scandinavian name like "Karen." Then we gave her the middle name "Darlene," that of her aunt, Vernane.

Spared For a Purpose

After being home for two weeks, baby Karen got sick with a bad case of diarrhea, so we took her to the hospital. Dr. Eshleman thought she probably was infected with one of the many African bugs to which foreigners are so susceptible. He ordered antibiotics and told Vera she could strengthen the formula. Vera had not been able to meet the baby's nutritional needs through breast feeding, so she had prepared a formula with cow's milk. Now we took Karen home and put more milk into the formula, but the diarrhea only got worse.

The next day, Friday noon, baby Karen stopped sucking. In the last few hours, she had gotten weak and lethargic and dehydrated, so we rushed her back to the hospital. This time they admitted her, and the missionary nurses took care of her. We went home.

We were young, inexperienced, and extremely naive. Of course, we were concerned about baby Karen, but we weren't really worried.

To us, babies did not die. If they got sick, you took them to the hospital, and they got better. With that assumption, we slept well that night. Obviously, the families we came from had never lived in Africa.

The next morning at six a.m., Elaine Stoner returned home from doing night duty at the hospital. Her report shocked us, "Your baby is still alive and showing positive signs that she may make it!"

During the night they thought they were going to lose her. By the time we had brought her in, she was so badly dehydrated that they couldn't find a vein to give her rehydration fluids by IV. They had taken turns throughout the night, with a medicine dropper, dropping rehydration fluid down her lifeless throat. By early morning, she had begun to show signs of recovery, beginning to suck again.

But they still did not know why she did not respond to the anti-diarrhea medications they had given her nor why she had gotten so sick in the first place.

After breakfast, we went in to see the doctor. By this time Karen was a lot better, and the diarrhea had stopped. But the doctor was puzzled about the cause. Stool exams revealed nothing.

I informed him that her mother had an allergy to cow's milk when she was a little baby and was raised on goat's milk. Could there be any correlation? It was like a light went on in Dr. Eshelman's head. Of course, allergies can be inherited, and the symptoms fit perfectly. He would experiment with goat's milk.

The good doctor got on his motorcycle and went around town shopping for goat's milk. He finally found a source, brought some home, boiled it and made a formula. Where else in the world would one get such personal attention from a doctor? Baby Karen tolerated the formula.

By Sunday morning she tried to pull out the feeding tube. When they removed it, she was ready to suck. She enjoyed the goat's milk formula and recovered. In a few days we took her home. She had lost more than a pound and a half through this ordeal, but soon she was back up to her birth weight.

After another three weeks or so Karen got diarrhea again. This time we took her off the milk formula at once, and she got better on sugar water. We suspected our milk source. Could it be that the goat was not giving enough milk and they, to keep their contract, were topping it off with cow's milk?

Our mission director, Paul Gingrich, heard about our problem and phoned Nairobi and had a few cans of powdered soybean milk substitute flown in for Karen. Again, she thrived on this artificial milk and had no more problems except abundant gas pains from the bean juice. She grew very fast and became our biggest, fattest baby.

After six months Karen was able to go onto full strength cow's milk without any bad effect. We were grateful to God for sparing our Karen that night while we slept and are so thankful that she became a strong healthy lively young girl that added so much fun and joy to our home. Obviously, she was spared for a purpose!

About two hundred meters behind our house, in the midst of a field, was a small, lonely weed-filled enclosure that held two neglected graves, the one of an evangelical believer and the other of a baby belonging to a Christian Indian couple who were schoolteachers. It being an Orthodox area, there was no proper burial place for those who were not of the Orthodox Tewahedo faith. I often looked out at that lonely place and thanked God that our Karen was not laid to rest there!

I have often reflected upon a conversation I had with my dad back in Alberta while we were waiting for a whole month for our visa to be approved to go to Ethiopia. We waited and waited, but the visa was delayed.

Dad was always reluctant to give his adult sons advice, but this time he asked me:

> "Carl, do you really know what you are doing? It is okay for you as a single person to go off to Ethiopia by yourself and face all the unknown risks, but you have a wife and children. Is it wise for you to expose them to all the unknown dangers and hardships you might face in far off Africa? Why don't you just forget about that and go to the municipality building in Brooks and apply for a teaching job in one of our schools?"

However, I was convinced that this assignment in Ethiopia was a call of God, so I would not listen to his word of caution. And now, here in less than a month, we almost lost our baby. How wise and right my dad was! And yet, we did not lose our Karen. We were not alone in our coming. Surely the God who called was also present and able to protect and provide!

Vera and Cindy, so thankful that God, with the devoted help of our missionary medical team, spared our baby Karen.

House Help

Mestawet Gebre Mariam came to us as an eighteen-year-old girl in mid-December. She knew a little English, so at least we could communicate with her. We promised to help her with English if she would help us learn Amharic. She seemed very happy to work for us even though the pay was low. She was a good and willing worker and very pleasant to be with. She was still young to be so far from her home, and she missed her family a lot. Maybe that is one reason she took to mothering baby Karen so diligently. She became very attached to her and called her, "My Karen."

This was our first real experience with having a "maid" work for us. We couldn't have found a better one. She was becoming a part of our family. Then she informed us that she would have to leave us to return to her dresser training. We felt sad to lose her, yet we knew she needed to prepare for her future, and she would be living back home with her family. Consequently, after being with us for about seven months, she left at the end of July 1968.

Because the Stoners completed their term and were leaving in June, their house worker, Belihu, agreed to help us out until the end of September. She had promised to work for Dr. Paul T. and Daisy Yoder when they returned in October.

Belihu brought to us her "cousin" Almaz, a single young woman with a small child, Ruthie, from Arussi. We decided to give her a chance. She was a good and dependable worker, but she was more withdrawn and private. We all missed Mestawet.

CHAPTER 3

A New Career

In Front of the Class at Last!

After being in Ethiopia for one week, the time came for me to take my place in front, facing my first class. After seventeen years of sitting among the many facing the one, now I was to be the one facing the many. Instead of being among the many absorbing information, now I was to be the one disseminating information.

This wasn't just an ordinary class of students. They all had very strange and difficult names. They were people with varying shades of black to brown skin, youths from a totally unfamiliar culture, people for whom English was a difficult second or third or fourth language. Would I understand them? Would they understand me? Would I be able to teach them, or was there much more that they would teach me? I hoped it would go both ways.

Although I approached the challenge of my first real job with a certain amount of reckless naivete, I harbored some deep underlying strains of self-doubt as well. Although I had been taught by teachers for seventeen years and could immediately spot a good teacher from among poor ones, I was not a trained teacher. I would have to learn how to plan lessons in such a way that the curriculum would be covered within the allotted time and that the students would be prepared to sit for the government's final examinations at the end of grade twelve. Should they fail those all-important exams, they would not only bring disgrace upon themselves, but upon their teacher and the whole school. Was I really up to the challenge?

My first assignment was to teach ninth-grade Introduction to Biology, tenth-grade Chemistry, eleventh-grade Bible Doctrine and

Public Speaking, and a twelfth-grade course on the biblical book of Hebrews.

I made my entry into the teaching profession by facing the tenth grade Chemistry class first.

As I stepped into the classroom, forty bright young scholars stood up together, facing me with proper respect, and in unison repeated: "Good morning, Teacher!" I was unprepared for this. We had never done such a thing in all my days of high school. What do I do now? I was quick witted enough to walk to the teacher's desk and face them with: "Good morning! You may be seated!" They responded appropriately with precision. At least they showed respect and obeyed; so far this was not difficult.

We had an opening prayer. Then I turned to the class register. I introduced myself to them and wrote my one strange Scandinavian name on the blackboard. I challenged them to be patient with me as they had only one new name to master while I had forty strange names on the register that my tongue had never tried to twist around before. Then I proceeded to read out each strange name such as "Alemayehu Assefa," "Aster Wolde Kiros," "Demelash Dejene," "Germatchew Belete," "Heywete Haile Meskel," and so on until I reached "Tesfaye Asamenew," and "Zenebu Derege." After I enunciated an approximation of each name, I had them repeat it properly, then I would say it again. Eventually, I was able to master each name and attach it to one of the 109 faces in our school.

Then I turned to the lesson at hand. I felt forty pair of eager eyes measuring this new *ferinj* teacher up and down. "Would he be as good as Mr. Beachy?" I had heard about the legendary qualities of this experienced science teacher who had returned home on furlough. He had taught the first semester of "Introduction to Chemistry." Now I was assigned to continue in his shoes teaching the second half of the course. Could I possibly make it as exciting as Mr. Beachy was reputed to have made the first half of the course?

This was my severest challenge. I dare not confess to the students that I was not only a new and inexperienced teacher, but that I had never studied the sciences in college and had never looked at chemistry since my own days in high school many years ago. That would be psychologically devastating for the students and would unnecessarily hamper the possibility of them respecting me as their teacher.

I told the students that since there were three new transfer students in the class and since they all had a two-month vacation, I felt it would be well to undertake a quick review of the first half of the course before we moved ahead into the second half. Of course, I did not tell them that I desperately needed that review so that I could catch up to where they already were, or there was no way I could have continued as their teacher in any meaningful way.

The clever students really grumbled, and I almost had a rebellion on my hands. They wanted to move ahead to new material, but I urged them to give it a try for a few days. I would assign a unit each day and give a tough quiz the next morning. I made sure the quizzes were tough enough that even the best students couldn't score 100%.

The scheme worked. The clever students were frustrated and humiliated, the ordinary ones strengthened their grasp of chemistry, and in a few weeks, I was on top of the pile having learned more chemistry than any of them. From then on teaching chemistry was fun.

I had no major problems with the other classes since they all started with new course material.

After about two weeks, the director called me into his office and informed me that some of the students were complaining that they couldn't understand my English. Maybe I was using too many big words. I was fresh from an American seminary, and now I was suddenly talking to high school kids for whom English was a difficult second language. I had to make some adjustments.

I found the students very intelligent and eager to learn. They asked a lot of questions and studied with amazing dedication. I found out later that they were rigorously evaluated and screened before they were accepted into our school. The competition for a seat in The Bible Academy was extremely keen. For everyone who was accepted, there were many who were turned away. Each one valued and guarded his seat lest he fail, and it be given to another more deserving. They were among the finest students in Ethiopia.

The dedication of the students to their studies was enhanced largely by the competitiveness of the whole educational system in Imperial Ethiopia. Students had to score passing grades on tough national government examinations at the end of eighth grade, and even harder ones at the end of twelfth grade. Failure to pass either of those examinations meant that one's academic career was blocked; he could not go on to high school or university.

Since space in the high schools and the university was extremely limited, these examinations were for the purpose of screening and blocking the vast majority from pressing on. Only the select few would be allowed to enter those sacred university gates.

Consequently, every ninth-grade student already felt the heat of the pressure to excel. Students would come to their teacher and express their anxiety that they were not moving ahead fast enough to cover all the material in the syllabus. School classes started at 7:45 a.m. and went until 12:30 noon, and again from 2:45 to 5:00 p.m. Then they were required to be in their classrooms for study hall from 7:00 to 9:00 in the evenings.

The students were very friendly, and most of them were well-behaved and respectful and co-operative. The rules were strict, and each student was given a "conduct" grade along with his/her academic grades on the report card that was sent home to his/her parents. Fear of this grade kept most of them on the "straight and narrow" most of the time.

There were a few exceptions. These had to be disciplined in some way. The worst form of discipline for most of the recalcitrant students was to send them home with a letter to their parents. That would ensure them of a thorough beating. We saw students fall down before the director with their faces to the floor begging to be given any kind of humiliation or punishment but "Please don't tell my parents!" Usually, if they were first time offenders, they got to cut grass in the yard for a few days or to clean the latrine. They were never whipped nor beaten, which was the usual form of punishment in African schools.

Professional Colleagues

At the heart of the success of the Bible Academy was its dedicated and capable staff. In all there were nine full-time and part-time teachers. Shemsudin Abdo was the director. Calvin Shenk was business manager and history and religion teacher. His wife, Marie, taught typing, English, and business subjects. Esther Becker was Dean of Girls and taught English and many other subjects. Alemu Checole taught Bible, English, history, and music. Gerald Stoner was dean and taught mathematics and science subjects. Nevin and Blanch Horst each taught a course or two. Ahmed taught Amharic.

Shemsudin Abdo, the director, was a very talented and unusual person. He was born into a strong Muslim home near Deder in Harar Province. His parents sent him to the mission school in Deder for his elementary education. It was there that he understood the Gospel and became an ardent Christian. He was the first Ethiopian to hold the post of director of The Bible Academy.

Shemsudin was used widely in the churches as a preacher and served on committees. After serving as director of the Bible Academy for two years, the Meserete Kristos Church called him to be the first Ethiopian to serve as its Executive Secretary. During our first year there, our relationship with him formed the basis for many adventures we were to have together later.

Another Ethiopian teacher on the staff that made a lasting impression on me was Alemu Checole. He was born into an Orthodox Amhara peasant family in northern Ethiopia. His earliest memories are that of a carefree boy herding cattle on the hills in the northern Wollo Province.

Then tragedy struck which radically changed Alemu's' life. He contracted trachoma and became blind. His father took his little son to Addis Ababa where he was enrolled in the new "School for the Blind" that was being started by Emperor Haile Selassie in cooperation with the Mennonite Mission. School was not to start for another few weeks. Haile Selassie took the little boy into his personal care. Until school opened, Alemu lived in the royal palace with the emperor! Alemu was about seven years of age. He thrived in school.

About fifteen years later, Alemu Checole graduated from the Haile Selassie I University with distinction with a bachelor's degree in teaching English literature. He was hired to teach at the Bible Academy.

Alemu was an outstanding man in every way. He had an attitude that was shaped and purified by his sufferings. He sometimes said that he had come to thank God for his blindness, for it was the means for him to escape the bondage of ignorance and illiteracy of the peasant life and to come to know the Lord Jesus as his personal Savior. For him, his blindness opened a whole new world of opportunity.

Everybody admired and respected Alemu. He had so many friends and treated each one as someone special. The students loved him, and we staff were all his special friends. He was good in music and taught piano and organized singing groups. He had a keen interest in theology and in world affairs.

Alemu Checole Teaching

During our third year, Alemu went on scholarship to the University of Syracuse in the U.S.A. where he earned a master's degree. He returned and continued teaching at the Bible Academy until it was closed in 1982. During that time, he married Abebech, and they raised a beautiful family of six children. He served many years as an elder in the Meserete Kristos Church and continued to teach in private schools and colleges as long as he was able.

International Students

Among the student body, there were two Somali students, three Tanzanians, and four refugees from southern Sudan sponsored by the United Nations. They provided a bit of international flavor and drama for the Ethiopians.

Said Sheikh Samatar and Herzi Ahmed were both born in the Ethiopian Ogaden but grew up in the Somali nomadic culture and were citizens of Somalia. They were sent to us as Christians on scholarship from the Mennonite Mission in Somalia. They were now in eleventh grade.

Said was a very sociable fellow and had a lot of interesting stories to tell. Instead of studying with the other students, he preferred to hang around the teachers and talk, if any had time to listen, which I usually did.

Said grew up with camels in the bush with his mother and her children. His father was a Sheikh, a nomadic leader who moved around a lot in the adult world and who had other wives and families who moved with their herds. Said remembers the first time he was introduced by his mother to this strange man who turned out to be his father. Said had forty-nine brothers and sisters. At that time, he said the oldest was fifty-two and the youngest was two.

He told tales of his childhood, of swimming with the other children in the Wabi Shebelle River among the crocodiles. Occasionally a croc would take an unlucky swimmer, hold him down until he drowned, then carry him off to some isolated shore where it could enjoy its meal in peace. Usually though, the other children would run to get the adults to help. Sometimes they recovered the body or parts thereof, and occasionally even killed the murderer.

He explained that if you were swimming and met a croc, the best way to prevent being taken was to remain in an upright position with hands straight down by your sides because a croc cannot bite with its head held sideways. It can only bite up and down, so if you stand upright as straight as a pole and leave no appendages for it to grab, it cannot open its mouth wide enough to get a good hold on you. I took this as very interesting survival information, but I deeply resolved that I would never put myself into a position of testing its veracity!

Said told tales of living and sleeping with the camels. At night they would put the camels in a thorn branch enclosure for protection, build a little fire outside to cook their tea, and then take turns watching while the others would sleep.

One night Said was peacefully sleeping alongside the enclosure when suddenly he was startled by the frantic shouting of the watchmen. Before he could get to his feet a huge lion jumped down right on top of him from the inside of the enclosure with a baby camel in his jaws. What a rude awakening!

Said still marveled at the power of that lion. It carried that little camel of perhaps two hundred pounds up over that eight-to ten-foot-high thorny enclosure and jumped down on the other side and ran off into the night without once losing its grip! Said was glad that the lion's jaws were already full when he landed on top of him!

Many Ethiopians scorned the Somalis for their use of camel's milk and meat. It is somehow a tabu for them. They claim that the milk will cause diarrhea if you are not used to it. But Said was a firm believer in the superior nutritional value of camel's milk. He said, as a teenager, he stayed a whole year with the camels eating and drinking nothing but camel's milk. He said he was healthy and did not even have one sick day that year.

When Said grew up, he found his way to Mogadishu where he enrolled himself in a school for adults, learned English, got a job, and somehow became a strong Christian in that very staunch Muslim society.

At the Bible Academy, Said ranked number two in academic standing for the full time until he graduated. He never stressed himself with studies like most of the students but could be found walking around looking for someone with whom to visit. He was satisfied to be number two on the list without the extra work needed to surpass Tenassi Nicola, who was always number one.

Upon graduating, Said returned to Somalia where he married the missionary, Lydia Glick, and served as a leader in the underground Somali church for a time.

Years later, the couple moved to the U.S.A. where Said studied at Goshen College and earned a PhD. from Northwestern University. He was widely recognized as a specialist and a professor in Somali literature and history at Rutgers University in New Jersey. He passed away in 2015.

The four Sudanese students were sponsored by the UNHCR, the United Nations Refugee Agency with all expenses paid. Though "Christians" from the south, they must have been suffering psychological damage from the traumatization they had been through in the civil war and the refugee camps. They were paranoid, suspicious of everybody and believed that all their suspicions were irrefutable facts. They simply could not get along with the other students. They imagined there were spies for the Muslim northern Sudanese Government among the students watching them.

One day Jonathan (not his real name), the oldest and most damaged of them, drew a knife and tried to stab Said saying that he was a Somali spying for the Muslims. Other students intervened and Said was spared but quite shaken. Jonathan would not be reconciled, even after Said, as a Christian, agreed to forgive him, so the staff suspended Jonathan for two weeks.

The Sudanese refused to accept his punishment. The other three showed their solidarity with their fellow national by stalking out of the school together after making a very nasty scene, cursing the staff, and insulting the school. We were sad to see them turn away an opportunity to better themselves for which many Ethiopians would have been glad to pay dearly. However, their departure made life simpler for the school, and everybody was relieved to see them go.

Staff

Slowly we got to know some of the support staff despite the language barrier. There was Ato Bedada and Ato Biru who were our security guards, one of whom could be found somewhere nearby to open the gate at almost any time during the day. Both had been in the army in their younger days.

Ato Bedada was a unique character in his own way. He was a habitual drinker and had a special way to try the patience of his superiors as he invented ways to be excused from his innumerable unexcused and inexcusable absences. As an old man, he had married a woman much younger than himself and had many children that were still of elementary school age. His meager earnings couldn't support both his habit and his children. Yet, having them proved very convenient and productive when he felt the need to finagle one more "last" advance on his wages from the wary but compassionate missionary.

Mammitu was the altogether efficient cook at the Academy, who along with Ato Fanta and some female assistants saw to it that the food was prepared in abundance and on time for the 109 students three times a day and that the dining room and kitchen was reasonably clean before the next meal. She was a good manager and loyal worker. She was married to Ato Belai and lived in a nice, new four-room house with a tin roof just next to our house. They had no children. Belai worked as a dresser in a clinic. He invested his money in "garis' and prospered.

CHAPTER 4

Adjustments

D uring those first few months in Ethiopia, our flexibility and adaptability were put to the test. Those were times of major adjustment to living in a completely new situation in a new country, with new culture, new language, new climate, new environment, new job, new roles, new baby with its sickness, new status, and new relationships all around. Maybe we were too naive or too dull and insensitive, but we were not bothered much by any degree of culture shock. My attitude was gung-ho, "Let's go for it!" and Vera's was one of willing cooperation. Life was an adventure. This was an adventure. God was with us, and we were enjoying it.

Addis Ababa

The capital city is found on the southern slope of the Entoto Mountain range in central Shoa. Spread out on the slope covering an area of over 100 square miles (250 square kilometers), its altitude ranges between 7,500 to 8,200 feet (2,300 to 2,500 meters). This location affords Addis Ababa a cool, pleasant climate with temperatures ranging from 4°C in the coolest nights to 20°C during the sunny days, and an average temperature of 16°C.

Established by Queen Taytu in 1886 as *"Addis Ababa"* (meaning *"New Flower"*) because of its agreeable climate and its hot springs, the infant settlement grew in popularity with the courtiers until Emperor Menelik II made it his official capital in 1891.

The later introduction of the Australian eucalyptus tree made the "New Flower" self-sustaining in fuel and building materials, thus assuring its permanence, and in the process immeasurably enhanced the beauty of this flourishing capital.

By our time, Addis Ababa was a cosmopolitan city with a population of over six hundred and forty thousand persons from all eighty-two ethnic and cultural groups within the boundaries of Ethiopia. It was the diplomatic capital of Africa, being the home of the United Nations Economic Commission for Africa and the headquarters of the Organization of African Unity (OAU), as well as boasting over seventy embassies and consular representatives within its boundaries. It was also "home" and headquarters to many international organizations, businesses, and non-governmental organizations.

This city was already the industrial center of the nation. Its factories produced steel, cement, building materials, plastic products, flour, processed foods and beverages, textiles, clothing, shoes, leather goods, and more.

It was the financial capital of the nation as well, boasting headquarters for numerous government and private banks and insurance companies. Its products, its population concentration, and its central location also made Addis the trading center where export/import and wholesale and retail businesses flourished.

By mid-November we felt the need for our first business visit to Addis Ababa. We, along with Dr. and Mrs. Roy and Esther Wert and Gerald and Elaine Stoner decided to go together. Some documents needed to be worked on such as driver's licenses, and some groceries and household supplies needed to be bought.

We set out early Saturday morning and shopped all day until 7:00 p.m. We were introduced to the office of the Mennonite Mission in Ethiopia, to the Menno Bookstore, and to Piazza, the downtown shopping area.

We were amazed at how well we could do business using the English language. Although Ethiopia had never been a British colony, everyone who went to school could understand and speak some English.

We found we could buy most anything we needed in Addis, for a price of course. Bambis was a favorite supermarket for the foreign community featuring everything they wanted, including frozen chicken from the U.S.A. However, we could find most staples in the many Arab and Indian or Armenian shops.

45

Street peddlers were in abundance offering everything imaginable. At first, we found their boldness and persistence intimidating, a lot like the pesky flies—they never seemed to give up. We soon learned to drive a hard bargain. It became a kind of game between buyer and seller.

Then there were the parking boys who offered to "watch" our car for a small token tip.

The most difficult thing to get used to was responding to the many pathetic looking and sounding beggars. But we soon learned that you can't help everybody, and that their survival does not depend on you alone. They were there before you came, and they will be there after you leave. Further, if they get too much, it will only become an incentive for more people to pursue begging as a lucrative trade. Therefore, one does not have to feel guilty every time one passes up an opportunity to fill a beggar's outstretched hand. It is safer to help the poor you know (and there are plenty of them), rather than the poor you don't know.

Homesickness

There were emotional costs in being away from our family and friends. We missed the times of family get-together. We had just missed my brother Paul's wedding in October where he had asked me to officiate, but I had to decline. Then we heard the news that Vera's aunt, Ida King, a single woman past fifty, married an older widower in November. Shortly after that Vera's widowed mother confided that she would be marrying Jacob B. Yoder, also a widower, in the coming summer.

At the same time her younger sister, Vernane, was finishing college and struggling with her feelings towards several boyfriends and was in the process of making a decision that would likely lead to another wedding in the near future.

Around Christmas the tug of home became stronger. We could suffer homesickness, ignore celebrating altogether, or create new traditions of our own as a growing family. At the school, December 25th was to be a working day. Ethiopia celebrated Christmas on January 7th. They did not make a big deal about it as we do in the West. For them "*Pascha*" (Easter),

"Timket" (the baptism of Jesus by John), and *"Meskel"* (the finding of the true cross) were the major celebrated holy days. In African culture, birthdays were not much celebrated nor remembered as calendar events. Most older people did not know the exact day or even year in which they were born.

We were willing to celebrate our Christmas with the Ethiopians on their day, January 7th, but earlier missionaries had set a precedent by making a big all-day get-together on December 25th. Who were we, junior missions associates, to challenge traditions hallowed by many years of observance by the pioneering spiritual giants of the past? So, we had to give way to established tradition though I deeply felt it showed gross cultural insensitivity. This year our missionaries from Addis and Nazareth were to gather at Good Shepherd, the interdenominational school for missionary children in Addis.

On the 25th, all us expatriates abandoned our school to the care of the few Ethiopian staff and went off to Addis for a full day of feasting and celebration that lasted from brunch at 10:00 a.m. through playing basketball, eating the traditional Christmas turkey dinner at 3:30 p.m., hiking, opening gifts at 6:00 p.m., then dessert and fellowship until 8:00 p.m. after which we returned home surfeited and tired and happy. It had been a "real Christmas," as genuine and as enjoyable as any we could have missed back home.

Back at school on Saturday, the 23rd, Emperor Haile Selassie had passed by on his way to visit the sugar estates of Wonji and Shoa. Upon his return, he found the students waiting for him on the road. Without the knowledge of the director or any teachers, they had stopped his motorcade and invited him in to visit their school. They proudly showed him their rooms all decorated for Christmas. He presented them with 300 birr "to buy candy for Christmas." However, the faculty decided to use it to put on a Christmas banquet with *"doro wat"* (chicken) for the students. It was the highlight social event of the year.

Some weeks later a high government official came to school and scolded the students severely for their bad behavior in stopping the emperor's motorcade. Such behavior was in line with ancient tradition and might still be excused in the remote rural areas, but it was definitely not becoming of "civilized" students! Our administrators apologized on behalf of the students and for themselves for not being vigilant on that Saturday afternoon. It did not happen again.

Over Christmas vacation the maintenance men started to build the kitchen cupboards in our house. I built some bookshelves in the living room and a sewing table for Vera. We went to Addis and did a bit of Christmas shopping, using a monetary gift from my folks to buy Cindy a tricycle and a doll buggy. I also made her a cute little doll crib and a cupboard for her dishes. On January 7th, the Ethiopian day for Christmas, we had our own nuclear family celebration.

Easter

I wake up on Easter Sunday morning. I hear the glad song of birds exuberantly voicing their morning "devotions" and the distant crowing of roosters. These are the sounds of the heralding of the dawn, of creation heralding the good news of the rising of the sun.

In a similar way, we Christians welcome Easter, heralding the rising of the Son from the darkness of the tomb to bring light to a dark world, to bring warm rays of hope to the despairing human heart. Death is defeated!

Our Easter celebration is a "crowing" of the good news of victory over death. Our mission in life is to ever "crow" this bit of good news every morning of the year. Roosters do not all crow equally well. Some proclaimers "crow" more eloquently than others, and some "crow" without eloquence. But we all can and must "crow."

The Seasons

In one sense, there are basically two seasons in Ethiopia, the dry season ("*buggah*") and the rainy season ("*krempt*"). However, altitude is the deciding factor in determining the great differences in the weather patterns in the different regions. Lowlands are hotter and dryer; Highlands are cooler and have more rainfall.

In Nazareth, at 5,000 feet, the long dry season begins when the rains stop in late September and continues into early June. We found the nights to be very balmy and pleasant. With only one light cover, we could sleep well with the windows open. The mornings were fresh and warm and invigorating.

However, around 9:00 a.m., a strong prevailing breeze would begin to blow in from the eastern desert. It would increase in velocity until it became a dry, scorching-hot, dust-laden blast over the zenith of the day. Around 5:00 p.m., it would begin to wane, and by 6:00 o'clock, when the sun touched the rim of the escarpment behind us, all was perfectly calm. This pattern started mildly in mid-September and picked up momentum until it reached its cruelest in May, with a possible exception known as the "small rains" which were usually very small indeed at Nazareth, during February or March.

The eastern winds were always dry, having blown up from the Arabian and Danakil deserts, while the western winds were cool and moist, having blown in from the Atlantic Ocean across the vast green west African jungles. They dropped moisture all along, keeping the jungles green as they gained altitude until they reached the Ethiopian highlands where they dropped the last of their abundant moisture for the crops. Then they continued their journey dry and barren across the eastern desert and over Arabia.

I did not like the prevailing east wind at all. I would leave our house after lunch all combed and washed. By the time I reached my classroom 400 yards away, I felt dirty and unkempt. My shoes needed shining, and my trouser legs had turned grey. The dust got into everything. Our eyes were usually red and sore. The books we picked up, the chairs we sat on, the table we leaned on, and the duplicating machine were dusty. Everything had to be protected or dusted before we could use it without getting dirty.

Outside the wind howled every day. It sucked all the sap out of the trees and plants. Trees and shrubs lost most of their leaves, the grass turned brown and blew away, and the flowers and even the weeds died. Every lorry or car that whizzed past left a billow of dust rolling off the road.

The big rains ("*krempt*") came from late June through early September, and usually provided enough rain to produce a good crop. Whenever the prevailing east wind changed directions and blew from the west, then we could safely predict that in three or four days there would be rain.

I was always amazed how that one first rain could transform our parched, dull, dusty, grey desert into a garden of Eden overnight. The atmosphere was so clean and fresh and the air so cool and pleasant. The smell of moisture and wet soil and of growing things was so refreshing.

Twelve hours after a rain, little shoots of green would show where the grey-brown grass had blown away. The birds and frogs joined together to sing their thanks. The farmers were out in their fields with their plows, turning the rain-softened soil, shouting encouragement and directions to their sweating oxen. There was more cheer in their greetings, more spring in their steps, and new hope in their hearts.

We loved Nazareth in the rainy season. It was transformed into a virtual paradise. We planted gardens and watched them grow and produce abundant supplies of potatoes, peas, beans, onions, pumpkins, and corn. The farmers quickly turned the dull, grey, sun-burnt fields into freshly plowed, clean, brown patches of soil where they planted their seeds. In a few days, these would turn a pale light green sheen as the seeds sprouted, then a darker rich deep green as the plants grew towards maturity. Tropical flowers and flowering shrubs as well as flowering trees turned many yards and even streets into a riot of color.

Most of the rain fell in the evenings or at night, leaving the days free for the sun and the farmers to do their work. Even though the rain was heavy, the light sandy soil could be plowed the next morning.

June was plowing and planting time, when all the farmers arose at 5:00 a.m. to get their oxen and plows ready in order to be in the field at the first streak of dawn. You could hear them whooping and hollering commands and encouragement to their animals and the frequent crack of the whip to reinforce with a threat where encouragement failed to bring the desired results. The oxen seemed to understand the directions, for the farmer steered his one-handled wooden plow with one hand and carried his whip in the other hand, depending only on his words and his whip to guide the team.

July and August were taken up with the tasks of weeding and cultivating the crops. This was all done by hand. Women and children were recruited to help with this back-bending and tedious task. Neighbors often worked together in groups to make work into a social event: "Today in your field, tomorrow in my field."

By mid-September, the crops were left to ripen. The rains stopped, and the atmosphere became very clear and sunny. The roadsides and wastelands blossomed out in brilliant gold-hued *"meskel"* daisies, marking the end of *krempt*, the rainy season, and the beginning of *buggah*, the dry season with all the excitement of harvest time. The flowers also reminded one that it was the Ethiopian month of *"Meskram,"* the first month of the Ethiopian calendar and the time of *Meskel,* when Ethiopians celebrated the finding of the true cross.

After Meskel, the harvest began. The peasants cut the grain with a short sickle, much the same as they did in the time of Abraham. This again was a man's job, and they often worked in groups, singing together as they worked. Women often helped to tie the cut grain in bundles and carry it to a central place to be stacked to dry until the threshing time. The work was hard and laborious, but the mood was usually one of joy and thankfulness. A good harvest spells life, and a poor harvest means hunger and suffering.

The threshing was also very hard work. First, threshing the grain, separating the seeds from its stalk or straw required the preparation of a "threshing floor." This was made by leveling a large circular area of ground near the stacks of grain, then smearing the circle with a mixture of fresh cow dung and water. This was usually the women's job. When this mixture dried, it formed a tight plastic-like seal that prevented the sandy soil from mixing with the grain.

Bundles of grain were then moved from the stacks and spread out on the floor. Cattle or donkeys were then brought to tread on the grain, walking around and around in circles, dislodging the kernels from the stocks.

After the grain was thoroughly trampled, the farmer would begin the task of separating the kernels from the chaff. Using a wooden fork, the farmer would rake off the loose straw and the smaller heavy seeds would remain on the pile.

Then, the process of winnowing began. Using a wooden shovel, he would throw the mixture of grain with the chaff into the air. Here he needed the help of a nice breeze. The wind, when it cooperated, blew the chaff and straw away, and the clean grain, being heavier, fell close by in a separate pile. The clean grain would be put into sacks and carried home to the storage place. The straw was stacked in neat piles to provide forage for the animals during the next dry season. All this work was done by hand.

Once the threshing operation began, the careful farmer would not rest or sleep at his house until it was completed. For as many days as it took, he would sleep with a few of his sons or neighbors at the threshing floor. If he did not, he could be sure that thieves would make his work lighter by removing the bulk of the not-yet cleaned grain before morning.

The few sacks that the farmer ultimately took home, minus a third for his landlord, represented most of his family's annual income, that which would feed and clothe his family and educate or buy medicine for his children. He must guard it jealously and desperately.

Threshing was usually completed by January. By this time, it was deep into the long dry season. The landscape had turned dusty grey, brown; trees kept only a basic facade of dull, dusty green leaves. Skinny cattle and goats accompanied by their dirty, tattered child-shepherds roamed at will, scavenging some remnants of grass or stalks of wheat or maize from the bone-dry and barren fields. The daily hot, searing winds sucked up all the moisture from the landscape. Water levels on the ponds went down by half an inch per day. One by one all the water holes dried up.

With the drying of the water holes, the cattle had to make the twice or thrice weekly journey from their homes as far as thirty kilometers to the river to gorge themselves with its warm putrid waters so they might survive until the next journey.

Every day, huge herds of complaining cattle and noisy goats made their dusty way slowly past our place, blocking traffic and causing a general commotion, going down to the Awash River in the morning and as slowly, returning in the afternoon.

Women, who were lucky and could afford it, paid a small fee which allowed them to carry clean water from the local town water spigot.

Now everything slipped into a survival mode until the next rainy season would renew hope and bring new life.

Ethiopian Cuisine

Some things were quite easy to adjust to, and one of those things was the food. Ethiopian cuisine is unique, special in this world. Its base is *"enjera"* which is made from *"teff."* Traditionally, teff is grown and used for human consumption only in Ethiopia, although it has been introduced in Kentucky and other states as excellent fodder for racehorses. Even its straw is very rich in protein and iron.

The teff plant looks very much like grass; although, it is actually an annual cereal grain. The mature plant stands from twenty-four to thirty-six inches tall and has a cluster of seeds at the top that looks every bit like a grass seed stem. In the husks are thousands of the tinniest seeds you ever saw. A seed is about one millimeter in diameter. One thousand seeds make about 0.3 grams. In fact, the word "teff" comes from a root which means "lost," for that is what happens when the seed is dropped. These seeds are harvested like any other cereal grain and ground into the finest flour.

The teff flour is mixed with water and a starter yeast making a batter that is allowed to soak and ferment for two or three days. This batter is then poured evenly over a hot clay *"mitad"* or smooth circular grill that is about eighteen to twenty inches in diameter. It is covered with a lid traditionally made with a mixture of cow dung and clay, fashioned and dried in a slightly conical shape with a handle on top. In a few minutes, a nice, thin spongy pancake-like *enjera* is ready to peel off the smooth grill. It is soft and flexible, like a quarter-inch thick foam napkin.

This *enjera* is eaten by breaking off a bite-sized piece with the right hand, scooping up some of the *"wat"* or sauce with it and popping it all into one's mouth. *Enjera* itself has a slightly sour, fermented taste and smell. Yet when eaten with *wat*, it adds a very pleasant flavor that asks for another bite.

There are as many kinds of *wat* as there are cooks, for each follows her own recipe inherited from her ancestors and maybe modified to suit personal or husband's taste. There are the very hot *"wats"* or sauces that make your eyes water and your nose run. These contain a lot of *"berberi,"* which is a mixture of several spices including a lot of small, dried chilies or red peppers ground to a powder. They also have an abundance of hot red onions chopped and cooked to a dark brown mash, spiced ghee or oil, and some meat such as chicken, goat, or mutton, and possibly eggs, or if there is no meat, perhaps just lentils or peas.

Then there are the "cold" wats which do not have the hot *berberi*.

These may have tumeric and look yellow. They may be a mixture of cooked vegetables such as cabbage, carrots, green chilies, onions, and potatoes, or cooked spinach, or they may be lentils or peas, or an uncooked salad of chopped up tomatoes, lettuce, and sweet peppers.

Enjera b'wat is served on a large tray with a diameter slightly smaller than that of the *enjera*. One or two *enjera* are spread out in the tray. Then the different *wats* are ladled out in little piles on top of the *enjera*. Sometimes a pile of fresh cottage cheese adds a definite something special to the spread. More *enjera* are placed along the edge of the tray like folded napkins. It is from these folded ones that the diners start their feast. The men in the family or the guests will be served first.

After washing their hands, the diners gather around this tray and begin breaking off pieces of *enjera* and scooping up *wat* and eating it together.

Sometimes to show friendship and good will, they make a very large handful of the *enjera* and *wat* (*"goursha"*) and pop it into their hostess or host's mouth as she or he stands by serving.

While the feasting goes on, the host or hostess or servant will add *wat* or *enjera* as needed. In the end they may eat all that is in the tray, though in good Ethiopian tradition, the tray should never be emptied entirely. The hostess should see to it that all are completely satisfied.

More will be added to the tray and fed to the children and women in the kitchen, then the servants will have their turn, and what they don't finish will be given to the beggar at the gate or to the dogs. Though it seems that food is there in abundance, really nothing is wasted.

Bureaucracy

Another adjustment was getting used to the antiquated system of bureaucratic red tape one had to endure in getting any service from the government.

Getting packages through the post office was a classic example. Whenever a package came, it was locked in a box by the customs department. They would put a notice in your mailbox. When you came to collect the package, you would first have to drive downtown to the customs office to collect the one and only official who was authorized to open the box in the post office. If he was not to be found present, then you could wait for him to show up, or you could go on your way and try again another day.

If this was your lucky day, and you could persuade him to leave his busy work to come with you, then you would take him to the post office in your vehicle. On the way he would remind you of how poorly paid government employees are, and of his many children and the high cost of living these days. He might even be so bold as to openly suggest that a gift was in order.

Upon arrival at the post office, he would shuffle slowly into the back room and slowly unlock the customs box and search for your package. Finally, he would bring it out, look at it slowly and ask you what was inside, even though it was written in clear print on the form what it was and that it was an "Unsolicited gift of no commercial value."

Then you would be asked to pay the eighty cents storage charge, and they would fill out some forms. Then you would take the customs man carrying your package back to the customs office.

There, after entering the inner security area, he would ask you to open it while he watched. Then he would call his colleague, and consultations would take place in their language. Finally, he would inform you that it was a very valuable thing you just imported and that there would be a very high tax on it.

It was then up to you to politely convince him that you did not order it, that you did not pay anything for it, that it was an unsolicited gift from your very dear mother-in-law who cares very much about you, and who out of her very deep concern for your well-being, took it upon herself to see that we did not have to suffer any longer for the lack of this thing. He knew from past experience that missionaries never paid bribes, so he eventually would give up and let us take the thing home.

Imagine this official's surprise when I prevailed upon my dear mother to send us two pounds of Alberta's famous Netted Gem seed potatoes by air mail from Canada in January. By the time I received the notice in the mail and got around to collecting the package, it had lain in the customs box for two weeks. The label plainly said, "Potatoes, no commercial value." There were millions of cheap little potatoes available in the local market. Why would this strange white man be receiving potatoes in the mail?

Puzzlement lined the official's brow, and deep suspicion shone out of his normally sleepy eyes as he handed me the smelly package and commanded me to open it. His now hawk-like piercing gaze fastened on the package as I carefully opened it, and his jaw dropped a bit in amazement when I unwrapped a soggy dripping plastic bag full of stinking rotten potatoes. The room was quickly filling with the odors of a town market, so the man, shaking his head at the unfathomable ways of the *ferinj*, hurriedly stamped the forms and sent me on my way carrying my precious dripping bag of stinking Netted Gems. No "gifts" or "something for tea" asked this time!

I still don't know if it was the Canadian cold or the plastic wrap in a hot customs box that made the potatoes rot, but there was still life in some of them, and I managed to put twenty-two plants in the ground. However, my hoped-for major scientific breakthrough was a disappointment. What is a horticultural marvel in the cool northern "land of the midnight sun" did not do well at all in the twelve-hour days at the equator! That which was "Netted Gems" in Alberta certainly were not "gems" in Ethiopia! That was one of my early lessons in tropical horticulture.

Security

I grew up in a community where we never locked our doors, not even when we went away on a vacation. Our house, tool shed, barn, automobile, even gas tanks were left unlocked. Usually, we even left the keys in the ignition switches on our car, truck, or tractor. We hardly knew the use of locks.

Now we were living in a "fortress" of a house with steel bars on our windows, locks on our steel doors, a high brick wall around our brick house, a locked steel gate at the entrance, and our lookout guard, Illihu, on duty until ten p.m. I really doubted if all this was necessary. Weren't we overdoing it a bit? The people seemed so good and friendly; surely, they would not stoop so low as to steal!

The first week we were in our new home, Vera washed a rug and put it out to dry on the front porch. Never mind that the day guard was not on duty, nor that the steel gate was open. A few hours later, she noticed it was gone. We decided we had better keep the gate closed during the hours the guard was not on duty.

A few days later after dark, the guard was on duty and the gate was securely closed, supper was over, and we were resting. Suddenly, we heard Illihu outside running towards the front yard and shouting; then there were excited voices and shouting in the street outside. We were newcomers and did not understand what was going on in the dark.

Soon Gerald Stoner came in and explained that a thief had crawled over the wall and had stolen the watchman's prized heavy coat that he had laid aside while he did some gardening duties. Illihu had just come around the corner from the back of the house in time to see the thief making for the wall. He hollered, then he noticed that his coat was not on the porch where he had laid it. Then he really shouted and ran after the thief. The thief sprinted over the seven-foot wall, knocking a couple of loose bricks off and falling on the other side.

Illihu's frantic shouting roused his neighbors who instantly came out and apprehended the thief. The thief resisted arrest, and there was a big fight until they beat him down into submission. He got a bad cut on his head which was bleeding. The thief cursed and swore at his arresters, slandering them as disloyal Ethiopians (Why should they stick up for and protect this disgusting foreigner while arresting a fellow Ethiopian?). Illihu wanted to take him to the police and charge him with theft of his coat. Of course, Mr. Stoner would drive him there.

First, they took the unsuccessful thief to the hospital and put several stitches in his scalp to stop the blood flow, then they took him to the police who were glad to have a thief brought to them without expending any energy on their part. Illihu would have to pay a "fee" of fifty "birr" to press charges. Such was Ethiopia's justice system at its finest. Now that was about two month's wages for poor Illihu, but he was adamant that the thief stole his coat, so he must be punished. The thief was kept in custody until Illihu could raise the money; then he was sentenced to six months in the local jail. Illihu was pleased. Justice was served!

Now we of the Mission should have been the ones to lay the charges and pay the expenses. However, we had a policy that we did not press charges for two reasons. First, we held to a peace theology that urges us to love and forgive our enemies and to do good to those that do us wrong. We couldn't quite see that putting a poor hungry unemployed thief in an Ethiopian jail for six months was really in line with the meaning of "returning good for evil."

The second reason was because we were "rich" guests in a country whose culture and connections we did not understand. If we became people who fought back, certainly we would generate enmity, and we could never predict how or when our unknown antagonists would strike back. For us it made better sense to suffer a little wrong now and again and live in peace with all in the society. When you are a guest in a foreign land, the best security is to have good relations with the local people.

Other missionaries talked of workers making off with little things like sugar, small tools, or articles of clothing. We never encountered that problem with those who worked in our house. If it happened, we never became aware.

However, one time when we were visiting our friend's house, their male worker made off with the pink bottom to Vera's two-piece swimming outfit. We found that to be a bit amusing, especially when we tried to imagine how and where he would wear it! But it was also quite annoying, for after all, bottomless swimming was not yet fashionable among missionaries in those days!

Traffic

I was impressed by the kinds of trucks that rattled or chugged or roared past our place. Ancient pre-World War II Italian trucks still hauled sugar or building stones to Nazareth. Some of them burned a distillate mix of fuel, oil, and water. Some of them seemed to be equipped with a kind of governor that made the motor alternate between a full throttle roar and then a brief relaxed idle, a regular persistent on again, off again, on again, off again pattern.

The more modern trucks were all European. They sometimes pulled very heavy four-wheel trailers, but there were no semi-tractor-trailer rigs. I understood why when I saw the kinds of roads they had to negotiate in the mountains to the north. Some places there were dozens of sharp switch backs where the road zigzagged straight up the mountain and then zigzagged straight down the other side. It was hard to imagine these big lorries making these hairpin turns at all.

Speaking of roads, the one connecting Addis to Nazareth would not have been so bad had it not been so overburdened with livestock. The Nazareth "big market" was a major collecting point for marketable cattle and sheep and goats from the widely scattered communities of the Awash Valley to the east and Arussi Province to the south. Cattle buyers would come from Addis and buy up thousands of animals and then herd them to the city in huge droves driven by herders on foot. These joined the ever-present abundance of regular pedestrian traffic, the homo sapiens, cattle, goats, sheep, donkeys, and dogs.

It was a three-day journey, and the tired animals would clog up the road to vehicle traffic. No matter how loud or how long the irate driver honked his horn, it had little impact on the tired, dazed animals as they shuffled along slowly to their slaughter like zombies in a trance.

Enterprising capitalists should have spotted a golden opportunity to launch a livestock trucking business. Surely the kilograms lost on each animal that made that grueling three-day trek without grass or fodder would have easily covered the costs of hiring the lorry. Additionally, the fatter, more tender meat would have brought a better price on the market. Certainly, it would earn the good will of the motorists who had to buck livestock all the way from Nazareth to Addis. The thinking of a greenhorn western capitalist!

Such variety and quantity of traffic made driving hazardous at best. In fact, in the three years we lived in Nazareth, we saw the remains of more road accidents than we had seen in our entire lifetime before. Besides these road conditions, the combination of drinking and driving had a lot to do with this heavy toll in loss of life and destruction of property and permanent disability. There seemed to be no restrictions on alcohol intake.

Another factor was the inexperience of the people with speed. Moving from the donkey age into the age of high-speed mechanized transport in one generation is a phenomenal adjustment at best. Drivers and pedestrians alike showed this lack of understanding of speed and how quickly it can kill.

One day a bus Vera and I were riding in struck a donkey. It

must have had its hind legs or back broken because it couldn't walk. Perhaps it was stunned, or it was slowly trying to think about what had happened. It just sat there on the road in resigned silence. A pitiful sight. Another time we chanced upon the scene of an accident where a lorry had plowed into a herd of cows. We counted at least nine carcasses scattered around. Several others were in various stages of woundedness to dying.

On the way home from a missionary conference in Addis Ababa one night, we came upon the scene of an accident. A big lorry had come around a sharp curve with considerable speed and plowed into a crowd of workers who had just come out from their shift at a textile factory near the bridge at Akaki. Five men were lying on the road. One had his face smashed and was dying. One was unconscious. One had an injured back and a broken arm. The others were battered badly. The driver was so drunk he could hardly walk.

On two occasions after our arrival, buses loaded with passengers had failed to negotiate the big curve where the highway begins its descent into Nazareth and went rolling down the steep boulder-strewn hillside. Several died, and many were hospitalized. On at least one of these occasions the driver was drunk.

It seemed to be the accepted practice to drink and drive. Every town had dozens of bars. People said that many truck drivers traveling at night would stop for a drink in every town to keep awake. One of the Indian teachers insisted that the reason the king granted licenses to so many bars was so that the poor can drink and forget their misery. It may be so. Later, we found out that the king also owned the St. George's Brewery!

It is sobering to remember that the official cause of the untimely death of the king's favorite son and Crown Prince, the Duke of Harar, was that his car was struck by a speeding drunken driver. An unofficial and more widely believed version had it that the Crown Prince was assassinated for playing around with a general's wife and an "accident" was manufactured to give a respectable cause of death for the noble gentleman.

A few months before our furlough, Almaz's little three-year-old girl, Ruthie, ran across the road from our gate without looking and was struck by a car. We first thought she would be killed, but much to our relief, she was only stunned and scratched. The driver of the car stopped and offered to rush her and us to the hospital.

An examination revealed that she was okay. We thanked God for that. It was a powerful lesson for our girls who were her playmates. They always looked both ways before crossing after that, and even if the coming vehicle was a mile away, they would not cross until it passed.

Medicine and Eye Teeth

I was furious. Because of not knowing the language, I had to call in a friend to help me scold Ato Illihu properly. Our guard's one and one-half year-old child was sick with dysentery, so we took him to the clinic. The nurse gave him a penicillin shot and told the mother to bring him back every day for five days for additional shots. The mother apparently decided that it might cost her too much money although our worker's medicine was free to them. They took the child to a local witch doctor instead.

This uncertified practitioner mustered all his inherited medical wisdom and extracted the four "offending" eye teeth. Since they hadn't emerged yet, this meant that he had to cut the gums first to dig them out. This he did with unsterilized instruments and no anesthesia! The poor baby still had dysentery despite such effective treatment. In addition, he now had such a swollen mouth that he couldn't even suck and was getting terribly dehydrated.

The overpowered, thoroughly chastened, and intimidated Illihu promised to take the baby back to the clinic. But would he? "A man convinced against his will is of the same opinion still!"

I was so angry that I could hardly eat, but after cooling down and thinking about it more deeply, I could see that his action appeared logical to him and was administered with the deepest concern and love that a father can have for his child. I reflected further that he was just as logical, and his chosen remedy was about as effective as some of the more bizarre beliefs and practices many gullible people in our society steadfastly live and die by.

The problem was that the peasants believed that modern medicine must work an instant cure, or it wasn't any good. Why come back tomorrow if it did not help today?

On the other hand, the witch doctor's cure takes considerable time, but it is effective in the long run. And it doesn't require coming back every day. Everybody knows that the time-honored remedy of removing the baby's eye teeth is effective in stopping dysentery. All adults are living evidence. They all had dysentery sometime in their childhood, and they all had their eye teeth removed, and they are all alive today, and they don't have dysentery now! So, who in their right mind would even think of questioning such overwhelming evidence and such plain logic? (Don't mention all the babies who died of dysentery, tetanus, infection, or dehydration after their eye teeth were removed. God had his own reasons to take them back that we ought not question!)

Another problem is money. They don't like to spend money on modern medicine and can hardly find even five birr when a child is sick. However, they always find something big like a goat or sheep that might be worth a hundred birr for the witch doctor! Isn't it logical that "You get what you pay for"?

Again, upon reflecting, it is really more a matter of confidence than absolute poverty that decides their preferences. The old ways are tried and true. The new ways may work for some but are riskier. A poor person cannot afford to take a risk. It is better to be content with the tried and true and leave the rest to God who has final say.

Political Unrest

A few weeks before Easter, April 1968, some university students staged a demonstration in protest of a western fashion show being held in Addis Ababa. Predictably, in true imperial authoritarian style which allows no protest save that which is designed and orchestrated by the government, police were sent in to stop it. Of course, a riot broke out.

High school and then elementary school students joined in. Then the street boys and gangs of hoodlums who don't go to school at all got involved. They broke into buildings, destroyed buses, and killed several people. Then the army was called in to put down the riot.

His Majesty ordered all the students (who weren't in jail) to go back to school.

The students refused to return unless their comrades were released from jail, so the authorities declared all schools closed until after Easter. That included all government schools in Addis, Nazareth, and other towns. The Bible Academy was not affected by this action, but things were tense for a few days. The authorities even called a squadron of tanks from the army base near the Academy to go to Addis as a precaution. Just think of it, tanks against students!

This was the beginning of a series of protests, demonstrations, and strikes led by students that re-occurred each year that would lead ultimately to the overthrow of the government several years later.

Students discovered that they did have a voice, that they may not be appreciated, but they were heard. They did not have to be simple "sheep" to accept whatever their rulers decided. Theirs was a political awakening that transformed them forever. Never again would they be simple loyal subjects without an idea or opinion of their own worthy of expression. The days of oppressive totalitarianism were by no means over, but they were numbered.

Being a recent arrival to Ethiopia, I was, at first, impressed by the people's seeming devotion to their beloved emperor. His portrait hung in every room of every public building and in many private homes as well. No one would ever say anything disrespectful of him. The tightly controlled press heaped adulation and praise on him, giving him credit for every achievement and every wise thought and decision. Buildings, streets, institutions, and monuments were built and named in his honor. Foreign governments honored him and brought a lot of aid to Ethiopia on his account. People thronged to every occasion where he made a public appearance lining the streets, waving flags or branches, singing, and ululating or shouting their loyalty.

Appearances can be deceptive. It was only after the student riots in April that we began to notice that all was not as it seemed on the surface. Men started talking in low muffled tones their deep dissatisfactions and fears. Students were much more open to share the gossip that was passing around underground.

I learned that books and magazines perceived to be critical were vigorously banned, that all press and radio activities were strictly censored, even mail was opened, and that His Majesty had three separate intelligence agencies doing their surveillance work throughout the Empire, even checking on each other.

We heard of detentions, disappearances, and mysterious assassinations. They said that after the big coup attempt in 1960, there had been at least three additional attempts that failed. Some of Ethiopia's best political minds were hanged. Now potential rivals saw the emperor's life as charmed and were only waiting for him to die.

In approved histories and magazine and newspaper articles, and in public speeches, the savagery and atrocities of the Italians was always played up, and the patriotism of the aristocracy and the Ethiopian people and the bravery and heroism of the emperor were always magnified.

Now, we heard unofficial versions of that history that were not available and not even allowed to be quoted or referred to. Critics accused the emperor of cowardice in having fled to England while the patriots remained carrying on the fight against the Italians from the forests for the full duration of the five-year occupation. They felt he should have stayed and fought alongside his brave people. They saw him as a manipulator who cleverly worked his way into favor with the Allies who defeated the Italians and installed him as their puppet king on the imperial throne.

To mollify the top patriots who felt bypassed in having any say in the post Italian era government, Haile Selassie bought their silence and their allegiance by giving them huge tracts of land, some as big as 15-25,000 acres with the peasants who owned them, and warned them that if they valued their lives, they would enjoy farming and would stay out of politics.

For the last thirty years, these peasants had been forced to pay high rent or share produce and labor for the privilege of living on and farming the land they and their ancestors owned since ancient times. I was assured by the students that those people had not forgotten this great injustice. To them, the Italians were less cruel, more dependable, fairer, and provided more benefits than the imperial "liberation" forces. Many of the non-Amhara people looked at the Italians as only another overlord, perhaps to be preferred to the Amhara as overlords. Rumors were that in some areas, peasants were secretly smuggling in weapons with the aim of retaking their land from the aristocracy by force.

CHAPTER 5

Understanding Ethiopia

I write this chapter with a certain amount of trepidation and feelings of vulnerability. As an outside observer, I realize that my perceptions are faulty at best and may differ from that of an insider. There is always danger of gross misunderstanding and generalization. The following is simply a snapshot, a single glimpse of what I observed and learned during my stay in that great and diverse land of eighty different cultures. The whole is so much more complex than my simple poorly informed outsider sometimes-biased observations.

Also, the feudal Ethiopia we experienced some fifty years ago has since undergone a revolution and much change as it struggles to become a modern nation. At that time, it was a nation with a population of twenty-eight million with a literacy rate of less than five percent and boasted one small university. Today most of the 115 million Ethiopians can read and write and it has at least thirty-five universities. Ethiopia today is not the same as it was fifty years ago.

Its History

We found Ethiopia to have a most fascinating and unique history, little known to the western world. The existence of Ethiopia has been known since the beginning of the Biblical record. Ancient Hebrews knew Ethiopia as the land of "Cush" mentioned in Genesis 2:13 as the land through which the second river of Eden, the Gihon, passes. It was named after the son of Ham whose descendants populated the southernmost parts of Arabia and spilled over into those parts of Africa known to the Hebrews (Gen. 10:6-8; I Chron. 1:8-10).

References in the Old Testament to "Cush" or "Ethiopia" are

usually general, referring to the darker race (Jer. 13:23) of people living in the furthest known lands to the south and southwest. To the Hebrews "Ethiopia" or "Cush" has no known southwestern boundary. Sometimes it is only the source of countless hordes of nameless hostile invaders (II Chron. 21:16; Jer. 46:9). Sometimes the name of their king is known (II Chron. 14:9-13; 16:8; Isa. 37:9). And sometimes they are real people with whom Israel shares something of her faith and culture (II Sam. 18:21-32). Moses, for example married a "Cushite" wife (Nu. 12:1) and was criticized for doing so.

Referring to Cush, the son of Ham in the Genesis account, the Chronicles of Ethiopia list the first kings, "and Cush begat Aethiops, and Aethiops begat Aksumawi...." Aksumawi is the legendary founder of the city of Aksum, the earliest capital city of Ethiopia.

The Greeks knew this region as "Aithiopia" (meaning "burnt face") which extended south of Egypt from the first cataract of the Nile through Nubia, eastern Sudan, and most of modern Ethiopia including both sides of the Red Sea. Ancient Egyptian inscriptions show that the Pharaohs used to send ships to the "Land of Punt" in the southern Red Sea and Gulf of Aden area to bring back incense, ivory, gold, and spices.

An ancient Ethiopian legend holds that Tamrin, a Sabean merchant, returned to his country and told Makeda, his beautiful and powerful queen, about a peaceful and powerful monarch in far off Israel who was famous for his wisdom. This queen was fascinated by the report and decided to pay King Solomon a visit.

Queen Makeda went with a caravan of 797 camels and mules laden with gifts worthy of the great Queen of Sheba that she was. After many days she arrived in Jerusalem. King Solomon was as impressed with Makeda's beauty as she was with his wisdom. He at once fell in love with her and said in his heart: "A woman of such splendid beauty has come to me from the ends of the earth. Will God give me seed in her?"

After staying for some time, she was overcome by Solomon's cunning and seduction and after returning to her realm, she bore a son by him whom she called "Menelik." She gave up the worship of the Sun to worship the one true God who created the universe. When Menelik was old enough, she sent him along with a number of sons of courtiers to Solomon's court to be educated by his father in the wisdom and traditions of the Hebrews.

After completing his training, Menelik returned to Sheba and was crowned king of the Sabeans. He expanded his empire across both sides of the Red Sea and promoted the Hebrew religion and customs throughout his domains (cf. I Kings 10:1-13).

Legend also holds that the original Ark of the Covenant was stolen by Menelik from the temple in Jerusalem and brought with him when he returned to Ethiopia. It supposedly still resides under the careful protection of the monks in a special chapel sanctuary in the Church of St. Mary of Zion in Aksum. In their zeal they will not allow anyone, neither the emperor, the archbishop, the priests, the people, the tourist, nor the scholar to view it. One priest/monk is ordained for life to guard it night and day and allows no one to see it.

Since the time of Menelik I, significant migrations of Semitic peoples from southern Arabia across the Red Sea to the Horn of Africa occurred. These Semites intermarried with the local Cushites, blending their races and cultures.

The ancient town of Aksum in Tigre, according to legend, was the capital of Makeda, the Queen of Sheba who ruled both sides of the Red Sea. After a long period of decline, in the first century A.D., its fortunes turned as it became the center of what was known as the "Aksumite Empire" which dominated the region for about seven centuries, more or less parallel with the Roman Empire.

A new written language known as "Ge'ez" evolved, which made the flourishing of their empire and civilization possible. They also accepted and promoted Christianity as the official state religion around 333 A.D. They traded with the Middle Eastern countries and India, minted coins of gold, silver, and bronze, built quality stone buildings, and erected monolithic, intricately carved stelae that stand as high as ninety feet. In the 4th century A.D., King Ezana added Meroe and much of Sudan to his empire. In the 6th century, King Kaleb occupied a part of southern Arabia for some time.

A subject of much curiosity has been as to whether the unnamed "Ethiopian eunuch" of the Acts account (8:26-40) could have been the one to introduce Christianity into Ethiopia. "Candace" was really the title given to the queen mother whose treasury he superintended, and who ruled a large territory from her capital at Meroe. This sizable city was located over 1600 miles up the Nile from Egypt in Sudan, about 200 miles north of Khartoum where the Blue Nile merges with the White Nile. To the Biblical writer, this was also a part of "Ethiopia" at that time.

It is only normal to assume that a government official, a literate proselyte, who would travel almost 2,000 miles by horse and chariot "to Jerusalem to worship" and back again over the same rough track, and who would choose the book of Isaiah as his recreational reading material to shorten the long journey, might also be a man who would enthusiastically promote the new insights he gained through his encounter with the evangelist, Philip, throughout his queen's empire.

Less certain but highly possible, a story circulated that the Apostle Matthew spread the Gospel as far south as Aksum in the first century.

However, it is widely accepted that Christianity was established in Ethiopia around 333 A.D. when Frumentius was ordained as the first *"Abuna"* or bishop of the Coptic Church in Ethiopia. He was known as "Abba Salama" or "Father of Peace."

It took many centuries for the new faith to become firmly established among the common people. In fact, the task was never completed. The translation of Scripture was limited to the Ge'ez version which was translated from Syriac.

Because of the failure to present the gospel in the different vernaculars of the many ethnic groups that made up the Ethiopian Empire, Christianity only very slowly penetrated deeply into their cultures. It was an imperial religion and was spread as much by conquest and cultural domination as it was by the monks who undertook the missionary challenge.

In less than a century later, the Arabs had spread their new religion of "Islam" across Arabia, the Middle East, North Africa, and into Spain and Portugal. Their method was "Jihad" or "Holy War," a bloody and fiery conquest that forcefully persuaded the Christian communities and pagans alike that it was in their vital interests to convert to the new religion of the day. Those that were not deeply rooted to the truth of the Christian Gospel were overpowered. Christians were reduced to small, isolated persecuted minorities in the Middle East and Egypt and across North Africa.

Even Ethiopia was not spared. In the centuries that followed, again and again, Islamic jihad was raised against the Ethiopians, or "Abyssinians" as they were then called. Again and again, the Ethiopians heroically resisted, and their highland plateau with its deep impenetrable gorges served its people well as a fortress. Ethiopia remained, to use Theodoros' term, "an island of Christianity in a sea of Islam." From time to time, the Empire was renewed by strong emperors such as Amde Zion, Kaleb, Zara Yacob, Theodoros II, Yohannes, and Menelik II.

Again in 1530-43, the fierce warrior, Ahmed Gragn ("The left-handed"), led a vicious holy war to take Christian Ethiopia for Islam. The Ethiopians were hard pressed and in desperation, appealed to the Portuguese for assistance. About 400 Portuguese soldiers came to their rescue and defeated the Muslims. Ahmed Gragn was killed, and Christian Abyssinia was spared.

Traces of Portuguese influence remains in a few Portuguese-inspired castles in Gondar, a small, sometimes-persecuted Ethiopian Catholic Church, some few Portuguese words adopted into Ethiopian vocabulary, and a deep suspicion and hatred for anything connected with the concept of "missionary."

Menelik II (1879-1911) expanded and consolidated his empire right under the noses of the colonialist powers who were dividing up the rest of Africa. When the European powers met at the infamous Berlin Congress of 1885, they divided up Africa on a map with rulers and pencils as though they were carving up a plump cooked turkey. Officially, the Europeans respected Menelik's new frontiers and included them on their new map of Africa. However, just between friends, they let Italy know that if she wished to do so, Ethiopia was in her "sphere of influence."

The Italians were feeling empire hungry, and since they already controlled the coastal provinces of Eritrea and Italian Somaliland, they decided to add Abyssinia. In 1896, they sent an army into Tigre and provoked an incident at Adwa.

Menelik led an army of about 40,000 warriors armed with their traditional weapons plus a few old guns against the Italian invaders who had modern weapons and were trained in modern warfare. The Italians were surprised by the bravery and determination of these wild highland warriors and were soundly defeated.

In 1887, Menelik II founded a new capital city which he called *"Addis Ababa"* (*"New Flower"*). He selected the site in the heart of Shoa

Province which is in the center of the empire. Up to that time, Ethiopian emperors had no large permanent capital cities because whenever a large population lives in one place for a long time, the supply of trees for building houses and cooking the food is soon exhausted. Where there are no roads or means of long-distance transport, maintaining a pleasant life in that place becomes impossible.

To supply an adequate source of firewood and building materials for his "New Flower," Menelik imported eucalyptus trees from Australia. These trees have an amazing capacity to coppice quickly after being cut down. On the cool plateau of over 8000 feet with abundant rainfall, the rich volcanic soil can produce a fresh harvest of eucalyptus poles suitable for building as often as every two or three years.

Today, life goes on in this bustling city of over five-and one-half million inhabitants because of the abundant supply of building material and fuel provided by the band of eucalyptus forests that surround it for many miles.

With the Italians controlling Eritrea, Ethiopia had no outlet to the sea. Menelik negotiated with a French company to connect Addis Ababa by rail with the French Somaliland port of Djibouti. As a result, construction of the Franco-Ethiopian Railroad was begun from Djibouti. It reached Dire Dawa in 1902, but it wasn't until 1917, some years after his death, that the heart of the ancient Abyssinian Empire was fully connected to the outside world for the first time with a rail link complete with telegraph and telephone services. The process of the modernization of the world's oldest empire had begun!

Ras Tafari Makonnen, son of Ras Makonnen, became regent in 1916 at twenty-four years of age. After Empress Zewditu died, he was crowned as "Emperor Haile Selassie I, King of Kings, Elect of God, Conquering Lion of the Tribe of Judah" on Nov. 2, 1930. He was said to be the 225th monarch of the Solomonic dynasty established by the Queen of Sheba and King Solomon. Within the following year, he gave his country its first constitution and abolished slavery.

Then in 1936, Mussolini's Italy launched a full-scale military invasion of Ethiopia with the most modern weapons of that time. Traditional Ethiopian warriors armed with swords and spears and a few old rifles, mounted on horses, were no match for the thousands of tanks and armored vehicles with hundreds of thousands of well-armed and well-trained Fascist troops. Italian airplanes swooped down on them with bombs and machine gun fire, and worst of all, the new dreaded mustard gas!

The Ethiopian forces did not stand a chance. They put up a heroic but futile resistance, dying by the thousands. Then they slowly retreated, some of them going into the forests from where they waged guerilla warfare throughout the five-year occupation. Despite their vastly superior military machine, it took the Italians eight months of fighting to reach Addis Ababa. They had to build a road for their heavy military equipment while fighting a running battle with the "patriots" hiding in the forests along the way.

When he saw that the cause was lost, the young emperor fled to Geneva where he made a very dramatic and moving plea before the League of Nations for the member states to come to Ethiopia's assistance. He received a lot of sympathy but no help. The leaders of the League were impotent to stop Italy's spree of aggression. Haile Selassie went into exile in Britain where he tried to muster support for his struggling people. In 1941, he re-entered Addis Ababa with the triumphant Allied forces who defeated the Fascist armies of Mussolini.

Following the Allied victory over Fascism in Europe, the United Nations awarded the trusteeship of former Italian Eritrea to Ethiopia. In 1952, Haile Selassie ordered a referendum to be held in Eritrea, and the not-undisputed outcome was that the Eritrean people chose to become an integral part of Ethiopia as the province of Eritrea. Now the Empire of Ethiopia reached its full historic dimensions and had full access to the Red Sea with the two port cities of Assab and Massawa.

Eritrea enriched the rest of Ethiopia in many ways. It had been under colonial rule for seventy years and had factories, businesses, schools, an infrastructure of good roads, and most important of all, an educated elite of doctors, professors, teachers, mechanics, technicians, drivers, and businesspeople that spread throughout the ancient empire where their services were highly valued.

Its Government and Social Order

Pre-revolutionary Ethiopia was an empire with an ancient feudal system. It was probably an over-simplification, but it was commonly said that the royal family owned one third of the land, the aristocratic families owned another third, and the Orthodox Church was said to own most of the rest. The emperor lived like a real emperor. He had at least fourteen palaces scattered throughout the empire so that no matter where he traveled, he could always rest in his own royal domicile. The aristocracy lived in fine style as well. They had luxurious houses, servants, and Mercedes Benz cars at their disposal. They traveled abroad and sent their children to the finest schools at home or abroad.

Following World War II, Haile Selassie I set his empire on the road to modernization. He chose capitalism as the road, and foreign investment and foreign aid as the means. He encouraged Christian mission organizations to open schools, hospitals, clinics, and dozens of other helping and training institutions. He encouraged multi-national corporations to open industries and businesses in Ethiopia. He traveled widely on the international scene, soliciting any kind of development aid he could get.

He also set up Ethiopia's first Constitution which provided for a Constitutional Monarchy and a bicameral Parliament which created and controlled all the proper ministries as in any modern government. The lower house of Parliament was elected directly by the people.

*His Majesty, Emperor Haile Selassie visiting the Bible
Academy, escorted by the director, Negash Kebede with
Million Belete and Shemsudin Abdo following.*

He also arranged so that the power to control the Orthodox Church
was transferred from the Coptic Church in Egypt by appointing the
first Ethiopian born *Abuna* or archbishop. Over 1600 years of Egyptian
domination of Christianity in Ethiopia was symbolically ended with
this appointment and the dropping of the word "Coptic" from the
name of the Ethiopian Orthodox Tewahedo Church.

The aristocracy adjusted well to the capitalist challenge. They
invested heavily in industries and businesses and housing. The cities
became thriving, bustling centers of commerce and industry.

However, in the countryside, the feudal system continued as it
had for hundreds of years. Peasants continued serving their landlords,
sharing their crops, giving free labor, or paying cash rent for the use
of the land.

The landlords would make periodic visits to their estates to collect
their rent or to see how their peasants were doing. They almost
always returned loaded with "gifts" of chickens, goats, grain, honey,
and maybe fruit that the peasant was expected to give above the
rent as a token of respect and gratitude for the privilege of being his
peasant.

Some of the smaller landlords lived on their estates and considered
themselves "farmers." We might call them "gentlemen farmers" since
they depended upon the labor of their loyal tenants.

One of our students was the son of such a farmer. He boasted that the four hundred peasants living on his dad's estate were quite lucky because they did not have to pay cash rent for the land on which they grew their food. All they had to do was work four days a week in his father's fields, then they could work the other three days for themselves on the land he so generously allotted to them! He had also built a church (Orthodox) for them.

I asked the boy if he made any provision for the health or education of the peasants and their families. "Of course not." Yet I knew that man had sent his own children to the best schools in Ethiopia and America. He also drove a nice American car, a prestige symbol in that country in those days.

The peasants who had their eyes open and saw the injustice and hopelessness of the situation sometimes would try to send one or some of their children to school, hoping that they could escape the vicious cycle of poverty. Others would encourage their children to go to the city or town to try to find a better way of life. Thousands drifted to the towns and cities desperately hoping, and thousands were disappointed.

Growing masses of the unemployed, desperate to find work at any price, guaranteed that the price of labor remained at bare subsistence level. Large slum areas grew up around the cities and towns. These formed ugly suburbs of rusty corrugated iron or cardboard and plastic shanties without any sanitation facilities and strewn with stinking garbage. These became breeding grounds for every kind of disease, vice, and crime.

The annual per capita income of the average Ethiopian at that time was about US sixty dollars. A construction worker at Nazareth felt lucky to earn fifty cents for ten hours of hard labor each day. A night security guard or a house worker would earn between twelve to thirty dollars per month with, perhaps, no days off, depending on the kindness of his/her employer. There was no way possible that one could provide even decent food, let alone house rent, medical help, or education for a family on that.

Since there were some very wealthy people with huge incomes, it was obvious that many others were not even reaching the average. The vast majority, eighty-five percent of the population, survived on subsistence farming. They hardly ever saw money.

The Ethiopia of Haile Selassie's day, as we found it, was an empire made up of at least eighty different tribal language groups, most of which have several distinct dialects. Each had its own unique history and culture, but in an empire, like in all the prevailing colonial systems, the language and the culture of the dominant power dominated.

In Imperial Ethiopia that dominant power was undoubtedly Amhara. Government policy was to create a national unity and identity through a process of Amharization. Amharic was the national language along with English. Students from all tribes were required to learn it. All government services used Amharic. The law courts used it. Trading was done mostly in Amharic. If a peasant did not know Amharic, he would be at a distinct disadvantage in the marketplace, in the government offices, and especially in the courts or police stations, even if he was in his home tribal area.

Books and printed materials including Bibles could only be published in the official languages of Amharic or English. If an Oromo peasant wanted to learn to read, he would have to learn a new language in order to find reading material.

Amharas were the rulers. His Majesty appointed his friends, relatives, fellow aristocrats, landed gentry, and favored military officers and retired generals to governing posts in the various provinces. There, they would rule as petty autocrats, acquiring choice plots of land for themselves, often by force or fraud.

In almost any sizeable village in the empire, one could find an elite core of Amhara or Amharized collaborators who represented the leadership in the community. There was sure to be an Orthodox Church, houses of Amhara landlords, Amharic-speaking police, and government officers, and perhaps, a school or a clinic with Amharic-speaking people in charge. In the towns Amharic was used, but in the countryside the local dialect prevailed. The elite tended to despise the simple peasants and did not hesitate to treat them as the underdogs they thought them to be.

Its Religion

The role of the Ethiopian Orthodox Tewahedo Church was very central to the shaping and preserving of the Ethiopian culture. In pre-Christian times, the Aksumites held to a religion that could be described as a combination of Solomonic-era Hebrew faith and ancient animistic beliefs. The acceptance of Coptic Christianity in the fourth century altered this basic religion but did not replace it. In fact, this underlying stratum of popular folk religion exerted a great deal of influence upon the shape of Ethiopian Coptic Christianity.

The Aksumites spoke and wrote in "Ge'ez" which has a lot of commonalities with the Hebrew of the Old Testament. The Ge'ez script was derived from but differed substantially from the South Arabian script. Instead of writing from right to left as did the Hebrews, Ge'ez is written from left to right. Also, where Semitic scripts did not indicate vowel sounds, the Ge'ez incorporates vowels into each letter so that each letter represents a syllable. What Latin is to Europe, Ge'ez is to Ethiopia. It is still the liturgical language of the Orthodox Church. It is the root of most Semitic Ethiopian languages such as Amharic, Tigrinya, Adare', and Gurage'.

Monasticism played a very important part in preserving ancient Aksumite writings through the "dark ages" and times of war and social upheavals. Monks lovingly and meticulously copied these writings and jealously guarded them. Even today, some extremely rare and valuable ancient manuscripts are being zealously guarded and preserved by monks living in ancient monasteries on some of the most remote and inaccessible "ambas" or plateaus in northern Ethiopia.

Even today, priests recite their prayers and lead their liturgies from books written in Ge'ez, and deacons memorize extensive passages whether they understand them or not. There is somehow power and mystery and merit in the very utterance of those sacred words, whether the one saying them or the ones hearing them said understand them or not. Somehow mysteriously, their utterance is for God's sake. And what is good for God is somehow good for us as well.

The liturgy itself is very meaningful, if understood. The priests lead in doing the liturgy inside the church building while the worshipers stand reverently inside, or more likely, as an act of humility and self-debasement, on the outside. Is one really worthy of entering the holy place?

Liturgy is mostly read from ancient manuscripts written in Ge'ez or recited or chanted in a slow rhythmic way from memory.

However, in recent decades Amharic is used more and more. The liturgy includes a lot of standing, kneeling, bowing, kissing icons, swinging smoking censors, while chanting prayers and readings from the liturgy.

The Eucharist is given to children and to older people. Young people between puberty and middle adulthood are excluded, assuming they are not likely to be free of sexual impurity.

The clergy often dress in long black robes and wear a black head gear or a white turban on their heads. For special ceremonies they may wear very colorful robes of purple, blue, yellow, white, or red that may or may not be elaborately decorated with gold or silver embroidery. They may carry colorfully decorated ceremonial umbrellas, fly whisks, and elaborately carved brass, silver, or wooden crosses.

Bishops may wear a shiny black dome-like head dress wrapped tightly in a special way. They sometimes form choirs of clergy moving and singing in a row, or they may face each other in two rows and sing and dance, swaying back and forth in a slow mournful chanting way, swinging their crosses or censers to the slow rhythm.

Ethiopian Orthodox Church buildings are often set on a prominent hill or high ground near a village and can usually be identified by a natural grove of mature indigenous trees surrounding them that somehow escape being cut down or defoliated because they are on holy ground. The buildings are often a modest one-and-one-half-storied structure laid out in an octagonal pattern with a two-storied center with sloping roof broken by a ring of small windows and then continuing down to form a porch on all eight sides. It has doors or windows on several sides so the people standing outside can appreciate what is going on inside.

The building is often surrounded with a large yard and fence that allows enough space to hold a burial ground, the sacred trees which are nice for shade, and a place for large crowds to gather.

Orthodox services are always favorite places for beggars to gather, for it is customary for recalcitrants to show their penitence for their sins by doing acts of charity for the less fortunate. Thus, beggars fill an important function by being present to assist the devout in working out their salvation as conveniently as possible.

The priests and deacons can marry once, and if that marriage fails through death of the spouse or through divorce, they may not marry again, but if they do, they can no longer function as clergy. Monks, on the other hand take vows of chastity and must never marry.

Ethiopian Orthodox Christianity did not reflect the whole of Ethiopia's religious cultural heritage. At that time, it was only the religion of the dominant Amharized culture, the 48% which made up the Christian highland core of the empire.

Besides these, another 32% of the population was Muslim. These were scattered in large pockets throughout the empire, especially in the trading centers. Many of the Eritreans and all the Afar and Somali peoples and the Oromo peoples that made up the whole eastern part of the empire were Muslims.

Then there were those tribes to the south and the Nilotic tribes to the west who were still following the traditional animist religions of their ancestors. It was among these that most of the Protestant missionary work was being done.

Finally, there were those other outsiders: the Catholics, the Protestants, the indigenous "Pentes," the cults, and the Falashas or indigenous "Black Jews" which together at that time accounted for less than two percent of the population. Those percentages have changed drastically over the past fifty years. Today those labeled "Protestant" make up about 20% of the population, thanks to the effectiveness of the "missionary" intervention.

Its Rites: Marriage

Three kinds of marriage were socially acceptable within the Ethiopian Orthodox community in which we lived. First, there was that which was solemnized in the church which was binding for life. Few young people were willing to take that much risk. Deacons and priests must have their marriages solemnized in the church.

The most common form of marriage was a civil agreement made with the families concerned for the man and woman to live together as husband and wife as long as both agree. Many times, they did not agree for long. Older men often divorced their wives when they ceased to bear children in favor of taking a young one. If such a marriage brought many years of satisfying relationship, the couple may decide to make it lifelong by solemnizing it in the church.

The third kind of marriage is hardly rated as a true marriage. It was a kind of private common-law arrangement between a man and his housekeeper in which the marriage bed was included in the contract. Such arrangements did produce children but were often temporary.

A great deal of emphasis was placed on the importance of the virginity of the bride while there were no restrictions on the men who marry them. Many fathers preferred to give their daughters to older men who were more likely to be patient with them and take better care of them and provide a more stable home life with honor in society.

There were occasional cases of wife stealing. One girl came to our school to escape from a plot to kidnap her. The idea is to kidnap the virgin and force her to have sex. Then, since she is "ruined" and no one will want her, it will be easier to negotiate a marriage with her parents.

With these kinds of marriage arrangements, it was not surprising that there were a lot of married women around without husbands and with a lot of children to support. Often these women faced economic necessity that pressed them into alcohol brewing or prostitution or both.

We were privileged to attend the wedding of a church elder and his fiancée. They were married after eight years of preparation. That preparation started when the groom chose a young girl and made an agreement with her parents. Then he put her in a good elementary school and sent her on through high school. Now she had reached maturity and was ready for matrimony. Hopefully, she had turned out to be the kind of girl he wanted. He had been working for many years and owned a house and a car. He had saved up enough money to put on a very nice wedding. They were married in the Bole Chapel and then had a big feast afterwards in a tent.

There was always an element of gambling in such arrangements. We knew of other men who did the same thing, choosing and educating their fiancée only to have the young maiden run off and marry some other young lover when her time came. Truly a risky investment!

Its Rites: Funerals

One of our school kitchen workers, an unmarried Orthodox woman, found herself pregnant. This was not uncommon, but it was disgraceful.

One Sunday night her time came, and she gave birth to twins at home. She bled to death. One of the twins died also. We were all shocked. Students talked. Some were sure that "God killed her!" because of her bad behavior.

The next day classes were cancelled, so we could all attend the funeral. We followed the coffin slowly as it was carried the three and one-half kilometers to the Orthodox Church on a small hill near Nazareth. Religious leaders chanted prayers asking forgiveness as the column mournfully wound its way. The people in the procession wept and wailed loudly, some running this way and that, flailing their arms, scratching their faces, and beating their breasts as they cried out in anguish and despair. Others simply wept bitterly, too exhausted perhaps, or overcome with sorrow and hopelessness or fear.

Now the procession finally arrived at the Church on the hill. The body which is considered impure was not brought into the sanctuary. Nor did we the people go in. The coffin, draped in a specially embroidered church cloth, was brought to the door, and lifted three times to a standing position so that the face of the deceased "kisses" the cross on the door. Then, it was carried to the burial place.

There, the priest read or recited scriptures and prayers from a Ge'ez prayer book. It seemed like a long time standing there in the hot noonday sun in that dry, dusty rock-strewn cemetery. Finally, he reached down and threw soil on the casket as he recited the end of the ritual. Then they buried it in a shallow grave about two feet deep outside the church yard, and a large pile of stones was heaped on top to keep the hyenas and dogs from exhuming it. Then we went slowly and sadly home.

How different from the behavior I observed at another funeral procession when a young girl belonging to one of our evangelical church families died. There the church choir sang songs of faith and hope and longing for the resurrection and meeting in heaven as they made their way to the burial site. Believers joined in the singing. A few Orthodox relatives or neighbors wailed loudly, but the elders encouraged the mother and family not to weep, for they would be reunited in heaven! Their procession was peaceful and orderly and a witness to the hope we can have through Jesus Christ.

In much of African tradition, when the news of death is broken, relatives and neighbors respond with loud crying and demonstrative wailing and breast beating. Then they quickly gather at the home of the deceased and share their sorrow together. After some time, the shock of death subsides a little and responsible adults begin planning for the funeral and burial. If they are near a town, close relatives or friends will buy a coffin. If not, local carpenters will prepare a rough one. The body is washed and perfumed, and all the orifices are stopped up with wads of cotton. Then it is wrapped up in a special cotton burial sheet which is tied shut at the head and the foot before it is placed in the coffin.

In the local community, every family should be a member of a burial society or "*ider*" that owns a large tent and mattresses and benches as well as dishes and cookware. This equipment is brought to the place of mourning and set up, perhaps while the family follows the corpse to the burial site. Society members bring food and help where they can.

Because there are no morgues or funeral homes and the weather is hot, the dead are buried the same day of their death if it occurs in the morning. If death strikes in the afternoon, burial is sure to follow the next morning. There will be no sleep that night, for it would be offensive and a sign of disrespect for the deceased to stop active weeping or to eat food until burial is completed. With a delay in burial, weeping or wailing becomes very hard work. Sometimes mourners faint on the way to the church or burial site from exhaustion and hunger.

After burial, the immediate family members shave their heads, put on a black scarf or cap, dress in black clothes, and sit with relatives in mourning in the large tent for three days and three nights. *Ider* members will bring them *enjera b'wat* and eat with them.

Neighbors and friends come and console them and sit with them for a while. They will be given "*nyphro*," a mixture of wheat kernels and beans softened and swollen by boiling in water or roasted on a skillet over fire. *Nyphro* is the food that goes with funerals "to dry the tears." These consolers may get up and leave to go about their duties

81

and later come again and sit some more. They don't have to talk, just be there to show solidarity with the family in their sorrow.

When the three days are completed, the tent and equipment are taken away by the society members, but the mourning isn't over for the family. They will move into a smaller shelter of branches if their house is too small and sit there on mats and mattresses for an added four days and nights. Distant friends and relatives will come and mourn with them there.

When seven days of mourning are completed, they will move back into their house, but they will not sleep on a bed for the next six months but on a mattress or a rug on the floor. They will continue to wear black for at least a year after. Some of the older mothers or widows wear black for the rest of their lives.

Then forty days after the death, the tent is moved back to the home for a big memorial feast. Several barrels of beer will have been brewed in preparation. A big ox is slaughtered, and a lot of food is prepared. Everybody in the community feels free to come to remember and celebrate the memory of the departed neighbor. The bigger the crowd, the greater the honor!

Before the feast gets underway, a special sheep that has been slaughtered and prepared and the finest of the food and beer are taken by the family members to the church and served to the priests and deacons and their families. This meal for the priests is called "teskar." The clergy, in return, are obliged to perform special prayers and liturgy for the departed soul of the dead. After the family members return, the feast can begin.

Again, at each anniversary of the death, some special effort must be made to remember the dead. Then at the end of the seventh year, another big and final feast must be made to honor the memory of the loved one. This is the final goodbye.

Its Celebrations:

"Meskel"

"Meskram" is the first month of the Ethiopian new year which starts on September 11. It also marks the end of the rainy season and the beginning of the harvest season when the humidity disappears from the sky and everything seems so clear and clean and fresh, and the roadsides and the hedgerows and the wasteland between the waving fields of ripening grain is covered with the large yellow daisy-like *meskel* flowers. This is the time when the big *Meskel* festival is celebrated.

"*Meskel*" means "cross." This is one of Ethiopia's most important and most colorful holy days and holidays. It is the celebration of the finding of the true cross. According to the legend, in the fourth century, Queen Helena, mother of the Roman Emperor Constantine, a very pious Christian, undertook a pilgrimage to Jerusalem to try to find the cross on which Jesus had been crucified.

Upon her arrival she lit some incense and prayed for divine guidance in finding the place where the cross was buried. It is said that heavy smoke from the burning incense rose into the sky and then descended as an arrow leading her to the exact location. When she unearthed the cross, she made a big bonfire on the top of a hill to signal to her son that she had succeeded.

So it is, each year on the eve of September 27th, Ethiopians in every town celebrate with singing and dancing and with parading around a "*demura*," a special tall pile of firewood stacked in an upright wigwam fashion and profusely decorated with greenery and the golden *meskel* daisies.

As the day draws to a close, the people of the community gather to take part. The priests gather with their colorful robes to sing and chant. A long parade of different groups of warriors, soldiers, police, elders, and youths pass by singing and shouting.

As darkness settles over the land, the *demura* is lit with a torch. Everyone watches as it lights up the night and slowly burns until it finally collapses in a shower of sparks and fresh flames. Everybody goes home to continue celebrating with food and festivities. It is a time of great rejoicing.

"*Timket*"

About two weeks after Christmas is the big "*Timket*" holiday. This is the annual celebration of the baptism of Jesus by John the Baptizer. Although it is celebrated in every community where there is an

Orthodox church, we decided to go to Addis Ababa where the big celebration took place.

Every Ethiopian Orthodox Church has an "ark" or "*tabot*," a nicely decorated replica of what was thought to be the original "Ark of the Covenant" which is believed to have been smuggled to Ethiopia when Menelik, the son of Makeda and Solomon, graduated from his father's training program and returned to rule Sheba, or was it when King Solomon's Temple in Jerusalem was destroyed? It depends upon which legend one wishes to believe.

The original "Ark of the Covenant" is said to still reside in the St. Mary's Church of Zion in Aksum. It is such a holy object that under no circumstances will the priest charged with its care allow any scholar to even see it, let alone examine it to authenticate its origin or its antiquity. All other arks are said to be replicas of this original one.

Considered a most holy object, this replica or *tabot* is kept inside the church all year. It is a small box that is carefully covered with richly embroidered cloths. Only on the night before *Timket* is the *tabot* carried outside the church on the head of a priest in a solemn procession into a meadow. There, in a ceremony reminiscent of the ancient Hebrew "Feast of Tabernacles," the priests spend the night in the field with the ark in tents. In the morning there is great pomp and ceremony and celebration as the ark is brought back to the church. The priests sprinkle the people with holy water, replicating their baptism ceremonially to remember the original baptism of Jesus at the hands of John.

In Addis Ababa, as the custom was, all the arks were brought out from all the local churches on Friday afternoon. Solemn processions of elaborately decorated chanting priests and dancing clergy along with somber officials and crowds of happy singing people slowly wound their way from every direction till they all converged at "Jan Meda," the meadow where they all would spend the night.

We and other interested *ferinjoch* joined the swelling crowd in the field at 7:00 a.m. the next morning. Almost immediately, the royal motorcade brought the emperor right past us. We were in close enough proximity to gaze at him and take photos of him and his officials for the next three hours as they rested in the shade of his royal red and gold pavilion, watching and taking part in the ceremonies.

In public appearances, Haile Selassie always presented himself every inch as an emperor. A lifetime of self-discipline showed in every move he made, and even in his sustained posture during the three-hour ceremony. He sat ramrod straight on the edge of his oversized throne chair, as if to compensate and stretch, making the most of his diminutive size, and giving full attention to the activities as if they really mattered. Never once did this seventy-seven-year-old man appear to sit back, relax, slouch, doze, show boredom, or let his gaze idly wonder from the central performance of the moment.

There was much singing and chanting of ancient liturgies by the various categories of clergy dressed in their finest gold-embroidered black, yellow, royal red, purple, blue, or pure white robes. Most carried exquisitely colorful gold-embroidered ceremonial umbrellas of green, purple, black, crimson, or royal blue, and large intricately carved crosses of varying designs of wood, bronze, silver, or gold. Some played ancient musical instruments or carried sweetly smoking censors, swinging them by short chain handles as they swayed rhythmically back and forth chanting their ancient Hebraic songs and prayers.

Here in the pomp and ceremony, in the dance and the prayers, in the tradition and devotion, one came nearest to the heart and soul of ancient Ethiopia. Without the presence of the legions of foreign tourists with their flashing cameras, and if the military vehicles could be seen as chariots, one could have sworn that he had fallen into a time warp that carried him back three thousand years to the field camps of David or Solomon, or even further to the orderly camp of Moses and Aaron in the shadows of Mt. Horeb.

The center of festivities moved to a large fountain. Here, there was more liturgical reading, singing, and chanting of prayers. The archbishop or *Abuna* dressed in black flowing robes and tightly wrapped black head dress officiated. The emperor stepped forward and knelt before him and was baptized with the sprinkling of holy water from the fountain. After that, the officials came and were likewise baptized. That marked the climax of the ceremony. The masses of the jubilant common folk rushed forward, some even jumping into the fountain and freely splashing each other with the holy water in a massive orgy of baptism.

Meanwhile, the clergy gathered their respective arks and

reformed their groups and began their slow winding processions joyfully dancing and chanting their way back to their respective churches. It was the beginning of a great religious holy day that would continue in the homes with much feasting and revelry and visiting throughout the day.

CHAPTER 6

Recreational Activities

B esides teaching, we found some recreational things to do such as going shopping in Nazareth or Addis, taking a day or a weekend off for swimming and relaxing at Sodere, taking a picnic lunch with some friends to the "hippo hole" on the Awash River, or going hunting with Calvin Shenk for guinea fowl or warthogs.

During school vacation breaks, we missionaries were expected to reserve up to three weeks for annual leave. This meant going camping at Lake Langano or taking the train to Dire Dawa and visiting Harar and our stations at Deder or Bedeno or joining with other missionaries on a major *"sheer-sheer"* north, visiting the historical sites such as Gondar and Lalibela. We got to do most of these things except the historic northern tour.

Swimming At Sodere

The routine of teaching was getting monotonous, a long weekend was coming up, and we were looking for an opportunity to celebrate Vera's birthday. Why not check out Sodere, a popular swimming resort famous for its mineral hot springs. It was only about nineteen kilometers from us. On Sunday afternoon we left baby Karen with Mestawet and took Cindy with us in the little yellow Opal.

Sodere was situated along the Awash River southeast of Nazareth a few kilometers off the Asella road. The road passes through some rather wild bushy forest area where some very traditional Oromo people live and farm or herd their animals.

Finally, we arrived at the gate where we paid a small entrance fee. We parked our vehicle and strolled around to survey the resort.

Inside, compared to the hot, dry country we had just passed through, this was really an oasis! Huge indigenous sycamore trees spread their shady branches overhead, while exotic and native flowering shrubs and tropical flowers added their flamboyant array of color to the irrigated greenery of the grass carpet beneath. We felt like we had entered the Garden of Eden!

Monkeys scampered across the grass and up the trees where they rudely interrupted the chorus of the singing birds with their uncouth noisy chatter among the branches. Gardeners and attendants were going about their duties tending the sprinklers, cutting grass, digging around the flowers, or picking up trash, which always seems to follow the paths where human beings trod.

We found two pools there, a small older pool, and a new large Olympic-sized pool with a shallow annex fenced off for children and non-swimmers. Most of the people were crowding into that annex. It had a sloping floor that was shallow at one end and deeper at the other end. The main pool was twelve feet deep the full length and was very long, but it had few people in it.

We then went to look for a room to rent for the night. There were different grades of quality for different prices. The highest was twenty birr per night, and the cheapest was five birr. Being frugal children of poverty all our lives, we had no choice but to rent the cheapest! One birr was about fifty cents then.

What we got for the $2.50 was a small room with a bath. It seemed rather drab and badly in need of a good scrubbing and a coat of fresh paint. The two small cots with worn linen and faded covers somehow matched the drab interior.

I was inspecting the bathroom when curious little Cindy reached to turn on the lamp that was standing beside the bed. Suddenly, I heard her scream in terror. I rushed out to investigate. She was standing frozen to the lamp with a jolt of 220-volt current going through her little body! She couldn't let go as the current controlled her nerves. Vera panicked and did not know what to do. Sizing up the situation, I ripped the plug out of its wall socket.

After a good cry, Cindy was okay. Of course, at her age there was no way she could understand what happened to her or why. We prayed and thanked God that our precious little girl wasn't hurt. Because of language, I felt helpless to explain to the staff on duty that the lamp was dangerous, so I dismantled it completely and left it on the table. I thought if they were smart enough to put it together again, they might be able to fix it, and if they weren't, then it would be better that it be thrown away.

Apart from the lamp incident, we had a wonderful time. We learned that the monkeys were excellent thieves at our picnics, but that they also would graciously receive a morsal if offered from our hand. Cindy was especially impressed by the mother monkey with its baby clinging to it and feeding from its breast.

We learned what an equatorial sun can do to very white skin in a very short time. The effectiveness of the sun's rays seemed to be enhanced by the heat of the water. At high noon it only takes about twenty minutes of exposure to bring a light redness to tender skin. If you stay in the sun for one hour, by evening you will regret it very seriously. We learned very quickly to do our swimming in the early morning or in the evening. It was especially refreshing to do it after dark when the air was cool, and the heat of the water was comforting instead of depleting one's energy.

Hunting

Many a Saturday or public holiday would find Calvin Shenk wrapping up his guns and carefully tying them to his big Norton. Then, sometimes alone but often with a companion, he would go "put-putting" out to Welenchiti or the wilds of the Awash Valley somewhere east of Nazareth. Often, he would meet his doctor friend, Rohrer Eshelman, or someone else with a motorcycle along the way. Years later, he usually went with fellow teacher, Herb Kraybill.

Parking his cycle out in the quiet bush, Calvin, the scholar, intellectual, and pastor would become a different person. Forgetting the pressures of modern life and yielding to his primitive instincts, he would prowl through the tall grass and thick undergrowth, re-enacting the role of his distant ancestor, ancient man as hunter, gatherer, defender, and provider, stalking unsuspecting game to feed his family, his "village," and to fill his freezer.

In the evening, be it five o'clock or sometimes half past ten, he always rode home in triumph to a hero's welcome. Workers, students,

89

and family gathered around to marvel at his trophies of wild pig, warthog, or guinea fowl and to hear his tales. Often, if it were not too late, there would be a barbecue that evening.

One evening he came home without the usual tasty provender, but only a very huge hyena draped across the rear of his motorcycle. There was much awe and wonderment, but no barbecue that night! However, certain parts of the ears and skin quickly disappeared to the curious and superstitious for their supposed charm and medicinal value. It is not every night that a mysterious and evasive hyena comes riding into your village on a motorcycle!

Camping At Lake Langano

We will never forget our first camping trip ever. Mr. Christodos was a science teacher from India on contract with the Ethiopian government to teach at the Atse Gelawdewos Secondary School in Nazareth. Since we were short science teachers that year, we contracted privately with him to teach in our school on certain nights of the week. I got to know him a bit while taking him home after classes. He was a Christian, a member of a rather strict indigenous group whose leader was Bhakt Singh. We found a lot of common ground between that movement and Anabaptist beliefs.

He invited me and my family to his house to meet his family and to become friends. They treated us to real Indian hospitality and a very hot Indian meal of rice and curry and other delicacies.

Our friendship was progressing well, so one day he suggested that he would like very much to take his family on a camping trip to Lake Langano, but he had no car. Since I had access to a mission vehicle, would we be interested in going on a camping trip with them and splitting the costs?

It was an intriguing idea. Vera and I thought about it a bit and decided to go for it. We had never camped before, and neither did the Christodoses, but together, maybe we could help each other muddle through.

I arranged to borrow an old green army tent and sleeping bags from the Horsts, and we gathered a few cooking pots and pans together and some food. We would leave baby Karen with Elaine Stoner.

Then on a sunny day in April during our Easter vacation, we loaded our things in and on the roof of the little yellow Opal station wagon and drove over to the Christodos residence in Nazareth to pick them up.

I was still a very inexperienced adult. I had never once given thought to the possibility that there might not be room in our little Opal for two families and all the camping equipment that they might own or borrow plus all the food they might wish to take along.

By the time we got Mr. and Mrs. Christodos and her adult sister and their three boys into the car plus all their blankets and bags and hampers of food, the sides were bulging, and the bottom was dragging to say the least. Also, for all of us adults to get squeezed in required considerable condensation. We kept our windows open and went on our merry way, fully enjoying our first camping holiday. Little did we know that this was only the beginning of our squeezing and our suffering.

Langano is one of several beautiful lakes found in the Rift Valley in southern Ethiopia. To drive there takes about two and one-half hours. Upon reaching Mojo, we turned left, merging onto the road to Sidamo Province. From there the then new asphalt highway stretched somewhat straight south through rather flat savannah land with grass and acacia trees and occasional clearings where farming was being attempted.

It was a smooth road with little traffic, the weather cooperated, the day was peaceful, and the scenery beautiful. Apart from the discomfort felt in our cramped and condensed bodies and the occasional complaint of a child or one of the mothers, we could say it was a very pleasant journey.

Upon reaching Lake Langano, we selected a suitable campsite in the shade of an acacia tree and erected our tent. We found the borrowed tent to be the barest of army tents, for it lacked a floor. This meant that we would be living on bare ground for sure.

Now the acacia is a thorn tree which has the habit of dropping tiny twigs with thorns from time to time along with its worn-out leaves, not exactly the most desirable material for making a bedroom floor! This material slowly decays leaving a ground cover of decayed particles of organic matter which cling to everything that touches it.

Furthermore, the soil upon which we were camping was a mixture of course sand and gravel. So, the floor of our living quarters afforded us the luxury of having a mixture of sand, organic particles, and partially decayed thorns tracked into our sleeping bags. Under us, a layer of large, uneven pebbles was waiting to annoy us sometime after midnight when the thorns had completed their work on our air mattresses!

After staking up our tent, we put on our swimming trunks and went to test the water. Lake Langano is a large and beautiful lake, but it is also very deep, so that even though it lies near the equator, its waters are amazingly cold. This was certainly not like Sodere. Also, the beach is more a course gravel than sand, and it is hard on tender feet that want to wade in slowly to get used to the cold water gradually.

Some of us did not find the swimming as enticing as we had anticipated. Though the water was so cool, the equatorial sun still relentlessly did its ripening work on our pale skin. This time we stayed out in it too long.

However, the children loved to splash in the shallow water and dig holes in the coarse sand. Mr. Christodos brought fishing poles, and his boys were excited about fishing and felt greatly rewarded when they caught even a little six-inch one. It had to be cooked for supper, and we each got a taste.

Arussi women came carrying bundles of dry firewood they had gathered in the forest to sell to the campers. We negotiated at length until there was an agreement. Then they wanted to sell their ornaments too. We were fascinated by their traditional Arussi costumes and hair styles. Finally, they begged us to give them any tin cans or containers that we had, all of this without more than a few words of a common language. We figured they were astute businesspeople, even if they did not read or write.

The Christodos women brought most of the food, and they did most of the preparing of it. They cooked over an open fire using the three-stone method so common to all of Africa and Asia. We enjoyed getting acquainted with Indian cuisine. That evening as we ate supper in the coolness of the lengthening shadows, we could say that it was really great to be at Lake Langano.

But then it was bedtime. Was there really room for five adults and four children in our little tent? We never thought of that question before. Who was to sleep where? The children were tired and fussed. The Africans say, "There is always room for one more!" So, when in Africa, do as the Africans? Yes, we managed to all get tucked inside. The little tent was full, wall to wall, just like the little Opal had been for so many hours earlier in the day.

By this time Vera's and my over-exposed bodies and faces were glowing and feeling like red-hot coals. We were sensitive to everything that touched us, including the sleeping bags. If we covered up, we felt like we were in a furnace. If we uncovered, the chill night air seeped in and reminded us that we were still in the highlands, and the mosquitoes seeped in along with the cold, adding itchy spots to the general burning. We rolled and tossed, but sleep would not come.

The Christodoses, being blessed with the superiority of darker skin, had one less problem than us, and being equally tired, were soon fast asleep.

We rolled and tossed and swatted mosquitoes and rolled some more. Then Mr. Christodos started to snore loud enough to shake our sturdy tent. Rowdy neighbors partied and danced around their campfire somewhere down the beach. Hyenas whooped to each other and laughed as they divided up the garbage at the dump at the edge of the campground. Sleep continued to elude us till the wee hours of the morning. Then suddenly it was dawn and time to get up and prepare breakfast.

Dawn on Lake Langano can be a rich spiritual experience. One becomes aware of its coming when the first bird's chirp breaks the stillness of the night. Across the lake above the distant Arussi mountains, a faint lightness echoes the bird's announcement and grows until it spreads over the whole sky, absorbing the stars and the fading blackness and then streaking the scattered clouds with every shade of pink and red and yellow until the rim of the sun breaks in golden brilliance across the purple mountains.

Meanwhile the birds, now fully awake, join in a mighty chorus of thanksgiving and worship to their Creator as they understand him, whether they know that he notices when any one of them falls or not. The birds continue with their morning worship for some thirty or forty minutes; then one by one, they dismiss themselves and go about their morning chores in their normal noisy gossipy fashion.

Then the sleepy campers crawl out of their tents one by one and stretch and yawn. Some poke around in the few smoldering embers of their dying campfires and maybe put on a few remaining sticks before going off to relieve themselves.

Others go down to the lake's edge to wash sleep out of their eyes. Still others just go down to the water's edge wrapped in a blanket or a shawl and sit on a rock just to meditate, perhaps absorbing something of the awesome grandeur and grace of the scene spread before them, with the sun now reflecting its glory in a line of brilliance shimmering off the plate-glass lake. This was a time for reflection and worship if you were a believer and a time to be dumfounded if you were an atheist.

The second day of camping went by quickly and enjoyably. That night we were even more sunburnt. Vera was in real agony by this time and was running a low-grade fever. She was very ready to pack up and head for home the next day when the time finally came.

Summer Vacation

Meanwhile back in Pennsylvania, pressure was building up for the modest wedding of Vera's mother to Jacob B. Yoder, a widower, on June 8th. Since we could not attend, we celebrated a little by going to Nazareth for a night on the town. We had supper at Franco's, the fanciest Italian restaurant in town (which did not exactly fit the expected definition of "fancy"!). Then we went to visit Dr. and Mrs. Roy Wert. Dr. Wert was very sick with hepatitis and was later sent home to the U.S.A. for recovery.

This was the same time we heard the tragic news of the brutal assassination of Dr. Martin Luther King. Certainly not all of this world's trouble spots were focused on Africa. America, too, was a dangerous place in which to live!

The coming of the big rains coincided pretty much with the end of the school year on June 26th. We gave some attention to plowing and planting our garden. Gerald and Elaine Stoner completed their three-year contract and were busy packing to leave, so we took over the task of fixing up our yard.

We planted fir trees, bougainvillea, orange and tangerine trees, some bananas, and even tried rhubarb and strawberries, which did not do well at all in that climate. We, with the help of some workers and students, planted 250 trees around the football field and other parts of the campus.

By mid-July, Herb and Sharon Kraybill had arrived and moved into the upstairs apartment. They both had just graduated from college in the spring, gotten married, and arrived to begin their new life together here with us as teachers at the Bible Academy. Together with them and four others, we started an eight-week language school at the Academy which lasted until mid-September.

We found the Amharic language a bit difficult for us. In the first place, its alphabet has 231 characters; that is thirty-three basic consonants each of which comes in seven forms or combinations with each of the seven vowels. Further, the sentences are turned around for us. To translate into English thought patterns, you generally start with the last word and proceed to unravel it backwards. That is all the modifying adjectives, adverbs, pronouns, direct and indirect objects, subordinate clauses, and phrases come first and the subject and verb are usually combined in the last word. In this respect it is a lot like Hebrew to which it is related. It is a very simple and logical language. What may take twelve words to say in English may often be said in three or four words in Amharic.

CHAPTER 7

A New School Year

When we opened school again, there were many changes. Shemsudin Abdo had been appointed as Meserete Kristos Church administrator-in-training. He was to replace Nevin Horst in his role after one year of apprenticeship. In his place, Calvin Shenk assumed the office of director of the Academy. Dwight Beachy had returned and resumed the role of dean and chemistry teacher. I was happy about that. Girma Mersha was hired to teach the Amharic classes. Janet Shertzer joined the faculty to head up a new commercial stream and to teach business courses. The two Kraybill teachers strengthened the teaching faculty considerably in science and English and music.

When Prayer Becomes a Crime

Who would have guessed that the new Amharic language teacher, the soft-eyed, quiet-speaking gentle Ato Girma Mersha was an ex-convict? Yes, after spending some time in jail, his presence on our staff was a politically sensitive issue. As a young graduate, he had been assigned a teaching position in the service of the Ministry of Education at Debre Zeit. He fell afoul of the powers that be by becoming a leader in the *"Semaye Berhan"* ("Heavenly Sunshine") movement.

It was a recent growing indigenous pentecostal movement among the youth which had earned the opprobrium of the Orthodox Church and so was banned by the authorities (although the Constitution guaranteed freedom of religion). Yes, of course, the emperor was an "evangelical" Christian. At least that was what some western evangelical Christians convinced the Billy Graham Association to believe. The *Semaye Berhan* students held a different opinion.

One day the police-approved crowd raided their prayer meeting and destroyed their meeting house. The Police held Girma, an adult and a government employee, responsible, and hustled him off to jail where he stayed for about three months paying for his "crime."

When he was released, Girma was ordered to a teaching post in a remote hardship area at a reduced salary as further punishment, but Calvin Shenk offered him a job, which he was glad to accept. In later years, Girma proved to be a pillar of wisdom, stability and strength as the Academy and the Church faced persecution.

We wanted to start church meetings for the people in our immediate community, but we found out it was illegal to have public meetings in Oromo, the language of the local tribe. A part of the imperial Amharization policy was that all tribes should learn Amharic, and that the local languages and dialects should die out. An Oromo version of the Bible had been published, but now it was illegal to have it reprinted. All Oromo peoples must learn Amharic before they could have access to the "Word of God." In other words, due to royal edict, God was no longer on talking terms with the majority of the people directly, only through the imperial language! Yes, that was the policy of the much lauded "Christian" emperor and his government!

Sheryl Justina

Shortly after midnight, the morning of November 6th, 1968, Vera informed me that she was beginning to feel mild labor pains. What should we do? Based upon past all-day labor experiences, she rested till 6:00 a.m., got up, got ready, and made breakfast.

After breakfast I took her to the hospital at Nazareth. Dr. Paul T. Yoder examined her and admitted her to the labor room. Peg Groff and Amy Pieffer attended to her, and I got in the way as much as possible.

After a total of twenty dreadful hours of painful labor, Vera added a 7 lb. 9 oz. beautiful little daughter squirming in the nurse's hands.

It was a Wednesday evening, and all the missionaries had, by this time, gathered at the doctor's house for our usual prayer meeting. They were very handy to rejoice with us and to admire the little beauty. Sheryl had fat cheeks and a head of dark hair which everybody made a fuss over. Who would have guessed that she would become our blondest daughter!

After some deliberations, we decided that we hoped she would embody the twin virtues of purity and justice, so we named her "Sheryl Justina" in honor of her deceased great grandmother, Justina Friesen.

Vera stayed at the nurses' house where three dedicated missionary nurses waited on her hand and foot. Mestawet was back with us when Sheryl was born and took care of the other two girls. They were very excited about having another sister. Sheryl was the first of a crop of six girls born to our missionaries that year.

Due to a certain streak of perversity on my part, we had agreed not to inform our families back home that we were expecting another child. We wanted to surprise them. And surprise them we did! Withholding this news till after the fact of birth was totally contrary to popular practice in our family culture. I think it took a while for our mothers to forgive me.

Mestawet with Cindy, Sheryl, and Karen – 1969

A Guest from India

A few weeks later, we received a letter from my brother George with the exciting news that he would be stopping in to visit us on his way home from India. We should meet him at the airport on Tuesday, December 11th, since he had no idea how to reach us.

Vera and I, the ever-frugal children of poverty from birth, decided to go to Addis by bus instead of the more expensive mission car. We started out in what we, through lack of experience, calculated to be ample time. However, in Ethiopia in those days, you climbed into the bus at the Nazareth depot and waited for all the seats to fill up before the bus would go. It was our day to find an almost empty bus. That meant waiting. And wait we did!

Finally, the bus was full, and we took off. Then, on the way the bus had trouble. More delaying and waiting. We were working on ulcers by now, desperately wishing that the plane would be late, or that George would be held up in customs, or anything.

We finally reached the city about an hour after George's plane was to have arrived. As soon as we reached the right junction, we jumped off the bus and hailed a taxi to the airport. We came rushing into the main entrance door to the arrivals section and almost bumped into George, who was just coming out with a taxi driver on his way to find a hotel.

He had given up on us, thinking we must not have gotten his letter. He would have to search for us by phone. If we had arrived thirty seconds later, we would have missed each other. God's strange redemptive timing!

Three years earlier, at age twenty, George had accepted a voluntary service assignment with our Mennonite Board of Missions as a maintenance person at the Shantipur Leprosy Hospital near Dhamtari, Madhya Pradesh, India.

Maintenance was too small a challenge for him, so he undertook on his own to do an agricultural project, farming, and teaching about fifty people on about fifty acres of land new methods of growing rice. Now, his term completed, he was on his way home where he hoped to study agriculture at the University of Alberta, and then, if God allowed, to return to India as an agricultural missionary.

George would stay with us for a few weeks, so we planned several "see Ethiopia" things for the weekends because I was still teaching during the week. One weekend we camped in Sodere.

Another weekend we went camping in the Awash Game Park in the Awash Valley and visited the Awash Falls. It is a beautiful, wild place with rough black volcanic boulders and jagged mountains protruding from a dry savannah plain with tall grass and scattered thorn bushes and acacia trees. Monkeys surrounded our campsite. The children loved to feed them. They even loved it when they stole our bag of marshmallows and carried them up a tree and ate them before our envious eyes.

That weekend, baby Sheryl had bad diarrhea with bloody stools, so we left her at the hospital while we went off on safari. She seemed to have this problem frequently. For a while we feared it might be the same allergy problem that Karen had, but this was bacterial. Finally, the doctor insisted that Vera feed the baby herself and not allow the worker to do so. That seemed to solve the problem.

Another time, Dr. Harold Houseman invited us to fly with him to Lalibela. He had a pilot's license and had access to a small plane owned by the Presbyterian Mission. It was a nice clear morning when George and Vera and I climbed into this little plane along with our pilot friend. We flew over some amazing countryside of mountains, plateaus, and deep gorges for a few hours. As time passed, the good doctor felt the urge to urinate and, there being no facility for such activities on this little plane, he decided to land at Dessie to relieve himself.

In those days, local air travel in Ethiopia was still in its infancy. The "airport" there boasted only a simple rough gravel airstrip. As the doctor brought the craft in nicely and touched down on the rough surface, somehow a bolt in one front wheel broke and the wheel locked sending the plane into a hair-raising sideways skid.

After it came to a stop, we disembarked and surveyed the damage. Only one broken bolt. But how were we to fix it, having neither spare bolt nor the tools to install it? Harold went over to a small makeshift shack that looked like perhaps it was the terminal building. He found one person there who had no way to help us. But there was a working radio. So, he called the terminal in Addis and was informed that the next scheduled flight to Dessie was not due for another week!

What should we do? We could leave the crippled plane there on the desolate runway and take a bus home to Addis. But that was not a desirable answer for a borrowed plane. We all had busy schedules to return to, so taking a forced "vacation" in a little dingy "hotel" in that remote town where we did not know a soul for a full week was not a pleasant prospect. Well, one thing we could do was pray.

Then, just a few minutes later, while we weighed the options, we heard the distinct sound of an airplane coming in. Wow! Where did that plane come from? Apparently, it was not on the official's schedule.

A slightly larger cargo plane came into view and landed. As it taxied up close to us, we noticed it had USA markings. Then it stopped and a crew of uniformed men came out. They identified themselves as on a "mapping mission" doing a survey of Ethiopia.

One of them was a German mechanic. While he examined our broken wheel and repaired it, the crew rolled out a dozen barrels of aviation fuel that they wanted to store to service their planes. In a few minutes, they were done, and our plane was fixed. The mechanic told us, "The bolt I put in place is not the right bolt, but I will guarantee it for one landing, Go back to Addis!"

Much relieved, we obeyed his orders, and abandoned our tour of the ancient rock-hewn churches of Lalibela. That would be left for another time, which turned out to be twenty-nine years later.

George made a lot of friends with the students. He was able to accompany Mr. Beachy and me as we escorted the senior class on their trip to Addis Ababa. It was a three-day affair which included seeing the Parliament building, the OAU building, the Trinity Cathedral, a national museum, and several factories among other things including the umbrella factory, a successful business which hired only handicapped people.

The time came too quickly to say, "Goodbye." George had to move on. He was to meet our dad in Denmark, spend two weeks there getting to know his relatives, then travel home.

It was forty-one years since our dad had left his home in Denmark to find a new life for himself in Canada. Now at age sixty-four he was going back to visit for the first time. What a reunion that would be! Then to have George join him from India—what an exciting conjunction of world travelers!

At the end of our class tour, I had to relinquish my grip on my beloved brother and allow him to board his flight out of Haile Selassie I International Airport. It was a lonely trip home.

Brother George Hansen joined the senior students on their class trip.

Unrequited Love

Sometimes I can be like those afflicted with "tunnel vision," stubborn and driven, who would tend to dig through a mountain rather than explore options like going around it or over it.

One night we had guests for a New Year's Eve party. After successfully bringing in the new year, the guests went to their homes, and we prepared to spend the first few hours of the new year in sweet slumber when Vera noticed that the yard light that normally illuminated between the back of the house and the servants' quarters was off. There were muffled voices back there. Since the night lookout guard was off duty at that hour, I had better go and investigate.

As I came around the corner in the pale light, I saw a dark figure slip almost noiselessly into the dark toilet room. The door was left ajar. Light was seeping out from under Almaz's door. I called, and she was inside, so I knew the furtive figure in the toilet wasn't her.

Fearing that the slinking visitor might escape, I rushed blindly into the dark room. He (Yes, it turned out to be a "he"!) saw that he was cornered, so he tried to slip out past me. I grabbed him and hung on.

Fortunately for me, he was a small fellow and though he struggled desperately, he could not escape.

Only then the thought flashed through my dull mind, how foolish of me to rush in. I had no idea who my intruder was, whether he was big and strong, or whether he carried a knife or even a gun. All I would have needed to do, had I been a bit clever, was to pull the door shut from the outside and hold it until help came. He had already put himself in "prison," why did I think I had to have physical contact?

I called excitedly to Herb Kraybill, our upstairs neighbor, and Vera phoned Calvin Shenk who came right away with a couple of security guards.

While they were coming, I continued to struggle in the dark with the now very desperate intruder. We seemed to be struggling on a broken bag of charcoal spilt on the floor, and the dust of the charcoal mixed with the stench of the not too clean "Asian toilet" (the squatting kind) nearly suffocating us and mingling with the sweat that was now pouring down over me in that over-heated place on that over-heated evening.

I was big and powerful, and my adversary was small and weak. I was also a teacher, an intellectual, unused to hard sustained physical labor, and my adversary (I learned later) was a brick maker, small but tough and hardened by years of relentless toil, and besides, desperate. I felt my power waning; I couldn't hang on much longer.

Herb arrived first with a rope, and we tied up the intruder. When Calvin arrived with security guards, we took him out in the light and examined him. He wasn't somebody we knew. Calvin interrogated him and found him to be a partially drunk laborer in the Italian's brick factory across the road, one of several hundred Welayta and Kambata men who migrated from their homelands in the south to labor there almost as slaves. They mostly left their wives and families back home.

Apparently, this chap had enough to drink to accentuate his loneliness and thought Almaz could help him satisfy some amorous urges that he felt. Almaz was quite upset and embarrassed. She said she had locked herself and her daughter inside her room for two long hours while rejected love stood outside pleading and begging for her to share her warmth!

Again, we decided not to prosecute, as the only thing he had done was to trespass. Besides, while we did not admire his tactics, who could judge him for being enamored by Almaz's charms? We threatened him very severely and warned him sternly to never trespass again, which stipulation he very readily and whole-heartedly agreed to comply with. Then we let him go.

I've often thought about that incident. "Fools rush in where angels fear to tread." I wondered if I would ever learn that "wisdom is the better part of valor"?

More Political Unrest

Again, in March, the university students in Addis planned to hold a demonstration to protest the inefficiency and corruption of the government and against the American influence in Ethiopia, i.e., their military base, Peace Corp teachers, miniskirts, drinking, smoking, and nudity. Of course, the secondary students would support the university students.

The emperor responded by ordering all schools closed and all students to stay at home. The Army and police were deployed to protect school property. Any students found in the streets were arrested and carted off to jail. Ring leaders were rounded up and put in the same place. Even the tanks from Nazareth were brought to Addis as a precaution and intimidation. With such a heavy-handed response, not much violence took place this time. Schools closed in sympathy across the nation. The Bible Academy was about the only secondary school that remained open.

After one week of this, on Friday, the emperor gave a speech ordering all students to return to their classes on Monday. On Monday, some of the students obeyed and returned to their classes, but when they found that their comrades were in prison and that others were boycotting school to protest on their behalf, most of them left again. By Tuesday, there were no students in the schools, and another week went by without classes.

Students from the government school in Nazareth called our students "girls" for not joining in the boycott and set out en mass to attack our school, but the police intercepted them on the way and sent them back.

Feelings were running high among our students, too. Was it really right for them to keep on studying when their fellow countrymen were languishing in jail? Would it be right for those in grade twelve to go ahead and take the final exams which were scheduled for the next month and move ahead while others sacrificed a year in the struggle against tyranny and oppression?

Finally, on the third Tuesday, our students did not come to class. They decided to hold a three-day sympathy strike to show their solidarity with their compatriots. It turned out to be nine days before we got school moving again.

When we just got started and the students were in an eager mood to get on with their lessons, trouble broke out again elsewhere, and the government ordered all schools closed until April 21st, after the Easter holidays.

The local governor called our director and ordered us to close our school, too. The students all had to leave and go home, wondering if there would really be any more school for the rest of the year.

The morale of our grade twelve class was especially low as their exams, which were scheduled for the following week, were "postponed indefinitely." Those were the crucial exams for which they had been cramming seventeen or eighteen hours a day. However. we teachers enjoyed the extended vacation!

For Easter vacation we decided to go camping at Sodere for a few days. We had bought camping equipment from Mr. and Mrs. Horst who were packing to leave Ethiopia in June. We had to bring all our food and drinking water along.

Getting all the food ready and frozen, while managing two babies in diapers when the house help was on vacation, was a major challenge for Vera and left her wondering if camping was really worth it. But camping at Sodere was extremely popular with Cindy.

The Somali student, Said Sheikh Samatar went with us for two days. He was such an interesting and sociable person. I related to him more as a friend than as a student.

We camped close to the pool, so it was convenient to swim in the evening when the babies were sleeping. It was so hot during the daytime that swimming in the hot mineral water was very tiring.

April 21st found the students returning, very eager to get on with their lessons. Most of the big schools in the empire remained closed for the year, but things had cooled considerably as the backbone of the resistance was broken for the time being. Only the seniors attended classes in the University. One teacher and five students were sentenced to five years in prison. Grade twelve students were allowed to take the crucial examinations in the first week of May.

A sense of relief and excitement ran high when graduation day finally came. Graduation was combined with Parent's Day which was on Saturday, May 17th. In the morning there were sports competitions while parents, relatives, friends, and officials trickled in by Mercedes, Peugeot, Fiat, or by bus. There were displays to be viewed and sales of things students had made such as sewing, embroidery, knitting, handicrafts, works of art, food, drinks, and baked goods.

The actual graduation ceremony began very late at 5:00 p.m. when the real important people finally arrived. Among the eminent guests were the governor of Shoa Province who lived in Nazareth and had a son in grade nine, and a special adviser to the king who was father to one of the graduands.

The parents were happy about our school and praised it for staying in session while most of the schools had been closed since before Easter. The adviser said he was going to send all his children to this school. But did we really want them? Our success in staying open and finishing the year would only increase the pressure we were already feeling from the aristocrats to place their children with us when we knew our best students usually came from the poorer classes.

Finally, the twenty-six graduands stepped forward one by one to receive a diploma, bow, and receive a congratulatory handshake. It was their day of triumph, an objective reached, a challenge conquered! Now they would have a well-deserved rest. However, their schoolmates, the undergraduates, would have to slave another month before completed exams would bring them respite. Furthermore, would there really be school to come back to after vacation?

About two weeks before the end of school, a girl in grade eleven tried to kill herself. Another girl saw her swallow a bottle of sleeping pills and reported it. She was rushed to the hospital at night in time to save her. She was deeply depressed.

She had been failing some of her subjects. When she went home for the weekend, her father, a Supreme Court judge, found out and became very angry and told her she was no good and threatened to kill her. This was more stress than she could take, so she decided she might just as well die and do him a final favor. A Supreme Court judge? What kind of justice could one expect from such a man?

For some of the remaining students, closing the year was disappointing, like the final judgement. They did not meet the minimum requirements for passing to the next grade.

Several students were informed that they were not welcome back the next year due to unsatisfactory conduct. Upon learning of the verdict, these latter ones showed their true character by getting drunk, smoking in full view, blaspheming their teachers, and even breaking a few windows.

In a way, that only made us glad to see them go, but on the other hand it filled me with a deep sadness to think that they were with us a full year yet did not seem to absorb any life-changing benefit, the sadness and finality of squandered opportunity.

Some months later we found that of our twenty-six grade twelve students who sat for the national exams, 40% or nine had pure passes. Another six passed all except math. Three failed almost all their courses. Tenassi Nicola was our champion with five A's and two B's. Overall, we felt quite good about our little school's performance in light of the fact that the total national intake into the university would be only 1000 students.

The next school year started out peacefully enough. However, just before Christmas vacation, the leader of the Student Council at Haile Selassie I University was murdered under suspicious circumstances. We were told fellow students went to the hospital and took his body to the university. The police wanted it back, but the students refused.

They began having a funeral service on the campus while armed police watched. The dead man's brother made a speech which the police did not like, so they shot him, and his body fell on his brother's coffin. Then the police bayoneted and shot others as they turned and fled over the walls. Others were arrested. The newspapers could not tell the truth, but according to consistent rumor, about forty students died. The University was closed again. Several plots to assassinate the king had failed or been exposed and thwarted during that year.

CHAPTER 8

A Harar Vacation

A Train for All Peoples

We decided to celebrate Ethiopian Christmas by touring some of our Church's mission points in Harar Province. On January 5th, 1969, we bought our tickets at Nazareth and boarded the eastbound Sunday morning special of the Franco-Ethiopian Railroad and headed the 400 plus kilometers east through the Awash Valley and the Danakil Desert to the city of Dire Dawa.

The station platform at Nazareth was crowded that beautiful morning when the train from Addis pulled in around 11:00 a.m. It was a short, narrow-gauge train which consisted of a small French diesel engine pulling about eight ancient-looking cars counting the caboose. The first-class car was a Pullman where one could sleep in privacy in enclosed compartments. The two second class cars were divided into several larger compartments which one shared with others. They had padded seats. The other major advantage was that they were not to sell more tickets than there were seats. Occasionally they stuck to the rules.

Third class included the rest of the train including the caboose. It was something else. It was the people's class—economy class—and there seemed to be no noticeable rules. For the modest price of 7.80 birr ($3.90) anyone, including his/her chickens and goats, who could manage to get at least one foot in the door and hang on was allowed to come along.

We, a family of five, only had to pay 15.60 birr or about eight dollars for the eight-hour ride. Children were free. For the ultimate adventure, we decided to ride third class. It was an experience not easily forgotten.

To visualize the following scene, the reader needs to understand that the "loading platform" was simply a strip of level ground alongside the track from which one needed to reach up about four feet to the floor level of the train car onto which one needed to climb to embark, or from which one needed to descend to disembark. Also, in that pre-revolutionary culture, queuing was not yet known. Queuing was one of the positive changes that was introduced and enforced by the Dergue government at a later date.

As the train slowly screeched and clanked to a halt, the crowd waiting at the station surged toward the open doors of the already nearly full third-class cars. A moment of madness ensued as everybody pushed and shoved and scrambled to get themselves, their children, and their luggage up in through the door at the same instant.

At the same time, those inside tried desperately to unload their things and get themselves down off the train through the same door. A pickpocket's perfect moment! Heavy Arab women traders, scruffy nondescript merchants, and "chat" chewing Adare men shouted orders and screamed and swore at each other while throwing boxes, suitcases, and huge bundles of merchandise of every size and description up to others on the train or down to others on the ground. Other would-be travelers scrambled desperately to get aboard between them with their bags and chickens or whatever possessions they hoped to take along.

There we stood, polite foreigners, timid and wide-eyed, holding our fragile two-month-old baby and our suitcases in our hands with two small timid and equally wide-eyed children clutching our legs as the crowd surged past. What were we getting ourselves into? A wave of despair rose within us! It would be impossible to make a "civilized" and yet timely entrance up the four-foot ladder-steps into the car before the train moved on and before the seats were all taken. We had been warned that we must push and shove like everybody else if we were to get on. But being told to do it and doing it were two very different things. For a moment we hesitated.

In the past year and a half, we learned that if you want to survive in a new culture, you must adapt. "While in Rome do as the Romans!" We had to forget we were "Christians," forget the "Golden Rule"! Desperately we threw our bodies into the clawing scrambling mass of mad humanity. Though gentle by nature, I can push and shove, too.

I made my way up to the opening and pulled myself up the ladder and then lifted the children up one by one along with the suitcases as Vera handed them to me.

Finally, we were all inside on a pile of merchandise and squirming humanity scrambling for the few wooden seats that were already claimed by far more people than could possibly fit on them. With one sharp blast of its horn, the train lurched slowly into forward motion. We were on our way.

My first thoughts were of horror and regret, expecting the worst in the long uncomfortable eight-hour ride to Dire Dawa, standing up in the swaying crowd or sitting among the smelly sweaty "chat" chewers and chicken crates on the chick-pea pods and already chewed chat stems that littered the floor. What did I get my family into?

Fortunately, we soon discovered that many of the passengers were short-distance travelers. Those who scrambled so hard to get on at Nazareth struggled just as hard to get off at Welenchiti. We soon found comfortable but hard wooden seats which we claimed for the rest of the journey.

The Franco-Ethiopian Railroad Company owned a fair-quality French restaurant in the little desert town of Awash, so it was in their interest to stop for lunch for one hour. Those of us who wanted and could afford it, disembarked, and ate a good French meal in the coolness of the open tree-shaded hotel. Others wandered to local cheap hotels.

Some remained on the train, nibbling on food they brought along or bought from the ever-present and ever-willing hawkers, some of whom set up their portable sidewalk restaurants and cooked it on open charcoal burners right there.

When the train crew had eaten well, they took their places, started up the engine, blew the whistle a few quick blasts, then took off, continuing down the track into the endless desert to the east.

In the dry season, the 400 kilometers of country between Nazareth and Dire Dawa is one vast expanse of hot, semi-arid desert with every species of thorn bush, ant hills, cacti, and some savannah grasslands. Along the way, the railroad crosses vast stretches of ancient black lava flows, barren moonscapes which support hardly a trace of life. It passes through the grassy Awash Park, lightly stocked with herds of kudu, antelope, zebra, and oryx. Other places the desert soil is marked with deeply eroded gullies that bear witness to the rare occurrence of heavy downpours of rain with the resultant flash-flooding during the rainy season.

As the tedious hours passed, my mind wondered, imagining the possibilities of flood control and rainwater harvesting that could be used to make the desert bloom, even in the long dry season.

Throughout the trip the train movement stirred up the desert dust that filtered in, covering everything inside the train until we, all one monotonous grey-brown color, blended nicely with our surroundings.

Scattered along the route, there were desolate settlements, each comprised of a small station building, a few workers' houses, a police outpost, a shop or two, a bar for sure, maybe even a little clinic, a small mosque or at least a whitewashed tomb of a Muslim saint whose remains have magical powers for healing or answering prayers, and sometimes an Orthodox church.

At several places where there was water for irrigation, there was some small fruit and vegetable farming. At such places, the train would stop for a few traders to disembark or embark. As the engine quieted and the train slowly eased into the station, we could hear a growing clamor of nondescript voices rising in intensity until we were surrounded by a sea of shouting humanity. Women, men, youth, and even children lined both sides of the train, urgently calling out their wares and holding up to the open windows tin plates in both hands stacked with bananas, oranges, paw paws, custard apples, "sambuusas," baked goods, or some other home-produced delicacy, and perhaps balancing larger baskets of the same on their heads. They even had "*soda cuzcuza*" which meant that the Coke or Fanta bottles were as "cool" as the warm water they were kept in.

A brisk trade ensued as the weary but hungry passengers bargained for the best deal for immediate consumption and for some extra to take to their destinations. One should never arrive at the house of a friend or a relative without bringing something in the way of food in one's hand. The bargaining went very quickly, for both sides feared the train would depart before they were satisfied, or proper change was made. Many deals were closed on the run. Sometimes change was never made, or fruit was never paid for. It was a business not without its risks.

Occasionally, we would pass Danakil herders or bare-breasted women struggling to hold their camels as the train whizzed by with its noise and dust, or quietly browsing their goats and cattle at a safe distance amidst the thorns and cacti and dry grass.

The Danakil, properly called "Afar," are famous for their handsome or beautiful features in spite of the rugged conditions in which they live. The women wear long skirts stained grey, brown with sweat and dust and often wrap a dark colored cloth around their heads to ward off the hot sun or to keep on hand to cover their bodies if it should get cool. They let their hair hang loosely matted almost shoulder length. Around their necks they wear one or two or three simple strings of locally made beads of different colors and shapes and perhaps a few tiny square leather pouches or amulets into which some local sheikh or shaman had sewn tiny portions of the Koran to ward off "the evil eye" or to bring good fortune. A few thick round or thin flat silver armbands or bracelets complete their adornment. They could often be seen walking stooped forward under a heavy load of precious water in goatskin bags strapped on their bare backs.

The men wear grey-brown wrap-around skirts and home-made rubber-tire sandals and carry a sheet draped across their shoulders in case of cool weather. They keep their hair long in a scruffy sort of "Afro" style. They wear a leather belt from which hangs a large scabbard encasing an evil-looking twelve-inch dagger. In their hands they carry a sturdy walking stick.

The Danakil are feared above all the other tribes as a fierce tough wild people, a logical product of the harsh environment in which they survive. Rumor has it that a young Danakil man is not allowed to marry until he has killed an enemy and brought the testicles to the prospective bride's father as proof of his manhood and his worthiness of the young lady's hand in marriage! The so-called "civilized" peoples of Ethiopia feared the Danakil, and the government's attitude towards them was that they were little different from the wild animals that shared the thorny desert with them. They could be shot by police or soldiers with impunity, and no one would be held responsible.

It was near seven o'clock p.m., and the sun had already set when our weary train began to slow down on the outskirts of the desert town of Dire Dawa. With mournful whistle screaming and wheels rumbling slower and slower, it crept into the station where it finally came to a screeching and clanking halt. We dusty and tired passengers suddenly came to life, all scrambling to get out at the same instant.

People shoved and pushed, shouting through the open windows to friends or relatives waiting outside, forcing their baggage through the opening to them. Families shouted to each other as they struggled to offload their belongings and keep their children together. While we were pushing to get out, coolies were crowding in to grab quick contracts to assist with luggage. Even taxi touts were falling over each other to be first to get in to finalize agreements with passengers before their competitors could reach them outside.

Dire Dawa

Before we reached the door, Mr. and Mrs. Robert and Alta Garber greeted us through the train window. They helped us extricate our luggage and ourselves from the seething mass and hurried us to their waiting Renault and whisked us away from the maddening scene.

At twilight, Dire Dawa was such a quiet, peaceful town. The evening air was a trifle hot, but laden with the scent of flowering shrubs. The streets, lined with flamboyant flowers and palm trees, were so clean and welcoming, assuring us that this was indeed a pleasant place to live. The streets were laid out in squares, and the well-built modern buildings spoke of the strong European influence in this railroad town.

We were soon turning into the Mennonite Mission compound and were welcomed by all the people there who were waiting to feed us supper. There was a small chapel, a youth hostel, a missionary's dwelling, a typing school, a garage, as well as a small guest facility with about five rooms. We will be staying in the guest quarters for a few days.

A most remarkable couple in their mid-fifties, Robert and Alta Garber were the very epitome of efficiency, industry, and grace. It is to unsung heroes such as these that the world and the church owe a debt of gratitude and admiring praise. Robert and Alta were among the pioneers whose dedication and total self-giving sacrifice made it possible for the first schools, clinics, and churches to rise and flourish in the hinterlands of Harar Province.

Now, besides being station head and host to the guests that stopped in now and then, Robert was pastor of the church, director of a Bible translating program, superintendent of all the Meserete Kristos primary schools in Harar and Shoa Provinces, the general "go-for" for the Bedeno and Deder mission stations, and a builder and mechanic for anything that needed to be built or fixed. Sometimes the overwhelming load of his various duties faced with the amazing incompetence or naivete of younger missionaries tested his patience most severely.

Alta was just as business-like and efficient as her husband. Besides helping him tend to all his duties, she was an excellent homemaker and hostess and ran the typing school. She also did a lot of pastoral work among the women. She was loved and respected for her hard work and loving commitment to the welfare of others and for her happy, cheerful disposition and firmness in times of trouble.

Dire Dawa, with its population of more than 60,000, was the third largest city in the Ethiopian Empire at that time. Yet it still had a special small-town quiet, peaceful aura about it. Not more than four or five blocks from the mission stood one of the emperor's fourteen palaces, the tallest building in the landscape, even though that was only a modest four or five stories. There was a Greek Orthodox Church and school, a theater, a Catholic Mission and school, several Italian restaurants, a few hotels, one place where you could buy ice cream, several Greek shops, and various small Ethiopian shops and businesses.

We soon learned it was a delightful treat on a warm evening for our children and us to walk down to the ice cream place after supper. The dimly lit streets were almost deserted, and very few cars were moving about. The air was still hot, but not burning like during the day. Additionally, the locusts and crickets added their endless songs to the night sounds as we walked together with our excited chattering children.

Coming to the restaurant, we would find a table on the veranda just off the sidewalk, order our favorite ice creams, then look around while we waited. Soon the tasty morsels were presented, and we all got excitedly busy taking small tastes to make the rare treat last as long as possible. There were always a few older Italian (or were they Greek?) men sitting at a table playing poker for small money, smoking, or drinking, and talking in their language.

We were most fascinated by the eleven-inch greenish geckos that chased flies up the walls. With their gravity defying logic, they ran upside down across the ceiling to assume strategic positions close to the fluorescent lights where they would wait completely immobilized like lionesses silently waiting at a salt lick for their prey. When a luckless visitor inevitably strayed too close, attracted by the light, the gecko would suddenly lunge forward, its long tongue flashing out with lightning speed and sweeping the hapless victim into its ravenous gullet where, presumably, it was absorbed into the gecko's essence.

After savoring the peaceful setting for as long as possible, Mother would announce that it was time for the children to go to bed. We would pay the bill and start our slow, happy walk back, carrying the youngest one on my shoulders to the Mission. She would inevitably be asleep by the time we arrived.

Dire Dawa started out basically as a railroad town, designed and built by the Franco-Ethiopian Railroad Company as a rail head in 1902. For several years it was the terminus of the Djibouti-Dire Dawa link while the stretch from Dire Dawa to Addis Ababa was under construction. In those days, a caravan route snaked its way through the desert from Dire Dawa to Addis. Thousands of ox-drawn carts ferried the merchandise between the capital and the railhead until the railroad was finally completed in 1917.

The next day we found that the clean, orderly town was only the "European" section known as "Kezira." There was another Dire Dawa, the real "African" town on the other side of the usually dry, sandy riverbed, the town known as "Megala," which sprawled out in typical disorderly fashion on the outskirts into the cacti and thorn bushes of the desert. It was the Dire Dawa of the Arab Muslim culture, the traditional Kefira market, the place of the Adare and Arab shopkeepers, the *chat* traders, the garages and lorry owners, and the mosques. It was the town of the cement factory, the cotton mill, the textile factory, and the garment makers that provided jobs to so many of the poor and paid wages low enough to guarantee they remained so.

This was the dwelling place of most of the population, a labyrinth of narrow, pot-holed, refuse-strewn, smelly, dusty streets squeezed between high stone walls. Steel gates protected the shops and hid the secure residences of the merchant class and their multitude of less enterprising relatives and live-in servants. These "fortunate" wretches kept no hours and knew no off time but derived their modest sustenance from their continuous service, which made the master's enterprise a profitable possibility.

The less fortunate ones lived out on the fringes and along the riverbanks in squatter camps, clusters of shelters made of mud and sticks, or branches and cardboard covered with waste plastic pieces. Some of the enterprising squatters lived in Somali-style hemispherical huts covered with a rust-blackened sheath of flattened kerosene tins. One can only guess what the interior temperature must have been at the peak of a normal sunny day in that hot desert environment!

Some of these folks made their living as low-paid factory workers. Others survived by trading in vegetables, *chat*, charcoal, kerosene, or a myriad of other essentials in the open market, under burlap-draped booths along the cluttered corridors, or by hawking their wares in the streets and even door to door.

Others offered their services as coolies, loitering in the streets with eye and ear alert to seize any opportunity to perform any kind of remunerable labor such as loading and unloading trucks, delivering merchandise, carrying purchases home for customers, disposing of garbage, digging, cleaning, guarding a rich person's car, or guiding a tourist.

Some devoted themselves to the dangerous and challenging art of picking pockets and snatching valuables from unsuspecting clients. This profession requires skill for long term survival and profitability. Failure could be extremely counter-productive.

Others simply engaged in the serious but less risky business of begging for a living.

Finally, there were the independent artisans, craftsmen, masons, builders, and mechanics who created works of art in their area of specialty to be offered for sale, or undertook contracts whenever afforded an opportunity.

We attended the January 7th Christmas service in the little yellow mission chapel on Tuesday. An Indian teacher gave a very appropriate Christmas message. He was one of the more than 500 teachers and one of the few Christians from India that were serving on government contracts in the schools of Ethiopia at that time. Only a few dozen people attended the service as the number of evangelical Christians was rather small in that Orthodox-dominated Muslim town.

Harar City

The following day we, along with two vacationing teachers from the Good Shepherd School in Addis Ababa, left the oppressive heat of the desert floor and drove up the escarpment to visit Harar City, fifty-four kilometers to the southeast in the cool highlands of the Ahmar Mountains. A narrow asphalt road snaked its way up the steep 800-meter incline for about twenty-one kilometers to Dengego.

Then, reminiscent of the fabled "Jack and the Beanstalk," we abruptly came upon a fabulous tableland, a verdant landscape of tall eucalyptus trees, green grass, terraced fields of coffee, sorghum, maize, and assorted vegetables. The contrast with Dire Dawa was impressive and refreshing, as if we had entered a different world.

We went ahead along a fine asphalt "yellow brick road" in this fantasy land for about nine kilometers until we reached the village of Alemaya (since then renamed "Haromaya"). There we stopped to visit the Alemaya Agricultural College.

This was a beautiful new campus built in the middle of a farming community near Alemaya Lake.

The College had been launched as a project aided by the University of Oklahoma, which left a profound impact upon it. Most of the faculty were Americans and lived in American style housing. They were pioneering in agricultural research in the Ethiopian context. They had a model dairy herd of Holstein-Friesians and a crossbreeding program. There was a small zoo with a hyena, some wild cats, a few gazelles, and a baby lion which was of particular interest to the children. We met and had lunch with two former Academy students, Sehenna Dejene and Tsehaitu.

Next, our journey took us to the growing city of Harar, spreading out over several hills overlooking a vast fertile plain beneath. As a provincial capital, Harar had offices and institutions representing every government department. Numerous green Peugeots and Land Rovers, police guards, military escorts, flags, signboards, and other symbols gave added evidence of the significant presence and importance of officialdom in this town. We slowly passed by military training institutions, educational institutions, hospitals, government buildings, and private businesses.

Finally, we came to the "old town," the famous historic walled city of narrow winding streets into which we could not drive beyond city square. The city of Harar was an important trading center since it was founded in 1520 by the Amir Abu Beker Mohammed who was murdered five years later by the notorious Ahmed Gragn (Ahmed the left-handed).

This was the base from which Ahmed Gragn launched his "jihad" against the Abyssinian Christians in 1530, a holy war in which he almost succeeded. Finally, he was stopped by Portuguese intervention and killed in battle in 1543.

Gragn's nephew and successor, Nur ibn al-Wazir Mujahid erected strong encircling walls to keep out the invading Oromo. For the next three hundred years, Harar survived and prospered as an independent city state. It was often militantly theocratic and a center for Islamic scholarship. At one point in history Harar was known as "the fourth most holy city in Islam." It had its own currency. An Egyptian invasion and occupation in 1875 put an end to its independence. In 1887, Harar was annexed to the Ethiopian Empire by Menelik II.

We drove in through the gate and parked the car in the little square and agreed with a boy to "watch" it carefully. We agreed with another young man to be our guide and set out on foot to see the city.

There was a marketplace or bazaar which reflected a blending of Middle Eastern and African cultures. The narrow random streets with overhanging balconies, intricately carved doorways, lattice work, and the many small mosques strongly reflected Arabic influence.

We toured some of the streets and entered several workhouses and shops of basket weavers. There, we left some of our money and went away with a nice assortment of very colorful grass-woven baskets.

After satisfying our craving for baskets, we left the inside of the city and drove around outside the wall. It was about two miles around the "old city." Built sometime in the early 16th century, this ancient five-meter-high wall was more or less intact, separating an ancient culture and way of life inside from the modern one outside.

Bedeno

Our visit to our missionary colleagues in Harar Province could not be complete without a visit to the Bedeno Mission. Some of the Bible Academy's star students originated from that remote town. Since the only transportation available was by lorry, we decided Vera would remain in Dire Dawa with the children while I undertook this adventure by myself.

Robert Garber arranged for me to go with Ato Nissre, a Bedeno merchant whom he often depended upon for getting people, supplies and mail into that difficult place. I should be ready to board Nissre's truck by 6:00 p.m. on Thursday. Thus began an experience in which I learned a lot about how trucks and truckers work in servicing the countryside.

First of all, it took a few hours to get the truck loaded and all the travel details in order. We finally got going at 9:30 that night. I was informed that we should be arriving at Bedeno in six hours. The distance by road to Bedeno was only one hundred kilometers, of which the first fifty were paved. But the remaining half was built by the Italians to enable their war efforts back in the late 1930's and had not experienced any major maintenance or improvements since. By now it was strictly limited to large trucks and four-wheel drive vehicles with low range capabilities.

Since I was a *ferinj* and "guest," I was forced, not reluctantly, to squeeze into the cab with the driver and a businessperson and several Arab women and children who occupied the bunk behind the seat on this Mercedes ten-ton lorry. The other fifteen or so less-fortunate passengers had to huddle on top of a high load of assorted merchandise hanging on for dear life.

As the lorry slowly left the town, it kept stopping periodically for police checks, picking up passengers, exchanging messages with shadowy figures in the dark, or to load or off-load more passengers. It took two hours to reach the fifty-kilometer junction where the rough road began.

Then the lorry really worked, creeping up steep inclines with engine roaring in the lowest gears, then shifting down applying air brakes intermittently as it eased down the other side. The road wound and twisted up and down along the western side of the massive

Garamuleta mountain, crossing boulder strewn mountain streams where bridges had long since been covered over or washed away, and rutted and eroded places where the road sloped at a frightening angle. Passengers on top of the merchandise hung on desperately as the truck swayed from side to side over the rocky and rutted terrain and passed under low hanging tree branches that grabbed at them in the dark.

Sometimes the way was so narrow that the one side almost grazed the jagged rocks of the cliff that rose hundreds of feet above on the left while the abyss gaped a thousand feet below just inches to the right. The uninitiated held their breath and helplessly clung to whatever was available to cling to and dug their toenails into the soles of their shoes, hoping and praying that the dark road was not wet and slippery.

Little did I realize that within a few years, I would become intimately familiar with every twist and turn, every rise and fall, every stream crossing, every mud hole, every rut and bump, every rock on that road, that I would know that road like the back of my hand and recognize the difference if someone changed even one troublesome stone or pothole on its entire length.

Finally, we passed the main body of the mountain and were ready to begin our descent on the southern slope. Bedeno was now only fourteen kilometers away. We should be reaching it in an hour and a half.

However, the driver got sleepy, stopped the truck, shut off the engine, crawled into his blanket and went to sleep. We had no choice but to do the same. Since I had been given a special position in the warm cab, I had loaned my blanket to a pitiable schoolteacher stuck up on the load. At two a.m., the air can be terribly cold on Garamuleta, which rises to 11,000 feet.

Quickly, I felt the truck cab cool off, and soon I was shivering helplessly in my light jacket inside the cab. I could not sleep. I wondered about the miserable wretches outside the cab clinging on top of the load. They must be freezing! Yet the driver slept on. How thoughtless of him! We were so close to the warmth and hospitality of the town. How we all would have appreciated if he could have endured a little longer to complete our journey, yet he slept on for four hours.

The sun was rising over a most amazing panoramic view of glistening mountains and dark valleys and forests and beautiful peasant farms as the lorry eased its way down the final slope and stopped in front of the Mission Clinic to allow me to disembark.

I was still shivering as I made my way up the steep lane to the missionary's house at the top. The exercise supplemented the sun's efforts to warm me up, and by the time I was seated in the Gamber's house, I was feeling much better.

The missionaries had started their work at Bedeno back in 1950. They opened and ran the first clinic and the first elementary school in the area. They built their buildings on a mountainside plot just above the road a kilometer before the main market area. The mountain rose steeply above their house for about one hundred meters. They had piped water from a good spring below a cliff directly to their houses.

Below the road a deep valley fell sharply to the south, and beyond that, vast rolling plains spread out and faded into the horizon as the land slopped downward towards the Ogaden wilderness of the Somali peoples.

At present Henry and Pearl Gamber were the only missionaries there. They were both elementary school teachers. Ethiopians made up the bulk of the teaching staff, and an Ethiopian dresser was managing the clinic. The school had produced graduates who became some of the best students at the Bible Academy and some of the best leaders in the emerging national church.

The Gambers were raising four children, the youngest of which were at this time in boarding school in Addis Ababa.

I was able to visit all the homes of our Academy students during the next two days. It was a new cultural experience. I was deeply moved by the poverty I saw and the way it affected the people's lives. The average farm family eked out an existence on less than half an acre of land, using inefficient traditional methods. Landlords exacted rent, even from the small income they did manage to produce.

I had planned to return to Dire Dawa on Saturday so that we could visit the Mission at Deder on Sunday. But the lorry went out on Sunday morning instead, so I learned that living in the countryside, one must accommodate his plans with the plans of those upon whom he depends.

Deder

The lorry arrived back at Dire Dawa at 4:00 p.m. and I immediately gathered my family and headed towards Deder in a public service Land Rover, arriving before 7:00 p.m. The level plateau that makes such prime agricultural land towards Alemaya becomes more mountainous as you go northwest. The peaks get higher and the valleys deeper and the fields get steeper, but they are still being farmed. Some enterprising farmers had begun to terrace their plots, but the feudal landholding system did not encourage that.

The town of Deder sits on the east side of a mountain at about 8000 feet and is cool, especially at night. The view at sunrise is particularly fabulous as the bright light glistens off the silvery hills and trees in sharp contrast to the dark shadows which seem to deepen the valley spreading north and south far below. The sun's first rays strike the shivering observer, adding warmth and peace and tangibility to the awesome beauty of the moment. The air is clear and pure, and the sky towards midday takes on a deep blue hue. The equatorial sun, even at that altitude, is burning hot, but when a cloud passes, or when it sets behind the mountain around 4:30 p.m., one feels an immediate chill in the air.

The missionaries were running a primary school and a small hospital. A small dresser school trained primary dressers or nursing assistants. There also had been a leprosy program and a leper's village remained nearby, in which the former lepers and their families lived.

According to the culture, once you were a leper, you would always be a leper, a social outcast. Even though, with modern drugs their leprosy was burned out, these people found it better to stay in this village rather than try to re-integrate back into their former home communities where the ancient tabu still dominated the beliefs and prejudices of the people.

There was also a small girls' boarding facility to encourage girls from a distance to attend primary school.

Dr. Harold Houseman and his wife Miriam were our host and hostess for the night. There were also two single female missionary nurses on the station, Martha Hartzler, Vera's mother's cousin, and Janie Zimmerman, both veteran saints who had given many years

122

of dedicated service to the sick in Ethiopia. Everything else was managed by the Ethiopian staff.

We returned to Dire Dawa on Monday afternoon and took the train back to Nazareth the next day. It had been a short, full, exciting, interesting, if not relaxing vacation. We had a very positive first impression of Harar Province. Little did we guess that God was preparing us for a time when we would call it "home."

CHAPTER 9

Church Growth

While the aim of the Bible Academy was not to proselytize, this school year we saw the students struggling to grasp spiritual realities more than ever before. Early in the new year, I gathered a group of twelve mature students who had expressed their faith in Christ and a desire to be baptized and began to have catechism lessons with them. Some of them were from mission elementary schools, and three of them were from Muslim homes. Some of them were active in teaching Sunday school or preaching in the nearby towns and villages on Sundays.

The Holy Spirit began to work among the students. About 78% of the students were of the Ethiopian Orthodox Church tradition and always considered themselves to be the true Christians. Now, they noticed some being truly converted to Christ, born anew of the Spirit, and obviously transformed.

This provoked a chain reaction. Others, seeing the changed lives, wanted to be changed, too. This, plus the Bible studies and teaching, provoked them to ask serious questions about their inherited religion. They were troubled by the discrepancies they found between the Bible and evangelical understandings on the one hand and their inherited Orthodox Tewahedo beliefs and practices on the other. One boy said, "I believe like a Protestant, but I am Orthodox." Another said, "I am not Orthodox, and I'm not Protestant. All I know is that I am a Christian!"

I learned that our petty divisive European theological arguments meant little to Ethiopians. I came to realize that our role was to teach them the Bible and then let them find their own way. Somehow an evangelical Ethiopian Church would emerge, and our denominations may be absorbed into it.

One day a young corporal from the army camp visited our Sunday morning service. He had been to the U.S.A. for technical training. While there, he had stayed with a Mennonite family in Paradise, PA on his days off. About a week before he was to return home, he accepted Jesus to be his Savior and Lord. Now a month later, he discovered that he was stationed next to a Mennonite school. He was excited. I asked him one day, "How is life?"

He replied, "Every day with Jesus is like Christmas!" He started to take his friends to church. He had been in the army for six years and still had one year to go. He said it was hard to be a Christian in the army, and he could hardly wait to be discharged and begin a civilian life.

Most of the Meserete Kristos Church growth had not come as a result of the missionaries' programs or attempts to evangelize or proselytize, but through attracting other groups who moved into the area. In the mid 1960's, Kambata and Welayta peoples had migrated to the Wonji and Shoa sugar estates as laborers and organized themselves into two congregations. Then, they negotiated to join the newly formed Meserete Kristos Church, swelling their membership from about 300 to approximately 600 persons.

In 1968, another group from the Metahara Sugar Estate joined, adding about 200 to the roll. These additions were mostly very poor people, recent immigrants to the area, laborers, poorly educated, and not deeply rooted in the faith. Therefore, they brought with them a lot of problems and a tremendous challenge. Their presence tipped the ethnic balance from a predominantly Amhara church to a truly multi-ethnic church.

I went with Nevin Horst one Sunday to visit this new church at Metahara about one hundred kilometers east. We found a group worshiping in a temporary structure made of a crooked pole framework covered over with grass for shade. It was hardly a roof to keep out any rain that might strike that desert town because it was flat. It was so low that Mr. Horst could not stand erect when he preached. The worshipers were happy, friendly southerner plantation laborers. After worship we were invited to dine at the leader's home. He was starting a small shop to make his living.

Sometime in February 1969, a delegation came to Nevin from a place called "Abadir" in the Awash Valley. They represented a little church of about seventy believers who had moved from their homes in Kambata to work on a cotton plantation. They had built their own building and had now come to see if they could join the Meserete Kristos Church as a group. In time their application was accepted.

A baptismal service for our students was finally organized right after school opened in October. Six of the original candidates were considered ready. They included the teacher, Alemu Checole, and five grade twelve students, Girma Tsige, Kalifa Ali, Alemayhu Assefa, Solomon Abebe, and Melaku Abera.

The candidates decided they wanted to be baptized by immersion this time, so we took them in a van down to the Awash River where we found an isolated spot where no enemies would see and report us to the authorities. It was still forbidden to baptize people who had been previously baptized as Orthodox. Five of these six were from an Orthodox background. Usually, Mennonite missionaries did not attend such functions for security reasons. The elders invited me, and I decided to break tradition.

When we saw how muddy the river was, the candidates had second thoughts about immersion. The traditional Mennonite way of pouring suddenly looked more attractive! They compromised and waded out into the water up to their knees. There in the river, they confessed their faith and promised to follow Christ faithfully the rest of their days, and there the elder in charge baptized them by pouring a handful of water on each of their heads. It was a very meaningful service.

Of these outstanding six, Melaku lost his faith in university, became depressed, and committed suicide. Solomon became a Christian university professor somewhere in the U.S.A.; Kalifa moved ahead to become the Executive Secretary of the Meserete Kristos Church for many years, served in prison for four and one-half years for his faith, and eventually died of cancer at the age of forty-two. Alemu and Alemayhu became faithful church elders in Nazareth, and Girma served as a faithful church elder in Addis.

Immediately after this baptism, we gathered a group of fifteen others who wanted to be instructed in the faith in preparation for baptism. This group swelled to about twenty-five as the year progressed.

Baptism was a big step for these young people. Those from Muslim homes faced the possibility of being disowned by their families and maybe even hearing about their own funerals. Those from Orthodox backgrounds realized that by being "rebaptized" they were hurting their parents and insulting their religion. It was not surprising when some of the candidates postponed the step.

By this time, the congregation at Nazareth was growing in numbers and in leadership. Since its beginning, it had always lurked in the shadow of the mission hospital being made up mostly of hospital workers and hiding in the hospital compound. Now the leaders felt it was time for the Church to cut its umbilical cord and stand on its own. They searched for land on which to build a meeting place of their own.

Finding the land and paying for it was one thing. Getting permission from the solid Orthodox State to build a "House of Prayer" for a "foreign religion" was something quite different.

It took a lot of prayer, a lot of patience, a lot of time, and a lot of diplomacy, but finally permission was granted. A groundbreaking ceremony took place at the site in March 1970. By the time they were ready to begin construction, the church attendance was growing so fast that the elders decided to change the plans and make it one-third bigger than the original plan. By the time it was completed one year later, the congregation filled the 350-seat building.

We could detect a definite moving of the Holy Spirit in Ethiopia and more specifically at Nazareth. There was increased attendance at our hospital chapel. Prayer groups were springing up around towns and on various public-school campuses. Students were excitedly studying the Bible and reading it to parents or any illiterate persons who cared to listen. The young began meeting with the older in homes to pray and study together.

CHAPTER 10

Vacation Ecstasy and Agony

A Garden Project

B y the end of my second year of teaching, I was becoming very aware of the causes and effects of poverty in Ethiopia and was interested in possible remedies. I came to realize that the two main resources Ethiopia had were its huge peasant population and its excellent arable land. If real economic and social development were to occur for the benefit of all, it had to begin with these two resources.

The coming of the multinationals with their industries was only exploiting cheap labor and making a few rich become even richer. Educating the children of the elite enabled them to become even more elite. It seemed to me at the time that the development taking place was really helping the oppressors of the masses become even more efficient oppressors.

If the real problem of poverty was to be addressed, it must speak to the plight of the peasant and his agriculture. This awareness grew on me, and I became interested in learning more about Ethiopian agriculture. I read a report put out by an Israeli organization which did a study on the agricultural potential of Ethiopia. Its findings showed that Ethiopia had the potential to feed one hundred and forty million people. At that time the country had a population of only twenty-eight million, most of whom were suffering from some form of chronic malnourishment, while she was a net importer of food.

I noticed that the Bible Academy had three hectares of good, arable land that was unused and only growing grass and weeds. I asked the director if he would allow me to use that land for some agricultural experimentation. He agreed. I contacted Ato Mulla, the local Agricultural Extension Agent, and with his encouragement and advice I began to make plans.

He would help us with a fertilizer test and demonstration plot near the road for all passers-by to view and admire and hopefully to emulate. In addition to demonstrating the use of fertilizers, we would use the latest scientific methods in growing tomatoes with chemicals, pruning, and tying them up on wires. We would test twenty varieties of wheat and different varieties of teff. We also included erosion control in our plan.

When some early rain fell in May, I hired a tractor to plow the three hectares, plowing down all the weeds and grass. Then when the rainy season finally started, I arranged with two students, Alemayhu Assefa and Girma Tsige, to farm one hectare. I was to be their financier, and they would repay me from their profits. The rest would go to their schooling the following year. We hired local oxen to prepare the soil for seeding. Alemayhu and Girma planted one hectare with Italian potatoes, lentils, and tomatoes.

I seeded one hectare of an improved variety of white teff, one-quarter of a hectare with wheat, one-half hectare with tomatoes, and planted the remaining land with beans. We bought commercial fertilizer for the crops. I hired five other elementary school students to learn by helping.

We transplanted 3,500 tomato seedlings and strung wires to tie them up off the ground and kept them sprayed with insecticide and fungicide. Alemayhu and Girma planted their 6,000 tomato plants the local way without chemical inputs, only to find that a fungal infection wiped them out completely. They only harvested a very outstanding crop of Italian potatoes that were bigger than any I had ever seen before.

The fertilizer demonstration was a success. One day Ato Mulla came to look at it and said it was one of the best and that he would bring the Minister of Agriculture out to look at it in a couple of weeks. Of course, we never saw the dignitary. I can only imagine that Ministers of Agriculture have weightier matters to occupy their time.

My tomatoes did well. To market them we went around to all the hotels and restaurants and made contracts where we could. Then we found local traders who would come out and buy at a reduced price.

In the end we were able to sell most of our tomatoes, though we did waste about ten crates.

Our teff crop was very good and yielded ten quintals of lovely white teff which we sold for a good price of forty birr per quintal. When everything was sold and all wages and expenses were paid, there was 140 birr ($67) to compensate me for my three months' work. You could say that I farmed for the shear love of it, but isn't that why every farmer farms? The students had earned something from summer employment and had learned some better agricultural practices, and I learned an awful lot about the struggles that a peasant must face if he is to survive.

Cross-Cultural Wedding

When the American maiden, Janie Zimmerman, nursing instructor of the Mission's Dresser Bible School at Deder, fell in love with the handsome young Shawle Whibe, Director of the Mission's Dresser Bible School at Nazareth, also a recent graduate of the Bible Academy, we all suspected that wedding bells or drums would be sounding soon.

The gossiping missionaries did not have to wait long, for soon the invitations were floating through the mail. The event would soon take place at the Mission Chapel in Dire Dawa, home of Robert and Alta Garber who were unofficial godparents to the beautiful Janie. We were not to miss the event of the summer for anything in the world!

Early, on a mid-July Friday morning, we along with nine other expatriate adult staff and three children stuffed ourselves and our luggage into the Nazareth hospital's VW Minibus and set out on a journey towards the rising sun. Our last journey was by third class train, this time we would be following the road. It would be a very different kind of experience.

The road out of Nazareth follows the railroad track through the same lava flow wasteland and past Awash Town through thorn brush desert to the dryland farming community at Miesso. There the road turns south and climbs up the long escarpment into the Ahmar Mountain range. It passes through the town of Asebe Teferi and climbs up and down the mountains and valleys, curving left and right around the ridges and gullies, and going in and out through all the important and unimportant towns and villages and trading points all the way to Harar City and beyond.

During their brief occupation, between 1936 and 1941, the Italians had built a nice gravel road between Addis and Harar. Then, just as soon as the road was completed, the British army, invading from the west, drove the Italians back east and out of the country. But, as the Italian soldiers retreated, in an attempt to slow the British advance, they blew up all the hundreds of bridges they had just built.

In the years following liberation, the bridges were rebuilt, and the road restored up to the town of Awash. But, from Awash on, twenty-eight years later, travelers still had to shift down to low gear and creep through the fords beside the ruined abutments.

We were thankful that it seldom rains in the desert though there were stories of cars being swept away by flash floods caused by heavy rains somewhere upstream many hours earlier. In those cases, the car and the head of the flood got to the crossing at the same moment, and the flood proved to be stronger than the car.

The rest of the road was rough. Even we from Alberta had never experienced so much "washboard" driving. Large potholes looked and felt like they could have been there since Italian times. The potholes were often half-hidden under a thick layer of light grey-brown talcum powder-like dust. Whenever we opened a window to cool the van in the desert heat, the dust filtered in through every screw hole and crack in the body of this ancient Volkswagen.

The road through the highlands was of more recent construction and had good functioning bridges. However, it was still gravel, rough washboard, full of potholes, dusty, twisting and turning, and stretched out over long, slow, steep ascents and short, fast, steep descents.

This road passed through some of the most breath-taking scenery in the world. To the left of the road the land fell away in steep slopes, deep gorges and valleys, and terraced farms with African huts and homesteads randomly scattered far down the mountainside, and from time to time we could look out over the edge to the vast brown desert far below stretching out until it faded into the northern horizon.

On the right side the slope went up with a continuation of the green fields of sorghum, maize, and sweet potatoes, and terraces of coffee and chat, the homesteads with the little round huts with grass roofs, and pasture lands and woodlots with tall, slender eucalyptus growing close together. In many places the mountain tops were still covered with indigenous forests of giant *"zigbah"* that rivaled the California redwoods for size.

Occasionally rivulets of clear water trickled out where the road cut through the rocky slope. Spring-fed streams cascaded down the ravines. The air was clean and pure and cool. The brilliant white fleecy clouds that contrasted so clearly against the close deep blue sky quickly evaporated and disappeared as they floated out over the distant desert.

We arrived in Harar City before 5:00 p.m. and moved into a hotel. After we cleaned some of the dust out of our eyes and nostrils and had something to eat, we went out for a night in the ancient town.

We drove around the old wall in the dark to see the "hyena man." This unique person had a special relationship with the wild hyenas of the area. Common belief held that people who were witches could and often did become hyenas at night and go around to terrorize and attack people. Some suspected this man to have a special league with the Devil or similar sinister personalities.

Every night he would bring a gunnysack of bones from the abattoir at a fixed time and find his place to sit in the dark outside the wall. A few tourists like us would gather nearby, sitting silently in their parked vehicles in the dark. The man would collect one birr from each spectator.

We paid and then waited in the eerie silent darkness. A few stars were shining overhead, and dogs could be heard yapping in the distant city. Somewhere a child cried, probably being spanked by its mother for spilling its supper. Our eyes grew accustomed to the shadows. We waited.

We did not have to wait long. Soon we detected movement in the bushes, an occasional grunt or snarl or a distinct hyena whoop in the distance as a latecomer was urged to hurry. Thus, the hyenas assembled as if called to a meeting at a specified time.

Then the man began his peculiar act. He took out one bone, called a hyena supposedly by name. The first shadowy hyena crept forward out of the murky darkness, the glowing fire in its eyes reflecting the dim parking lights of our VW as it glanced cautiously in our direction while it reached, taking the bone out of the man's hand, and quickly faded back into the dark cover of the bushes and began to chew.

Then the man took out another bone, called another hyena, and placed one end of the bone in his own mouth and leaned backwards. The hyena crept forward leaning right over the man and took the offered bone from the man's mouth, while tourist cameras flashed, then retreated into the shadows. The man then held a third bone in his hand behind his head, called another hyena, and let it walk right over his body to claim its bone.

As though controlled by rigid though unwritten rules, each eager hyena cautiously awaited its turn, crouching with the others in the darkness at the edge of the bushes, eyes occasionally flashing to let us know they were there, alert, and ready to be called.

This exercise went on until the sack was empty. It gave one an eerie feeling to be sitting in a car surrounded by a large pack of maybe fifty mysterious carnivorous beasts crunching and chewing bones in the dark.

I couldn't help thinking of the power in those jaws crunching those leg bones of matured oxen as if they were candy canes! What chance would I have if I should be met on a dark path far from home some night by a very hungry hyena? The shiver I felt wasn't from the cold.

Saturday morning found us up early, heading for Dire Dawa. We stopped at Alemaya College for a brief visit on our way. In Dire Dawa we checked into the Continental Hotel downtown since the Mission guest house was full, and the Garbers were preparing to leave for a year's furlough the day after the wedding. After lunch we all got ready for the Saturday afternoon wedding.

It was a simple yet marvelous event, a blend of Western, Evangelical, Orthodox, and Ethiopian customs. Loose tongues clicked freely and ineffectively weighing the pros and the cons of bi-cultural and bi-racial marriage in general, and gravely measuring the chances for the survival and happiness of this marriage. Only time would reveal their wisdom and their ignorance. In the meantime, the happy couple were to establish their first love nest in Nazareth where they both would work in the program of the hospital.

The next day after church, we had dinner with Mestawet who was living in Dire Dawa at this time with her aunt. Following that, we and the Beachys headed back west to Deder where we visited and spent the night.

Our other travel mates took the Sunday train back to Nazareth. We were assigned the privilege of moving the family of Beyene Mulatu from Deder to Nazareth. As Hospital Administrator, Beyene was being transferred from the Deder Hospital to the Haile Mariam Mamo Memorial Hospital at Nazareth.

We arrived home the following afternoon to find that Paul Kraybill, the Overseas Secretary of our mission and Arthur Miller from our mission board were visiting the projects in our area. We also learned that Mrs. Clyde Shenk, a pioneer missionary in Tanzania, was killed in an MAF plane crash in the Ngong Hills just outside Nairobi.

Vacation Fun and Horror

In mid-August we organized a second camping trip to Lake Langano and south to Awassa. This time we had the old green army tent we bought from Nevin Horst, but he had sewn a good canvas floor under it. Additionally, we bought a lot of their camping equipment. Using cardboard boxes and sawdust, we made an icebox in which we could keep frozen meat cold for most of the week.

We loaded everything into and on top of the little yellow Opal along with enough drinking water and set out for Langano. By this time, the Christodos family had moved to Zambia, and we were alone as a family except we left baby Sheryl home with Almaz, and we took along a young boy to guard our place and to help with dishes and errands. We were somewhat experienced by now. We selected a nice site under an acacia tree close to the lake.

We found that our friends and colleagues, the Daniel Ness family and the Dwight Beachy family were there, too, sharing a cottage. The children enjoyed playing together in the sand and swimming though the lake was very cold. We had fun together until they left.

One day we left the boy to watch the camp and drove further south past Shashemene to Awassa. South of Langano we entered a rich agricultural area of great beauty. There was a huge sisal plantation and lush fields of maize.

Further south we entered the "enset" culture area. Sidamo people live in large, rounded grass covered houses where the rounded roof simply slopes down getting steeper and steeper until it blends in with the wall.

These homes are surrounded by large plantations of the enset plant often called "false banana" because of its resemblance to the banana plant. This enset plant does not produce bananas as fruit. It is the roots that are eaten. A starchy substance is scraped off the fibers and is processed and fermented in holes in the ground for periods of up to seven years. Finally, the product is made into a kind of flat, heavy, rubbery-textured bread called "kocho" that forms the staple diet of the Sidamo people. It is a very labor-intensive way to prepare food and is starchy and low in protein, but when eaten with a special blend of ground meat, spices, and cottage cheese, it is surprisingly tasty.

A few weeks after returning from Langano, we joined a group of the teachers and their families going to Sodere for an evening swim and picnic. I played with Cindy, dressed in her yellow bathing suit, for a while in the crowded kids pool and then put her in her little black inner tube that just fit snugly under her arms. She was used to paddling all over the deep pool with that tube, so I could trust her. I told her to keep it on while I go with the men for a swim in the big pool. Vera was holding Karen, and the other women were in there too with their little ones. There was nothing for me to worry about.

Cindy was just tall enough to stand on the shallow end of the sloping floor of the kids pool and still keep her mouth above the water. Apparently, she noticed that her younger friend, two-year old Dwayne Shenk, did not have a tube of his own, so, in true missionary spirit, she took hers off and shared it with him. She thought she was big enough to go without.

But the water has a way of lifting the body from a firm footing when you stand in it up to your chin. Cindy found herself sliding deeper till the water covered her nose. None of the women saw her. When she opened her mouth to scream, water poured in. She couldn't scream, and she couldn't get herself out! When all her oxygen was used up, she simply fainted.

By God's providence in that crucial moment, Esther Becker noticed something yellow floating under the water and reached down to investigate. In shocked amazement, she pulled up our blue-faced Cindy, unconscious!

After a few laps across the big pool, I heard Esther Becker screaming for help as she was carrying something yellow out of the pool. Instantly recognizing that it was Cindy, I climbed out of the water as fast as I could and raced over to the crowd that was fast gathering around her. We laid her on the grass. I had never seen such blue lips and tongue! It was awful!

Remembering the rules, I had learned back in first aid class connected with attempting to resuscitate drowning victims, I was prepared to administer mouth to mouth artificial respiration. The first step is to roll the victim over on his/her side and give a sharp slap on the back to dislodge any possible vomit, water, or obstruction in the bronchial passage before blowing air into the mouth.

The sharp slap triggered her breathing function, and Cindy opened her eyes. Then she started to cry. That cry was the sweetest music we had ever heard!

The swimming party was over. We all put on our clothes and carried Cindy to the car and took her to the hospital to check her out. She vomited a lot of water on the way and then went to sleep. Dr. Roy Wert checked her over and declared her okay. She had swallowed a lot of water but had not inhaled. She had held her breath until she went unconscious, a natural defense against drowning, the doctor explained. I had never heard such a thing before.

Years later Cindy told me that she cried because she thought I was spanking her for taking off her tube when I had told her to keep it on. Yes, there is a price to pay for disobedience. It could have been fatal!

This was one time I was glad for having had swimming lessons and the Life Saver's Course. Even though I did not really have to use it, I, at least, knew what to do. It could have been so much worse. It is hard to figure out how a person can drown in a pool full of people. Anyway, we were profoundly thankful to God that Esther did turn around and notice that yellow thing floating under the water!

A Motor Cyclist's Brief Career

Several of my more affluent American missionary friends had motorcycles. On holidays or Saturdays, they often went out into the countryside on hunting expeditions or just exploratory joy rides. I felt left out.

I fell into irresistible temptation when I heard that Fred Yoder, an American University exchange student, was going home and wanted to sell his slightly used bright blue Suzuki 100 c.c. street bike for a bargain price of only 800 birr. He had paid 1400 birr for it a year earlier. I rushed to Addis to close the deal.

Although I hardly knew how to ride a bicycle and had never driven a motorcycle, I naively assumed I would just get on and drive it the ninety-five kilometers home to Nazareth, even if evening was fast approaching. No big deal. In the mission yard, I mounted the seat of this slick beast and kicked the starter. It roared to life. I suddenly realized it possessed a power I was unprepared to control.

To tame this beast required a multi-tasking skill that I had not yet learned. As I struggled to manage the clutch, the gearshift, the brake, and the flow of fuel, while keeping it balanced on its two wheels and steering it in the desired direction, I experienced a paradigm shift. Was I prepared and wise or even able to take it out in heavy rush-hour traffic and make it safely home? I swallowed my pride and submitted. "Wisdom is the better part of valor!" I arranged to have this untamed beast transported by the mission van to Nazareth at a later date and took the bus home that night.

When the motorcycle arrived in Nazareth a few days later, I took it out on the football field to teach myself to drive. It was then that I realized how foolish I was to even think of driving it home under Addis Ababa's congested road conditions, especially at night!

After a few minutes of practice around and around the football field, I drove home and offered to take Vera for a ride. Of course, Cindy was all excited about going along. Vera was a bit naive too, or maybe it was overconfidence in her fine husband who could do so many things?

Vera mounted behind me, and with Cindy straddling the fuel tank and hanging on in front of me, I started the motorcycle and drove a few kilometers toward Nazareth. Then we started climbing up the escarpment which required shifting down. As we came to a sharp curve, with my lack of experience, I lost control and tipped over doing a power dive onto the pavement. Cindy was scared; I was scratched; Vera was trapped under the little monster; and the beautiful blue machine's headlight and fender were scratched.

My ego was deflated the most, and my gross naivete was diminished considerably. How totally irresponsible to take my family, my most precious loved ones on my maiden voyage on the back of this unfamiliar, yet powerful mean machine! I now saw it would take some time to get intimately acquainted with this wild blue brute.

One fateful day some weeks later, while I was driving the motorcycle down the main street of Nazareth at a decent clip, a man driving a Volkswagen "beetle" approaching on the other side of the boulevard decided to make a U-turn right in front of me as if my presence did not exist. A collision was inevitable despite the length of rubber I laid. My front wheel lodged tight between the front fender and the bumper of the Volkswagen. I was ejected through the air, landing about twenty feet in front of the "beetle" which had stalled on the spot.

I picked myself up, unhurt, and saw the man sitting in his car sort of stunned and sheepish looking. I did not know if he knew English or not because he did not say a word, but I found some unsanctified vocabulary somewhere deep in the uncleansed caverns of my mind and left it ringing in his ears as I jerked the wheel free from his car, jumped on the starter and took off, never mind that the impact bent the last four inches of his bumper completely around. Later, I sincerely hoped that he did not recognize me as one of those "missionaries."

One Saturday in November, I decided to take a little weekend journey with Mergia, a grade twelve student, to his hometown of Bekoji, about 140 kilometers south in Arussi Province. After crossing the Awash River, the road climbs continuously up a gentle incline all the way to the Arussi highlands. Overloaded with two grown adults plus luggage, this long steady climb was too much for the little underpowered machine. All at once, about ninety-five kilometers into our journey, the engine just quit running, and the cycle quickly rolled to a dead stop.

We got off and checked the fuel and oil. Everything was in order. I tried to start it again. The motor turned over easily, too easily, but would not emit even a cough. I checked the spark plug. It worked fine. We waited until the engine cooled off enough so that I could touch it. When I removed the head, I found there was a big hole burned completely through the aluminum piston. This would take more than a Nazareth garage to fix. Would spare parts be available anywhere this side of Japan?

Fortunately, Mergia had a friend who had a house and hotel just a kilometer away. We pushed the cardiac case down the hill to that place, decided to store it there, and took a bus home. So much for our trip to Bekoji. I never did get there.

The next day we took the Academy's Ford Taunis van back to collect the stricken motorcycle. It was many months later that we got a spare piston through Herb Kraybill's connections with his brother, Dr. Harold Kraybill in the U.S.A. Yes, this medical doctor could fix most anything, even the "cardiac" problems of a motorcycle!

By that time our term was up, I was ready to sell the Suzuki. I did not advertise, just mentioned my intention to sell and had a buyer almost at once. A young graduate who had his first job at Koka Dam thought it would be ideal for cheap transportation to and from work. We agreed on a price of 850 birr, but he would need to take out a bank loan. Would I hold it for him for some days while he went through the lengthy process of getting the loan application filed and approved? I preferred cash since we would be leaving before the week was out. Reluctantly, I promised to hold it for him.

Two days later Abdi Nur, a Christian Somali student, brought a merchant who was determined to buy the motorcycle. The merchant had heard about it via a friend and had traveled all the way from Dire Dawa with cash in hand to take it home with him. Abdi helped as translator for the negotiations.

"You have come too late," I informed the man, "The motorcycle has already been sold! There is nothing to discuss!"

Assuming I was trying to drive a hard bargain he asked, "Have you been paid?"

"Not yet" I acknowledged, "but the buyer is arranging a loan, and I am committed to give him time!"

"Are you sure that the bank will approve the young man's loan?"

"No," I admitted, "I'm not sure."

"Then why not take real hard cash on hand rather than wait on a young man with a shaky promise?" the man reasoned with irrefutable logic as he pulled out a roll of bills and counted out 850 birr in cash.

"No, it is already sold and that is final!" I replied.

"Don't you know that an African's promise is nothing? He will never be back with the money!" he chided scornfully as he added a fifty, making it 900 birr.

I was beginning to resent this man's intrusion and the assumptions he was making about my integrity. I emphatically insisted, "I have given my word to the young man, and I cannot go back on it for any amount of money!"

Not quickly to be defeated, he finally added three hundred more to the pile saying: "I have come this far at considerable cost in time and expense and simply cannot go back without the motorcycle!"

By this time, I was getting annoyed at this man's twisted morals and demanding self-interest. Why should he be pressuring me like this? Did he not have any respect for me or my integrity? Why should the rich always get things their way, ripping the opportunities out of the hands of the poor?

I finally looked him coldly in the eye and said, "I have explained to you that I have given my word to the young man, and there is no amount of money big enough to persuade me to break my word. My promises are not for sale to the highest bidder! I did not advertise my motorcycle for sale, and I did not ask you to come, and I am not obliged to entertain your demands!"

At last, he recognized intransigence greater than his own and turned away in anger, muttering in his own tongue, "I have never in my life seen such a strange fool as this blind "ferinj"!

The clash of cultures and the clash of "kingdoms." How can a nominal Muslim merchant bred and grown in a cut-throat capitalist world understand "kingdom of God" values? How could he know of the simple principle to live by that goes, "Let your 'Yes!' be 'Yes!' and your 'No!' be 'No!'; anything beyond this comes from the evil one."?

After he left, Abdi, who had been helping as interpreter, was puzzled as to whether I had made a rather foolish decision. For him, it was a shocking lesson in practical application of Christian ethics and integrity. Now what if the young man did not turn up as he promised on Friday with the money?

Friday came, and the young man came without the money. He

was having some delays with the bank procedures. Could I wait a little longer? He was trying his best and needed that motorcycle badly. Our time came to leave, and we left Ethiopia without seeing the money or selling the cycle.

A few weeks later, a letter from Herb Kraybill informed us that the young man was so very proud to be driving that blue Suzuki and the money was safely in our account—a happy ending to the story for all of us except the rich merchant.

An Easter Vacation

We decided to fly to Somalia for our 1970 Easter vacation. For just twelve dollars and ten cents extra per adult we could add Mogadishu onto our tickets home. Why not do it? It would be great to visit our two graduates, Said Samatar and Herzi Ahmed. We would also like to visit the missionaries there and see the places mentioned in Omar Eby's books *Sense and Incense* and *A Whisper in a Dry Land* including the grave of Merlin Grove, the first Mennonite martyr in that land. We planned to leave on Friday, April 24th.

On April 22nd we went to the Somali Embassy to get our visas. They promised they would have them ready for us to pick them up by 4:00 p.m. on Thursday. Well, that is cutting it pretty close, but what are the alternatives?

When we came to pick up our visas on Thursday evening, we were informed that there would be no visas for us at this time. There had been a coup in that unhappy land. They had received a telegram from Mogadishu that morning ordering them to not grant any entry visas for Somalia without first sending an application and getting clearance from the government at Mogadishu. This ritual would take another week. That is how the new revolutionary government went about "improving" the tourist trade!

There we were after all the bureaucratic red tape, headaches, organizing, and anticipation, with our suitcases packed, tickets in hand, reservations booked for the next morning, lacking only little visa stamps. "Wait a week!" Just like that, our plans were added to that vast rubbish heap of wasted efforts and unfulfilled dreams and promises. What could we do now?

The first thing we could do was to telegraph our friends in Somalia: "Visa Refused. Trip Canceled."

We never did get to Somalia. Instead of going to the airport the next day, we took the bus home to Nazareth. After some quick reorienting of our thoughts and planning, we packed our tent and camping equipment into a car with about five days' supply of food and set out for our favorite vacation spot, Lake Langano. The children were not disappointed at all. They just loved to camp and play in the water and dig in the sandy beach.

Karen was so excited that while reciting Psalms 23 the night before leaving, she said: "He makes me lie down in a tent!" Camping can be a cheap wholesome way for a family to take a vacation.

Family camping at Lake Langano, 1970

On the Exploitation of Labor

Our school received a grant of $108,000 or 268,125 birr from Inter-Church Co-ordinating Committee for Development Aid, the Protestant aid arm of the government of Holland for a building project that would give us a modern science building with three classrooms, a chapel-auditorium that could seat three hundred, a student center, a library, and a latrine block. Building was to begin the summer of 1969.

Calvin Shenk organized a crew that made thousands of cinder blocks of volcanic ash and cement. Blueprints were drawn, and a contract was awarded to a local construction company. Construction got underway in late fall.

The contractor hired about forty laborers to dig the foundation trenches by hand and to pack in the fill after the blocks were laid. They had to work like slaves for ten hours per day for which they were paid the paltry sum of one birr (about forty-five cents U.S.). While those slaved away, sweat pouring down in the hot sun, a hundred other men waited patiently outside the locked gate, hoping for a chance to be hired.

If any worker slacked in his pace of work or tried to snatch a little rest, the boss at once fired him on the spot and sent him out. He knew there was a pool of desperate humanity waiting outside the gate from which he could pick and choose the best prospect for an effective laborer to take the poor worn-out man's place.

To me it was completely inhumane and unreasonable exploitation. I was ashamed to have this kind of treatment of fellow human beings associated with the school with which I was working, but we had given the contract to the contractor. Now it was Ethiopian exploiting Ethiopian. There wasn't a lot we could do to make it a kinder arrangement. The poor laborers seemed to accept this treatment with dull accustomed resignation as their normal lot in life. They were eager to keep their job, as meager and unpleasant as it was. They would be back at sunrise tomorrow.

CHAPTER 11

The Metamorphosis of a Development Worker

"Teach me to do your will, for you are my God;
may your good Spirit lead me on level ground."
–Psalms 143:10 (NIV)

A Growing Vision

While my mind was turning towards development, dozens of different schemes suggested themselves to me. First, I visited a farm project run by the Swedish Mission for lepers on a large tract of land in the Awash River Valley east of Nazareth. I was impressed that 500 lepers who had been outcasts and beggars were now being rehabilitated, earning their own living while learning to do farming as well as other trades, having a church and a school for their children, and having their own community where their dignity was being restored.

A vision, a dream began to form in my mind of a similar home for the street children of Addis Ababa. I recalled a scene I could never forget.

It was on a street in Addis Ababa one cold wet morning, I noticed six little street boys who at the same instant spotted a few overripe bananas on a garbage truck. In one split second, they all jumped up on the truck of reeking garbage, grabbed the bananas and stuffed them into their mouths. The banana of one of the boys was so overripe that it came apart and fell into the wet muck on the street. The boy scooped it up and popped it, muck, and all, into his mouth! That is hunger!

That was only representative of the way hundreds and maybe thousands of children existed from day to day. What future did they have? I began to explore the possibility of obtaining a tract of land for such a purpose.

A Coffee Plantation in the "Alps of Ethiopia"

About 150 kilometers to the south of Addis, on the southern slope of Gugu Mountain in Arussi, lived an eighty-two-year-old Swiss engineer, Ernest Baumgartner and his wife, Helen, and a fifty-four-year-old crippled daughter, Betty, on a coffee plantation he carved out of the wilderness about forty-five years earlier.

Preparing for his inevitable demise, Mr. Baumgartner had made a trust or foundation to which he gave all his property and named the Mennonite Mission in Ethiopia the trustee of this foundation. The Mission was to take care of the family until they all died and to continue the work of the clinic and to use the rest of the property and money in such a way that it would benefit that community.

The Mission accepted the estate and was looking for a volunteer couple to live there and manage it according to the plan on a self-supporting basis. The place had been neglected and would take at least three years to become self-supporting again. I took some interest in this as a possible solution to my dream.

In early December 1969, I was invited to accompany Shemsudin Abdo and Daniel Ness on a trip by Mission Aviation Fellowship (MAF) plane to check out the Baumgartner property and proposal more deeply. We flew out of Nazareth up over the escarpment into the Arussi Mountains and straight towards Mt. Gugu which rises to 11,887 feet. Down over the edge of the mountain, 6,000 feet below on the southern side, we found the Baumgartner house and coffee farm and made several low swoops to let them know that we would be coming and to get a sweeping view of the place.

We landed about twelve kilometers from the farm, on a little airstrip near the little town of Gololcha. We walked for two and one-half hours up the hill before we reached the farm. It was high noon. We arrived very hot and sore and tired, but the very warm and hospitable welcome we received renewed our spirits.

Ernest Baumgartner, an engineer, had built his house along the lines of a modest but adequate Swiss chalet. It was a two-story structure made of sawn timber inside and out. It had a lot of glass windows and was surrounded by a bougainvillea hedge. He had built it himself out of timber cut on the farm and sawn into planed and tongue-and-grooved boards on his own water-powered sawmill.

To power his tools, irrigate his gardens, and meet all their domestic needs, Ernest had installed a pipe from a spring 1,000 feet up the mountain that brought the water down to their home under very high pressure.

Helen served excellent meals with her own Swiss-style cooking and all the kinds of vegetables and fruits that they grew in the garden. Meals were served on a table set with fine china, silverware, and crystal on a linen cloth complete with serviettes—keeping their own Swiss traditions in this African wilderness. They had many beautiful flowers and flowering shrubs in the yard. Hedges and grass were well trimmed.

The Baumgartner farm was located in a region that was almost untouched by modern development. The road connecting it with the outside was passable only in the dry season by four-wheel-drive vehicles and trucks. Its high, rugged mountain peaks and deep gorges and fertile valleys and long green forested slopes earned it the title, "The Alps of Ethiopia." Its fertile soil was excellent for growing coffee and fruit and most food crops. Springs gushed out of mountainsides that could be harnessed for power and irrigation.

The neighboring Oromo people were subsistence farmers and very little of the land's potential was being utilized at that time.

The farm consisted of about 350 acres, mostly of natural forest with only 7,000 coffee trees planted.

Mr. Baumgartner, an engineer, had built a road six kilometers long with seven switchbacks up the mountainside for cars and trucks to connect his farm both to Gololcha below him and with a road above him going to Asella and Nazareth. Using his own resources and local labor, it took him twenty years to complete.

Now, with erosion, the road was in a state of disrepair and hardly usable.

The Baumgartners story was very interesting. Ernest came to Ethiopia in 1905 as a young man of about twenty years. He served briefly as a tutor in French, having the young Tafari Makonnen, the son of Ras Makonnen the Duke of Harar, as his student. A bond was established that did not break, even after his student/friend was later crowned as Emperor Haile Selassie I.

For some years he ran a transport business using fifty oxcarts and 800 oxen to ferry goods, anything from whiskey to guns, between the rail terminal at Dire Dawa and Addis Ababa (a distance of about 450 kilometers). This was before there was either railroad or road. A round trip would take about three months. This business closed when trains started to reach Addis in 1917.

During that time, he went back to Switzerland and brought back his bride, Helen, a trained nurse. They were religious people of perhaps Huguenot background. For a while he worked as an engineer with the construction of several roads in the mountains.

Upon reaching forty years of age, Ernest decided it was time to settle down. Menelik II had given them the land, but it took them eighteen years to get a clear title deed. This achievement required making two separate visits to seek Haile Selassie's help.

We asked him why he did not choose a farm closer to the capital and roads? He answered, "At that time there were no roads anywhere. This place was as good as any. They chose the wrong place to put the capital!"

During all those forty-five years, Helen Baumgartner stayed home and ran a small clinic, the only clinic in the area. She said that for twenty years she had never seen a white face except those of her husband and daughter. She was respected as a healer or medicine woman. The people called her "our mother" or "the woman with the healing hands." They had great faith in her. If she said to a sick person, "I have no medicine for your sickness!" they would say, "Oh no, just place your hands on me and pray and bless me and I will be well!"

Now she was about eighty years old and stooped and white-haired, but still serving the sick. The average number of patients was about thirty-five per day, and on market days, Helen could see as many as sixty. Few of her patients ever paid for their medicines or treatment. The Baumgartners subsidized their clinic from their own income. Despite the extreme isolation and their advanced age, we found them all bright and quite aware of events in the larger world.

As we were walking on the road, Shemsudin stopped to talk to a man and a woman in Oromo. The woman said, "Why don't you come and help us, and teach us what we don't know?" Shemsudin said to me later, "Maybe this is like the call Paul received from the man from Macedonia!" Maybe?

On the third day, Mr. Baumgartner arranged for mules and an escort to return us back down to the airstrip where the MAF plane picked us up in the afternoon.

In the days following, I mulled this opportunity over in my head formulating the possibilities. My dream was to make the farm into a self-supporting school/clinic/ church complex where students would come from the villages and study reading, writing, arithmetic, and religion as well as agriculture and a trade such as carpentry, mechanics, or smithery. Each student would work a few hours every day on the farm or in the shop. They would also learn health and hygiene and would take the new ideas back to their villages and teach their parents and neighbors. The produce of the farm could support the students and staff. If it was a success, other such programs could be started in other areas. I prayed that we might have the wisdom to know what God's will was for us in this.

An Exploratory Visit to Bokay

The question of our future loomed larger and larger as we approached the end of our three-year contract. As we began our final semester at the Bible Academy in 1970, we had an official invitation to return for another three-year term of teaching after a three-month furlough. Somehow, I was tired of teaching and was looking for a way to get involved with grass-roots poverty-relieving activity of some undefined sort. I had sent applications to about five different graduate schools to pursue a degree in development.

Then at the end of February, Shemsudin invited me to travel with him to "spy out the promised land" in the Chercher District of Harar Province where there was supposed to be a large tract of land open for settlement. Shemsudin's brother, Mohammed, a local chief in Deder, was given a plot of 20,000 acres by the government to distribute to peasants he could persuade to move there from the over-crowded Deder community. Of course, I was interested in accompanying him.

We traveled by train from Nazareth the four hours to the town of Miesso where we took a taxi the twenty kilometers uphill to Asebe Teferi. There we visited in the home of one of Shemsudin's friends, a Christian who was running his own dispensary and was leading a small group of evangelical believers.

Like a lot of middle-class Ethiopians, he had kept a handgun within reach of his bed, "just in case!" He had the sore misfortune of waking up one night seeing a figure moving at the foot of his bed. Instinctively he had reached for his gun and fired a shot at the figure. It slumped to the floor. When he found a flashlight to examine the hapless "intruder," he found it to be his wife! Dead! So much for the protective value of handguns!

We rented a Landrover that took us another twenty-seven kilometers south to the town of Bedessa where, as I described it in my diary:

> We dined and bedded down in the swank luxury of Bedessa's best hotel. We each had a private room of about seven and one-half feet by seven and one-half feet with a bed, a chair, a stand, and a candle. We enjoyed the comfort of an open-air washroom—the courtyard—and a rather closed-air toilet. It was a bit muddy in the washroom and odiferous in the toilet, but the bed was good, and the food was tolerable.

In the morning we negotiated with Landrover owners to hire a vehicle to take us out to "the place." Most Landrovers were busy, and only one was available at the exploitative price of 150 birr for the 120 kilometers journey into the unknown. We negotiated for the man to lower his price, but he insisted that "the place" is "far and unfamiliar" and the "road" is "bad and dangerous." If we did not want to pay him well, he would be perfectly happy to stay home.

After breakfast and searching in vain for alternate transport and seeing that this man was resolute in his demands, we had to decide. It was getting near 10:00 a.m., and the day was passing. We had come this far, and if we wanted to reach our goal, we would have to pay, so we finally capitulated.

Bedessa was the last town before "the place." From there the road soon became a trail blazed by the military some years ago to contain unrest among the Somali people inhabiting the Wabi Shebelle River basin and the Ogaden to the southeast. It was still passable in the dry season. For the first thirty kilometers, we passed through cultivated fields to a hamlet called "Bokay Tiko."

From there the "road" continued over a rocky stretch, and then over a vast empty expanse of gently undulating grasslands studded with occasional stunted thorn trees. There were no farms and no dwellings to suggest any human habitation. We were told that the Somali nomads grazed their herds there seasonally.

Four hours after setting out, we arrived at our destination, "the place," which we were told went by the name of "Bokay Teffe." Here we found a tiny settlement, a village of grass and stick shelters built in a circle with a tractor and a plow and wagon and a few fuel barrels and other equipment lying in the center. A small plot in the middle had been plowed, and a thin crop of healthy-looking maize and beans was growing.

The settlement had been started two months ago with ten farmers involved with three tractors. Already they had plowed about 200 acres. The soil looked like a variety of black cotton soil. It was likely quite fertile, but no one had ever done soil tests nor collected rainfall and temperature data out there, so we just couldn't know for certain what the potential was. There were very few trees in this area, just perhaps a sign that rainfall was quite scanty.

Mohammed's group had plans to eventually settle the whole region, build a town with mosque, clinic, and school, and a church, too, if we would come into the picture. It reminded me of the challenge of pioneering in the prairies of western Canada seventy years earlier. They offered to reserve 1,000 acres for me if I would be interested in joining their community or starting a project there. It was an intriguing challenge!

Having seen our "future home," and since we had a driver and rented vehicle, we returned the four hours back to "civilization" and spent another night in the same luxury hotel as the previous night.

God's Leading

A week later, on March 6, 1970, I was called to a meeting with representatives of Mennonite Economic Development Associates (MEDA) and the Eastern Mennonite Board of Missions in the Ethiopia Hotel, Addis Ababa. Among those present were Don Jacobs, Nathan Hege, Daniel Ness of EMM, Lloyd Fisher, Ivan Martin, and Orie Miller of MEDA.

I presented a preliminary plan for a self-supporting agricultural demonstration and training project based upon the likely location of Bokay. The project objectives included assisting peasant farmers to resettle on newly available crown land; combining an evangelical witness with social activities with the intent of extending the Body of Christ in a new area; training young men and women in rural skills; networking between newly settled population and the development efforts of nation and Christian church; and assisting nomadic (Oromo) peoples in the area with simple medicines and education, as much as possible.

The proposed project was to be sustained by mechanized cereal production on the 1,000-acre plot for self-support and for program support. It would take considerable capital to get started. I was hoping this might be covered with a MEDA loan.

A brisk and frank discussion followed. The group was affirmative, especially Orie Miller. Yet, they raised serious questions: Is the area envisioned suitable for peasant cereal farming? Is there adequate rainfall? Is the soil fertile? Would not the lack of roads make it economically infeasible? How could it be financed? Is the self-support cum program-support concept realistic? Would high intensity mechanized farming have any educational value for the peasant masses?

The consensus of the group was that they recommendation to Paul Kraybill, the Overseas Secretary that EMM plan for a program in which the Hansens could be supported as "Development Missionaries" whose entire efforts would be put into assisting peasant farmers to settle, training as possible in rural skills and rudimentary education along with an evangelistic, pastoral program.

The acceptance of this proposal would depend much upon Paul Kraybill's attitude towards it. The location of the project could be at Bokay or at Baumgartner's farm in Arussi or at another site yet to be decided.

CHAPTER 12

Home Interlude

The end of the school year in 1970 brought the end of our term of service. We flew out of Ethiopia on June 23rd, still not certain of the year ahead.

Nairobi, Kenya

This time flying was not such a novelty for us, but it was a great adventure for the older children. They were impressed by a lot of things, but what impressed them most was having our meals brought to us in our seats in little neat trays with little dishes that would be excellent for feeding their dolls!

Our journey home took us to Nairobi, Kenya, where we were unduly impressed with the greenery and beautiful flowers. Quite a contrast to the dry desert conditions and dust laden June winds of Nazareth.

Like every good tourist worthy of the name ought to do, we spent a day viewing the animals in the Nairobi Game Park on the outskirts of Nairobi. It was especially exciting when we came upon a pride of lions relaxing in the sun. They did not mind those four carloads of tourists circling around them, snapping pictures. They seemed to know that they were the "king of the beasts" as they laid back, yawned, and went to sleep. Tourists can be so boring!

Rome

Having enjoyed three days in Nairobi, we boarded our plane heading for Rome. As our plane took to the air, we noticed there was a loud thump below us as the landing gear was retracted into the body of the aircraft. No explanation was given, and we took no further notice.

But, when we came into the Leonardo de Vinci Airport, we were surprised to see at least twenty firetrucks and ambulances lining the runway. And we were even more surprised when they all started up and escorted our plane as we approached, following us into the unloading terminal. We found out that when the plane took off, the one landing gear, while retracting, got jammed in the cover which apparently cut the tire, or they were afraid it might have. To be on the safe side, they wanted the rescue squad to be ready just in case there was a problem with the landing. Thanks be to God, who always has his hand in our affairs and protects us!

It was kind of shocking coming out of the airport to find all the bus and taxi drivers were big burly white men. It was even more shocking when they talked to us in the Italian language. We found ourselves responding to them in Amharic. We had gotten so accustomed to the slender brown Ethiopian taxi drivers, for a moment something seemed wrong. Culture shock!

We were real greenhorns when it came to the refined art of being a tourist. Now we decided we would join a tour group to see the famous Vatican Museum with its vast treasure of priceless works of art. People looked at us twice, clucked their tongues and gave each other knowing glances as we lugged our three squirming kids up the steps into the tour bus with all the adults.

When we got to the museum, we found its one and one-quarter miles of elegantly decorated hallway packed with thousands of tourists moving in hundreds of tour groups. Group guides raised their voices in every language imaginable as they competed for the attention of their followers. The June 27th Mediterranean sun was melting the asphalt in the humid city streets outside, while the endless throngs perspired their radiant heat inside the ancient edifice. I sometimes wonder whether the accumulated human sweat of thousands of tourists on the hot days of summer would not have some impact on those precious fine works of art.

In those hot halls, Vera and I struggled to keep up with our guide while keeping our oldest two from disappearing in the throng as they wildly shouted, "Look Dad!" while pointing and running towards whatever took their fancy in different directions. Forget about hearing the guide, let alone reading the inscriptions!

In a short time, the youngest two became tired and needed to be carried. While Mom struggled to carry the sleeping Sheryl, I controlled the whining, tired Karen, and grasped the sweating hand of Cindy fearing lest she disappear among the thousands of legs. Needless to say, that which promised to be an interesting expedition quickly degenerated into a three-hour endurance test, then an unending nightmare.

When the marathon trial was finally over, we hunkered down in Hotel Canada for the rest of the day to recuperate. That was to be the last guided tour for many child-rearing years to come.

The next day we took a leisurely stroll with the kids down to the Colosseum, the Arch of Titus, and the park around the Roman Forum. I could wander around the ancient ruins and soak up the sights and sounds of history and commune with the spirits of the martyrs while Vera relaxed in the nearby park with the kids.

Standing there at the actual Colosseum, I found it even more awe-inspiring than anything portrayed in photographs. How those Romans, without the advantage of motor-powered tools, could erect such a massive structure with such huge stones staggers one's imagination. It shows what power the emperor had in those ancient days.

Then I had to think of the Christians, who, by the thousands, died for their faith. We were challenged once again by their memory. Will we today even live for what they died for? May it ever be so!

For some unexplainable reason, the girls and their mother were not overly fascinated by the history-laden rocks and bricks. By the end of the day, I gave up on ever seeing the catacombs. Perhaps on another journey when I am old and alone!

London

Our journey took us to London where we were given accommodation overnight in St. James Place, a classy hotel downtown right in the heartland among the seats of power.

That evening we walked over to Westminster Abbey where we

saw the graves of some of England's greatest such as Livingstone, whose heart was buried in Africa. His body was dried and carried by his African friends over one thousand miles from the interior to the coast by foot so that it might be shipped home to England and laid to rest in this most sacred shrine. Where can one find such loyalty today?

The Abbey is just a stone's throw away from the House of Commons and Buckingham Palace. This proximity symbolizes the European marriage of Church and State. The House is overshadowed by the famous Westminster Tower with Big Ben, the world's biggest clock by whose chimes a billion people around the world set their watches in relation to "Greenwich mean time." But time was not there to allow us to visit these monuments of history. Yet it was impressive just to be near this nerve center of the once glorious world-wide "empire upon which the sun never sets"!

The Victorian architecture and decor of our hotel blended well with the elegance of its renowned surroundings and met well the expectations and comforts of its upper-class society. How strangely out of place we felt! Our more-than three-year-old "missionary closet" clothes, bleached by the burning equatorial sun and worn by the sand-laden winds of Nazareth, flashed our conspicuousness like oscillating neon signs. Our overgrown home-done sun-bleached haircuts and deep-tanned dry skin betrayed again what our clothes obviously suggested. To further their suspicions, the behavior of our three curious and uncultured kids confirmed beyond a doubt the nature of our occupation: "Another missionary family going home on furlough, taking advantage of the airline's largess!"

English dinners are served late. We had traveled all the way from Rome and had turned the clock back two hours. Our children were hungry and tired and so were we. The hour finally arrived when Big Ben struck eight, and we could eat.

We timidly made our entrance into the dining room, then almost retreated. The elegance of the Victorian furnishings, the elaborate gold and ivory moldings of the ceiling and massive brass and crystal chandeliers, the antique Persian carpets, the finest silverware and bone china on the tables, the formal uniforms and stiff manners of the waiters, and the expensive suits and fine evening gowns of the guests almost screamed at us: "You can't come in here!"

But a waiter beckoned encouragement to us and led us to a table. I fortified myself with the reasoning that we had paid as much for our tickets as anyone else and should not be ashamed to accept the same treatment as anyone else regardless of appearance. In Ethiopia we had always been the well-to-do, the privileged class. Here, suddenly we were the paupers. Another evidence of reverse culture shock!

We got our wide-eyed children settled long enough to order the meal of the evening, "Stewed English Duck." We were probably as wide-eyed as our kids in this exotic atmosphere. We soon noticed that we were the only ones in the dining room with children. We felt eyes peering at us as we ate and as the children squirmed and dropped utensils and picked at each other and fussed and refused to eat and made loud comments. The duck was absolutely delicious and, coming from a land of hunger where nothing is ever wasted, we parents ate more of the children's share than we should have. It was difficult to sleep that night!

We later learned that dining out for the English is not like going to "MacDonald's." They do not take their children to formal dining settings.

I did manage to walk over to Buckingham Palace at six o'clock the next morning, alone with my little Hawkeye camera, just to stand and gaze dumbfounded, and to reflect. There it lay before me, glistening in the radiant light of dawn, imposing, a massive yet silent grey hulk, a giant jewel lying in the center of a vast green carpet.

It wasn't the time of day for taking a tour, so I could only imagine our beloved Queen somewhere in those 900 plus rooms in her crimson petticoat standing before her golden sink brushing her royal teeth with her diamond-studded toothbrush, or maybe snuggling under her sheets for "one more wink," or perhaps in her private chapel saying her prayers? Could she possibly notice that she has one early visitor standing outside her royal gate, one loyal Canadian subject admiring her house, one unknown traveler paying his respects fresh from a distant dusky Empire in the south ruled by a dynasty 2000 years more ancient than hers?

Home

We arrived in Canada at Malton International Airport where Vera's family and my brother Paul and his wife, Irene, met us. It was great to be back with family.

What amazing changes can occur in three years! Paul was single when we left. Now he and Irene had a son, Kevin. Vera's sister Vernane had married Dick Stutzman and they had a son, Preston. Vera's brother and sister-in-law, Sanford and Mickey had added a second son, Linford. Vera's aunt, Ida, had finally married the elderly widower, Tom Rinard. And Vera's mother had married the widower, Jacob B. Yoder, who had three sons and two daughters-in-law of his own. The family had multiplied, and now we were adding our own contribution, bringing two new daughters home. There were a lot of new relationships to set up and a lot of old ones to revisit.

After spending the night in Hanover in Paul and Irene's home, we drove south across the international border to Vera's home in Belleville, Pennsylvania the next day. Three days later we went to Lansdale to visit my uncle and aunt, David, and Esther Friesen, for four days. While there we attended "Mission '70," our denomination's big continent-wide missionary conference.

Surprising Turns in the Road

"Whether you turn to right or left, your ears will hear these words behind you, 'This is the way, follow it.'"
–Isaiah 30:21 (Jerusalem Bible)

At the conference we met Paul Gingrich, the former director of the Mennonite Mission in Ethiopia. He had ended his work two years ago and had just graduated from the Associated Mennonite Biblical Seminaries (AMBS) in Elkhart, Indiana.

Paul was excited to see us and had a lot of questions about Ethiopia. Then he asked what our future plans were. I explained about our tentative plans to study at the University of Alberta. Suddenly, he exclaimed, "Carl, you must go to AMBS and finish your M Div."!

It seemed like a light went on. That had been my original plan when I had left for Ethiopia after studying two years at Eastern Mennonite Seminary without completing the degree. Since then, my mind and ambitions had wandered far from that goal. Perhaps he was right. Could this be the voice of God? Would it not be wise to finish what I had started before branching out into untried new things? I would have to think seriously and pray about this. I must be prepared to discuss this possibility with the Mission Board officials when we meet them for debriefing in a few days.

Discerning God's will had always been a struggle for us. It seemed we followed a pattern. God would allow us to pursue his inscrutable will blindly, following a maze with sudden sharp turns to left or right. We would find ourselves agonizing and struggling about a decision until we began feeling right about it and making plans around it, only to find, at the last minute, a whole new dimension slipped into the picture and the plan completely changed, but the new direction was unmistakably clear and satisfying and right.

The Mission Board officials were very open to this new twist in unraveling our future. The Board decided to help us finish the M Div. Degree at the Associated Mennonite Biblical Seminaries for one year and then, decide about the university options later.

It made sense to us, but it also meant postponing my newfound passion to study development for a whole year. This was already the second week of July, and school would start in September. But we hadn't even applied to the Seminary. Would we really be accepted?

We decided to go for it. If it was right, God would open the way. We began the process of applying for a place in the Goshen Biblical Seminary which was "associated" with the Mennonite Biblical Seminary at Elkhart, Indiana, and in faith rearranging our plans for the summer.

We would first buy a car with the little money we had, which was less than $900. We prayed for God to lead us to the right car to fit our budget and meet our need. Then we went with our new step-father-in-law to check out the used car lots of Lewistown. All the small compact cars within our price range were old rusty oil burners that looked like they would not even make it to the inspection station without major outside help. I was quite discouraged. This wasn't going to be as easy as I had thought.

We drove into the last dealer before calling it quits for the day. I told him we were looking for something decent in the compact line like a Chevy II for example. He did not have anything in the compact line.

We were about to go. Then he remembered, a woman had come in yesterday to have a 1965 Chevy II appraised. Her eighty-year-old father had passed away about three weeks ago and she was trying to settle his estate. He had only driven his car about 8,600 miles. It was still like new. It was appraised at $850. We took her telephone number.

Soon we were driving a nice maroon four-door Chevy II that fit our little family perfectly. We later found it was really a 1966 model and could have sold. for $1,100 or $1,200. Of course, God knew we only had $900 to spend on a car. It served us well for the year, and we were able to recoup our investment after driving 24,000 miles. God provides!

A Worthy Detour: Back to Seminary

After a nice visit with family in Alberta, we made 504 Garfield Avenue our home in Elkhart, Indiana, for the next nine months while I completed requirements for the M Div. Degree.

It was a busy, but in many ways, relaxing and refreshing year. Cindy began her academic career by enrolling in kindergarten. Vera responded to the challenge of sales ladyship and combined it with environmental concerns by spreading the fragrances of Avon throughout the community. I undertook a course of supervised preaching in the famous Belmont Mennonite Church. We entertained friends and relatives that passed through the area from east and west.

We visited my family in Duchess, Alberta, over the Christmas break. There Karen spent four days in the hospital with pneumonia. What a place for a three year and two-month-old to spend Christmas! The children enjoyed getting acquainted with relatives that visited us. They experienced for the first time the double joy that snow brings to children, joy when it comes and joy when it finally leaves.

In my studies, I found this "detour" back to academia very beneficial in many ways. Besides giving me and my family a time of refreshment and social growth, I benefited directly from my courses.

The theological and biblical studies reinforced the foundations upon which I had built my faith, my value system, and my life ministry.

Especially, I was moved by an in-depth study of the major and minor prophets, particularly the books of Amos and Micah which highlight God's vision and purpose to which he calls his people. The very essence of God's will for us is "*To act justly and to love mercy, and to walk humbly with your God!*" (Micah 6:8 NIV).

This is reinforced in the New Testament by Jesus summarizing the will of God for us in his two-fold commandment: "Love the Lord your God with all your heart and with all your soul and with all your mind and with all your strength ...." and "Love your neighbor as yourself." (Mark 12:30, 31 NIV).

What are the implications of that for us who live as well-to-do in a larger world neighborhood with its masses of poor, illiterate, superstitious, disadvantaged, exploited, oppressed fellow human beings? I found this study to reinforce what I was developing as a rationale, a biblical basis for Christians to be involved in development. This helped to shape my future ministry. The "good news" includes the "cup of cool water" given in Jesus name and acts of compassion for the poor, the hungry, the cold and naked, the prisoner, the sick and the dying, as well as the good news that God forgives sin and makes a way for us to reach heaven after this life (Matthew 25:31-46 NIV).

As spring and graduation approached, we began again the anxious quest to define our future. In March we received word that my application to the Graduate School of the University of Missouri for a place in the field of community development was accepted. I was getting very homesick for Ethiopia and finding the thought of another year in academia was not appealing. I just did not sense God's leading in it.

Finally, we received a formal invitation from the Meserete Kristos Church in Ethiopia inviting us to return to "work with the Church in development." We felt God's nod of approval. "This is the way, walk in it!" We agreed to a four-to-five-year term, going out in early August with one stipulation, that we be given one year for study of the Amharic language. That request was approved.

After graduation on May 28, 1971, we spent the next seven days buying supplies, packing four barrels to be sent to Ethiopia, selling our furniture, packing the rest of our earthly possessions into cardboard boxes to be stored in "Grandma's attic," cleaning up the house, saying goodbye to all our new friends, and loading everything into and on top of a U-Haul trailer. Finally, at 8:00 p.m., June 5, our house was completely empty, and our 4' x 8' trailer was completely full, and our car was sagging to the dragging point as we crept out of Elkhart heading east into the dark, closing another chapter in the story of our lives.

We were exhausted. We only drove about twenty miles that night until we found a camp site where we pitched our tent, ate supper, and lowered our weary bodies into our sleeping bags and slept like the dead. The next day we made the 500 miles to Belleville, Pennsylvania without difficulty.

Then followed a round of visiting in Ontario, Eastern Pennsylvania, Virginia, and orientation at Salunga and a commissioning service. We returned to Elkhart where we sold our car to a friend and boarded a train at Chicago going west on July 14th. We were met at the station at Whitefish, Montana by our uncle and aunt, Ed, and Faye Friesen, and whisked to the annual meeting of the Northwest Conference of our denomination.

When the Conference was over, my brother Peter came and collected us in his big new Chrysler and brought us home to Alberta.

After a month of visiting friends and family in Alberta, the time came to say sad and long farewells once again. This time our flight took us northeast across the Mackenzie District, Hudson's Bay, Baffin Island, Davis Strait, southern Greenland, southern Norway, arriving at Copenhagen on August 26.

Denmark

Having been notified by my dad, my elderly aunts whom we had never seen, Jensine "Sina" Ragborg and Kristine Severinsen, were waiting for us where we disembarked. They were quite recognizable because they resembled family. They brought a woman and an Arab man to help translate. They gave us coffee and helped us find a hotel in town two blocks from the railway station. They thought we should stay in town the first night and then come out to see them in their homes.

We slept in the hotel for a couple of hours, and then the aunts came and took us to Tivoli, a lovely amusement park, where we spent the afternoon being amused. They went home by train that evening. We followed them the next day to Aunt Kristine's home in Hojby where we were introduced to more family.

The following day Aunt Sina went with us across the channel by ferry to Jutland and welcomed us to her home in Silkeborg. They arranged for us to travel to my dad's birthplace in Bur near the west coast. We saw the house where he was born and the little church where he was first baptized as a baby in sound Lutheran tradition.

Denmark is such a beautiful place. The towns and the countryside are exceedingly neat and clean and prosperous looking. Everybody seemed to be growing flowers. Technology is appropriate and efficient. The modern somehow blends with the ancient. The trains and buses run exactly on time and are so clean. No slums or trash or garbage dumps were visible anywhere. It seemed to me that the Danes lived better than the Canadians or Americans even though they may not make as much money or drive such big cars. They find life to be in order and dignity and grace rather than in opulence or ostentatious display of wealth. They live closer to the socialist dream of enough for everybody's needs and moderation in meeting everybody's wants.

I was impressed. I really wondered what it was that motivated my dad, back in 1927 at age twenty-three, to turn his back on all this and forsake his family in exchange for a lonely rundown bachelor's shack on the barren wind-swept wastes of Maple Creek, Saskatchewan? It is a deep mystery that only the pioneer spirit can comprehend!

CHAPTER 13

Living with Language Learning

Arriving in Addis Ababa, we found that the Meserete Kristos Church had arranged for us to live in the city for the year of language learning. They had rented a very nice, modern three-bedroom house for us in Kazenchis, not far from the Ministry of Agriculture, and placed an almost new Toyota Corolla at our disposal. But they had to make temporary arrangements for our accommodation elsewhere while our house was being prepared.

Alice Snyder was a slightly past middle-aged pioneer missionary who had given many years of service in the School for the Blind and more recently as manager of Menno Bookstore. She was well known for her friendly concern, honesty, intense dedication, highly competent business acumen, and meticulous efficiency.

Arlene Kreider was a not yet middle-aged missionary who had left a schoolteacher's job in Pennsylvania to join the team at the bookstore in 1967. Her cheerful, friendly disposition and eager willingness to help won many a customer for the store. Her courageous spirit and philosophical sense of humor carried her lightly over many troubled waters. More than anything else, it was the common dedication and diligent efforts of these two single women that made the Menno Bookstore the stunning success it was.

According to long standing tradition, the Mission saw fit to "punish" them for their singleness by requiring them to share a house. Obviously, the Mission Board policy makers were married males!

Also, according to established precedent, in lieu of the fact that the Mennonite Guest House had been closed, it fell to the single women to open the doors of their shared home to the aliens, the sojourners, and newcomers such as us with our pack of restless curious kids and all our luggage. Yes, we would be spending our first week imposing ourselves with our noise and clutter upon the kind and generous hospitality of these remarkable colleagues!

Perhaps because our arrival coincided with the darkest, wettest days of the rainy season, we found the house to be dark and dreary and cold. No wonder the sisters found so much joy in their long hours of work at the store! Our invasion together with our three kids provided them with a double portion of joy, joy of new companionship in their rather bleak and barren house when we came, and joy of relief when we left!

House Help

We needed someone to keep the children while we were in language study and to help around the house. Abebech was a pleasant, thin young woman, a mother of four, whose unemployed husband could not support her. She had been working for the Mennonite Guest House until it was closed, so we were glad to give her a job when she needed one. She was quiet, happy, diligent, faithful, and she related well with our children. Her cheerful service and support made our adjustments much easier. We appreciated her so much and found it hard to leave her behind when it was time to move on.

From the Mission we also "inherited" a security guard, Ato Germatchew Wolde Gabriel (not his real name). We had to pay for our own house help, but the Mission supplied the guard. No one in their right mind would think of living in Addis in a house like ours with all the wealth we owned without having, besides the significant stone wall and locked steel gate, at least one night security guard. Most had day guards as well.

This young father of three would come around 5:00 p.m. every day, water the flowers, dig in the garden, cut grass with a sickle, or clean the yard until dark. Then he would put on his great coat, bundle up his head in a cloth, and prepare himself to battle the cold and inevitable drowsiness as well as any potential thief that perchance might approach that way through the long night vigil. Inevitably the cold and sleep won their battles, but much to the credit of his shivering slumbering presence, or despite it, the expected thief never materialized. Except for one time.

We agricultural developers couldn't wait to reach the countryside, so we bought ten one-day-old chicks and were raising them under the warmth of a light bulb in our basement. Actually, they were the children's Easter project.

They were growing fine until one day the door was left open for ventilation purposes. A criminal cat crept in with wicked intent and massacred all the innocent little peepers. Although this crime was committed in broad daylight when the guard was off duty (but really in the shadowy recesses of the dark basement, for evil "loves darkness rather than light"), Germatchew took the deepest offence at this vicious barbaric act of ultimate feline cruelty.

As he mourned and meditated upon the heinousness of the crime, his agile brain formulated a scheme for ultimate revenge. He left the dead chicks as bait, fixed up a wire noose and laid a trap. He left the fatal door ajar just a crack, knowing that the thief would return when hunger pangs would overcome the fear of possible retribution. With the patience and cunning of a leopard, he crouched down shivering beside the car in the dark driveway outside the cellar door, holding the fatal wire in his left hand and a lethal club in his right. With steadfast determination Germatchew waited. The vision of those cruelly mutilated chicks burned in his mind and steeled his resolve, keeping him awake and alert and silent through the long cold night.

We were turning in our bed, slowly waking to the first rooster crows of dawn. Suddenly, we heard a loud crash and the scream of a cornered cat. Then there was a furious scuffling and whacking sound as vengeance rained down upon the hapless villain! And then there was silence!

We bounded out of bed to investigate. There stood the conquering hero out in the driveway holding up the remains of the vanquished foe, crushed and bleeding, by its lifeless tail. The smile of triumph that shone on his visage was even broader than when he received his monthly paycheck!

Our watchman was not just an ordinary guard. Germatchew was a man of principle, a devout Orthodox Christian, a man who feared God. As the new day progressed, the glory of his gory triumph began to fade as his sensitive conscience began to criticize him. Did he really know that he got the guilty cat? Did the cat not belong to some close neighbor? Maybe a pet to some child? Perhaps they depended upon it to keep their home free of mice and other undesirable rodents. Was it really wrong for cats to eat chicks? Perhaps it was more the fault of the master of the door whose carelessness tempted the cat beyond the endurance of its feline conscience!

Germatchew decided he must do penance. He went up to his favorite church, *Kidus Uriel,* and confessed his rashness, his presumption, and his violence to the priest on duty. What must he do to gain God's pardon? Well, it was true that he had done a rash and violent thing, and no amount of penance could restore the life to the unfortunate cat, but he was lucky that God is merciful and would likely overlook his transgression if he would say forty-nine prayers and give alms to seven beggars. Of course, it was only right to give the priest a little something as well. When he returned that evening, he was a much happier man. Forgiven!

We really appreciated Germatchew as a person as well as a friend. After battling the cold and drowsiness all night, as soon as daylight overpowered darkness, he would get out the cold garden hose, and start washing our car. He was determined that we should be driving the cleanest car in all of Addis. Whether we drove anywhere or not, every morning that car must be washed again. His fingers stiff with the cold, elbows aching with arthritic pain, and breath floating away in thick clouds of fog on the cold morning air, Germatchew was never happier than to be caught washing that car when we got up with the first morning sun to greet him.

At about 7:00 a.m., his morning chores all done, he would cheerfully bid us a good day and, with walking stick across his shoulder in true Wello Amhara style, stroll out the gate eager to get home to wife and family and breakfast. He would spend the hot part of the day recuperating in bed. Such was the life of the faithful Germatchew, seven days a week around the year.

If a special holiday demanded his absence from work, Germatchew had to argue long and steadfastly to obtain release from his employer. His salary of forty birr per month was not enough to pay the seven-birr rent for his little hut and supply enough teff and beans for the table, let alone pay for clothes and medicines for his often-sick children. The three-year old son suffered chronically from scurvy. His parents could not afford to give him the green vegetables and fruit he needed to grow up normal and healthy.

Vera found excuses to send some small "leftovers" home with him from time to time "for the kiddies" of course! I complained to the Mission Director. But policy is policy. He finally got a modest increment of ten birr. I was angry. Even rich mission organizations can be very bureaucratic, stingy, exploitative, and unfeeling. What does Jesus think?

For Easter we bought our workers each a big red rooster from the modern poultry farm. These European birds were about seven times as big as a local rooster. In fact, they were about the largest roosters I myself had ever seen. Germatchew could hardly get over thanking us. He said his family did not get meat to eat even once in a year. Then they got this huge bird. His wife said it was "as big as a goat!"

A New School

Upon arrival we at once enrolled Cindy as a day student in grade one at Good Shepherd School, a primary and secondary boarding and day school for missionary children jointly owned and run by Lutherans, Presbyterians, General Conference Baptists, Mennonites, and Southern Baptists. We would escort her to a nearby bus stand every morning and wait until the school bus came and whisked her away. In the afternoon we would meet her at the same place. The first thing she learned in school was that she did not like school after all. She wished that she was eighteen so she could quit!

Perhaps she was not that much different from her parents. Instead of going to a language school, Vera and I opted for a self-guided program of language study together with Marie Thomas in her home. Marie was the wife of Mel Thomas, the young business manager of our mission. They had one child, Audrey, who played well with our daughters.

We hired a young Ethiopian informant who had been trained to teach American Peace Corp Volunteers using the Peace Corp method which concentrated on oral rather than written Amharic. The program could have been quite good, but its success depended too much on the personal motivation of the learner and his ability to direct the teacher.

All three of us were exceedingly lazy language students. We would rather do anything else besides concentrate on language learning. We became geniuses at finding ways to delay, shorten, or cut the hours spent in diligent language study each day. Even a 3000-piece jigsaw puzzle became a consuming passion in comparison. We bought carpet remnants and scraps, cut, and glued them together in the most interesting designs. Anything to keep our minds from the torture of language study.

We needed the discipline of a fixed schedule and the challenge and stimulation of others to urge us on. As soon as our teacher left after his daily three-hour session, we would turn our minds to more pleasant things. Marie dropped out after a few months for domestic reasons. The daily drudgery moved to our house.

A Technical "Home" in Deder

The exact nature and location of our assignment was still unclear. The period of language study would allow time for the Church's vision to solidify. For the sake of gaining a work permit so that we could have a residence visa, they had to create a job description for us. It was decided that I would be called "Station Manager" for the Deder Mission. This meant that we would need to travel to register in Dire Dawa and in Deder.

One morning in mid-October, we left Cindy off at our mission director, Nathan Hege's house. She would remain behind to attend school. The rest of us boarded the train. The next morning in Dire Dawa, I went to the local government office where I was given a work permit.

Immediately we took public transport for a two and one-half hours trip to Deder. We were warmly welcomed by Dr. Harold and Esther Kraybill and were hosted by them and their three children from Tuesday to Saturday morning. We had to register with the local officials there since Deder was the seat of government for Wobera Awraja (county). Since there was a strong possibility that we would come to live there, we were keen to learn as much as possible about the people and the general situation at Deder.

At 8000 feet, Deder sits high on the east side of Wobie Terrara, a large brush and tree topped mountain, a perfect hideout for hyenas and many other wild animals. From that lofty position the view is absolutely breath-taking. The mountainside falls off sharply into an intensely farmed valley thousands of feet below. The far side of the valley is an amazing patchwork of small fields of variegated shades of green and brown and black desperately clinging to the steep hillside and generously sprinkled with small randomly placed homesteads with the usual huts and fences and trees connected by crooked paths. Some of the fields are neatly terraced for coffee or chat production, others covered with sweet potato vines, and others simply showing the residues of cereal production.

Eastward, beyond the valley and the sharp ridge on the other side, one can see the hazy blue Garamuleta mountain, towering distantly aloof from the peaked ridges in between. The mountains drop sharply to the lowlands in the south which gradually fade off in a distant hot haze where sky merges with the Ogaden desert. Deder is a small town at the end of an all-weather gravel road one hundred and five kilometers west of Dire Dawa. It is a center through which all trade passes between the city and a vast heavily populated hinterland to the south and east and west.

From the center of the town, several "roads" or trails branch off leading in several directions to the different valley communities. These "roads" are limited to four-wheel-drive vehicles or lorries, and then only in the dry season. Vehicle traffic is rare in any case. The roads are used mostly by donkeys and mules and of course the hundreds of thousands of pedestrians who find some reason they must walk the great distances to the Deder market.

The founders of the Mennonite Mission, like the government, had seen that Deder is a strategic location for penetrating the back country, and indeed ten schools and several clinics had been started from the Deder station in valley communities such as Harawacha, Soka, Koba, Kio, Karamakala, Genemie, and Karamela. We learned that the population was very dense, and the farms were very small. All arable land was utilized including steep slopes that should have been terraced or left with natural cover. People were living in extreme poverty and perpetual hunger.

The inhabitants of the Deder community were mostly Muslim of the Oromo ethnic group. Amhara were present mostly as landlords, government officials, government employees, soldiers, freehold farmers, or businesspeople. A few Arab merchants kept shops in town.

Deder Mission Hospital

The Deder Mission was running a little hospital, the only one between Asebe Teferi and Dire Dawa. A vast population area of perhaps a million people was served by this little hospital with one doctor, two expatriate nurses and a small Ethiopian staff. This doctor was also supervising the few small clinics scattered out in the lowland areas. Besides this thin network of modern medical aid, the people still largely depended upon the services of the traditional medical practitioners.

The Mission had also introduced the first modern school into the area. Although there was now a large government school in town, the mission school still had 220 primary students.

Now the Meserete Kristos Church was considering sending us to this community to start something in rural development. We were assessing the situation to see what could be done. It seemed to me that the biggest bottleneck in the path to development and prosperity for the rural population was the feudal landholding system. Most of the land around Deder, including the Mission compound, was owned by the royal family. Most of the rest was owned by other absentee aristocrats. Rent charges were linked to production. Any success in agricultural development would raise the cash or in-kind rents and thus greatly increase the risk factor for the poor peasant. Perhaps prophetically and certainly revolutionarily I wrote home:

> *Communism couldn't be any more demoralizing and dehumanizing than this wicked feudal system. Until the revolution comes, we must find ways to help the farmer that will really help him. May God guide us with the shrewdness and wisdom to find that way! This is Russia before 1917. This is Israel in the time of Ahaz (Isaiah 1-5). I can clearly see God sending a terrible judgement upon the high and mighty of this nation! May He spare the poor!*

Christmas

Back in the city, it was getting near to the Christmas season. Subtle signs of creeping cultural colonialism began to appear as some stores put up decorations including Santa Clauses in their Nordic suits and European "Christmas trees." Culturally mystifying songs about the virtues of riding in "a one-horse open sleigh," the strange exploits of a Germanic "red-nosed reindeer" called by its German name, "Rudolph," and someone's fantasies about a "white Christmas" blared out over crackling loudspeaker systems. It was completely un-Ethiopian and, to me, culturally insensitive and inappropriate. I was embarrassed.

Some of the missionaries from various organizations began practicing singing a Christmas Cantata, also un-Ethiopian. It was a tremendous release from language study for Vera. They worked hard and gave an excellent performance in several churches. They even had it recorded in the TV studio for broadcasting.

Then they were invited to the emperor's palace to sing for him. They made sure that they did not include the full two hours of it. His Majesty listened intently, thanked them graciously, extended his royal handshake to each one individually, and served them tea and cookies. Their hands were glowing with a royal aura for weeks thereafter!

Christmas also brought vacations and visitors and memorable

activities. We spent most of the week camping as a family at our favorite spot at Lake Langano. On our way back, we camped some more at the Bible Academy over a weekend.

That was the weekend for weddings. On Saturday, Negash Kebede and Janet Shertzer were married. Negash was the director of the Bible Academy, and Janet was a business teacher at the same school. They had worked together for a couple of years. They shared a lot in common, and we thought they made a well-matched couple. Vera had done a lot of the sewing of the dresses for the bride and her attendants.

Then on Sunday afternoon, another wedding took place in the Nazareth Chapel. Another teacher, Woudineh Habteyesus and the beautiful Talamau were wed in a simple solemn ceremony. Like in the story of Jacob of old, seven years of engagement and agonizing waiting thus came to a final blissful conclusion. She was working as a nurse at the hospital in Nazareth. There was a supper for invited guests at the Academy at 8:00 p.m. Afterwards someone brought an African drum and the guests joined in singing traditional wedding songs. We all had a great time watching or joining in wedding dances which represented a broad variety of tribal cultural practices.

CHAPTER 14

Narrowing the Focus

A Visit to Manz

While enduring the drudgery of language study, we found ways to spice up our lives a bit. One of these ways was to study development in third world countries. I read all the books I could find on the subject and visited all the projects I could reach to learn what was successful and what was not to be repeated. By the end of February, we still did not know where the Church was going to send us. The choice seemed to have narrowed to three possibilities, Deder, Bedeno, or Baumgartner's farm in Arussi.

One of these educational fact-finding trips took Vera, Sheryl, and I by plane to Mahal Meda in Manz.

Five years earlier, the Southern Baptist Mission had started a development project 300 kilometers north of Addis Ababa in Manz, a stronghold of conservative Amhara Orthodoxy. Their team consisted of five couples, each with previous experience elsewhere in Africa, and each with a determination to avoid the missiological mistakes that they knew too well. They would pioneer something new and make new mistakes if they must, but they were committed to avoid repeating the old ones.

First, they avoided building a missionary "ghetto" often called a "mission station" or "mission compound." They scattered the five families out over the countryside not less than four kilometers apart.

Second, they refused to start a new denomination in the area. As far as it depended upon them, no "First American Southern Baptist Church of Mahal Meda" would ever be found here. They worked for the renewal and growth of the existing Ethiopian Orthodox Tewahedo Church.

Third, they took a comprehensive approach to community development. The team consisted of a doctor, a veterinarian, an agriculturist, an engineer, and a handicrafts specialist. All of them were serious Bible teachers, preachers, and evangelists.

Fourth, they worked with the relevant government officials and ministries as much as possible, and worked with the utmost respect for the community, its leadership, and its culture.

Now they were five years into this grand experiment.

Dr. Sam Kanata took us in his plane. On the way he told stories of flying to the different airstrips the people had built on the different remote *"ambas"* or flat plateaus that were completely cut off from any road transport by huge ravines thousands of feet deep. The people on these *"ambas"* welcomed regular clinic visits from the flying doctor. He tried to keep to a schedule so they would count on him and bring all the patients to the "clinic" on the given day. They also brought their sick animals, for Dr. Jerry Bedsell would come along to treat them while Dr. Sam Kanata would treat the humans. While the doctors were busy, Mr. Gross, the agriculturist, would talk to any who cared to listen about farming problems and solutions.

Flying in the *"ambas"* was interesting, for the airstrips were often squeezed for space so that sometimes the end of a runway opened out over the cliff. In the hot part of the day, these cliff edges were subject to powerful down-drafts which made landing and taking off a bit tricky.

One day at one particular airstrip where the runway ends at the edge of the abyss, Dr. Kanata with two other doctors took off over the gorge. A sharp downdraft sucked his plane down into the abyss. He managed to regain control and brought it up and out over the other side, but it had lost so much altitude that he nicked the rim of the facing canyon breaking one wheel off as the plane shot out over. They missed certain death by inches! A miracle! A few feet lower, and they would have been plastered against the rock wall a thousand feet above the valley floor.

So far, so good. They were able to fly the crippled plane on to Addis Ababa, but with only one wheel, how were they going to get it down when they got there? He radioed advance warning. Their wives and colleagues were called to emergency prayer. When they reached Addis, the ambulances and fire trucks were lined up to welcome them. Fire retardant foam was sprayed on the runway. Another plane went up to meet them, flying under them to assess the damage. Yes, one wheel was missing! Nothing more! And nothing less!

Finally, when all the preparations were in place, Dr. Kanata circled once more, as they once again committed their lives to God, and came in for a crash landing. He brought the craft down carefully balancing the weight on the one wheel at first and then finally leaning it slightly until the one wing tip skidded in the sea of foam. They got in all right, minus a bit of paint! Another miracle!

This time we had a less stressful landing and were met by someone with a Land Rover and taken to one of the missionary's houses.

At about 10,000 feet altitude, this part of Manz is bleak and cold and inhospitable. There are few trees, and the cold wind sweeps across the plateau making warm homespun clothing a necessity. The depleted black cotton soil is divided up into very small plots from which the hardy peasants eke out a meager subsistence.

The Amhara people of this region are extremely conservative, staunch Orthodox, overbearingly proud, fiercely independent, and willing to spend much of their time wrangling in court with their closest neighbors over endless boundary disputes. It was reported that the peasants had just burned the government's new sheep breeding station because it was seen as an "alien intervention"!

It seemed that one of the Mission's most successful projects was the wool rug-making project. Manz has a lot of red and black and white hairy sheep. The craftsman had taught about twenty deacons how to make beautiful rugs out of the sheep's hair. Now they came together every day to make rugs and were earning four birr per day.

At the beginning of each day, there would be a fifteen-minute Bible study. The aim was that the religious deacons might get hooked onto Jesus in their eager pursuit of mammon, that they would come to really know Jesus as the personal center of their faith rather than just one of the distant mystical members of the celestial hierarchy to which they gave their blind loyalty.

It seemed to be working; Dr. Bedsell was excited to report: After five years of faithfully attending the mass at the Orthodox service, going through all the rituals, like kissing the priest's outstretched cross, Jerry was finally invited by the priest to preach to the people assembled outside the church after the service one day. Slowly a breath of new life was stirring in the rigid minds and hearts of the tradition-bound deacons and priests. Some of them were genuinely "born again" of the Spirit and became fiery preachers of a re-discovered ancient gospel. Others opposed, and persecution set in. Can new "wine" really be put into "old wineskins"?

We spent the night in the missionary's home. Their house was typical American with all the American fixtures, furniture, and gadgets, really an alien biosphere, a shelter from another world in that rugged Abyssinian preserve. The fact that these Americans were allowed to live in peace in this ultra-conservative environment spoke volumes about the rightness and wisdom of their development policies. It was the most enlightened and successful development project we had found in our travels in Ethiopia.

Our mission directors, Nathan and Arlene Hege joined us that afternoon, having driven the 300 kilometers in six hours by car. They brought us home the following day.

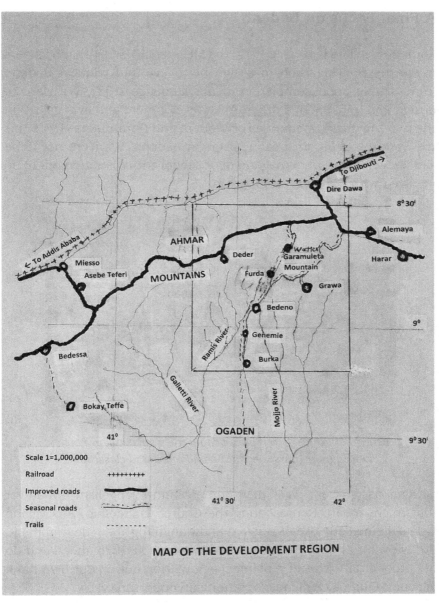

A map of the development area in Harar Province

A Final Focus on Bedeno

Sometime in late February 1972, the Meserete Kristos Church leaders made the final decision to assign us to live and work at Bedeno immediately upon completion of our language study. We were to design and implement a program in development and evangelism in the two *"Awrajas"* or counties of Wobera and Garamuleta. To do this we were to set up our headquarters at Bedeno. We were not to be saddled with station management or school administration nor to be involved with the medical program.

Bedeno Mission - l. to r. barn behind trees, missionary house, clinic, garage, nurses house behind trees, and classrooms

Our assignment was "development and evangelism" whatever that might mean. Representing the Church leadership, Ato Million Belete defined our job: "We do not know anything about development, but we want to do it. We are depending on you to go ahead and do it!" I took it as a sort of a blank check written out on our own bank account. Quite a challenge, and quite an opportunity!

Living in Bedeno would not be easy for us as a family. The challenges were many.

The treacherous road dictated a certain amount of isolation which would be particularly difficult for Vera. It also dictated a certain amount of physical strain and stress and danger and offered the strong possibility of mechanical breakdown each time we were obliged to travel on it.

The Amharic language we were studying so diligently was not widely known or used outside of the marketplace and government circles. We should have been studying "Oromo," the language of the Oromo people rather than Amharic.

The house we would inhabit was standing empty and needed extensive repairs.

Our children's education would be a problem. We would try home-schooling with Cindy in the first year.

And above all, the Oromo people were Muslims conquered and ruled and exploited by "Christians," and their resistance to anything with a "Christian" label was legendary and understandable. "Evangelism" may sound easy in a job description, but it would not be a simple assignment.

After twenty years of missionary investment in time, labor, prayer, tears, finances, suffering, and self-giving to keep the medical and educational programs running, the Church at Bedeno had only five members. Four of them were teachers, and the other one was the dresser. Hardly an outstanding "church growth" success story to write home about.

As is sometimes the case, the statistics sounded worse than the story really was. Since the school was the real base upon which "evangelism" occurred, almost all of the "converts" naturally graduated out of the community and went to the towns and cities for more training or jobs. In fact, our best students at the Bible Academy quite consistently came from Bedeno, and a large portion of our Church leaders had their origins in that town and their primary education in that school.

Yet we had to admit that we had failed to establish a grass-roots church in that Islamic community. Would a serious program in rural community development be a catalyst to enable that to happen?

The town of Bedeno

On the other hand, Bedeno was a strategic place to begin a new work in development and evangelism. Having been there for twenty years, our mission was well known and accepted in the area. We had a school that frequently ranked number one in the province in the percentage of passes in the national primary school-leaving exams. Our clinic was the first of its kind in the county and still served the community well.

Bedeno was located on the southeastern slope of a hill at the head of three separate fertile valleys. Its location made it a gateway to the vast Somali Ogaden region to the south. It served the government as an administrative headquarters on the *"Wereda"* or sub-district level to govern the dense population clinging to the steep hillsides and living in the valleys below.

Bedeno served the people as the main trading center and link with the outside world. It had a malaria control unit stationed there, and a new government primary school had just been built with assistance from the Swedish International Development Cooperation Agency (SIDA). The town had a population of about 2500 residents.

There was a very thick limestone cliff that formed a kind of backstop to the town's growth up the hill. From under this cliff came a strong spring of pure water. A German agency had installed a durable system that piped pure water from this big spring to various watering centers in the town.

The Oromo were a conquered people. Menelik II extended his imperial rule over them late in the 19th century. The best of the land with its people was apportioned to buy off rival aristocrats, to reward favorite generals, and to pay loyal soldiers. These conquerors ruled their estates as private fiefdoms, collecting rents from the indigenous peoples who labored in the fields which historically had belonged to their ancestors.

Rents could be as high as 50% of the crop plus a lot of extra services. Peasants were expected to work on the landlord's fields without compensation when he called them, which inevitably was always at prime time when conditions were just right to be tilling their own fields. Besides that, custom demanded that the peasant show his gratitude to the landlord with "gifts" of chickens, sheep, goats, milk, or honey whenever he came to visit or to collect the rent. Sometimes they preferred a simple cash rent which afforded greater security to the owner in times of crop failure and greater risk to the peasant. Besides this, the rulers often showed contempt for the local population and considered them as little more than uncultured "animals."

A typical Oromo neighbor's house

The peasant population was extremely poor. Squeezed into tiny plots averaging less than an acre per family, taxed almost to death by the landlords, humiliated and dehumanized by their superiors, harassed by the officials looking for bribes, worn by their toil and sweat, their lives were no more hopeful than slavery. Starvation was chronic. Life expectancy was about forty years for men and thirty-four years for women. Even in non-famine years, about 20% of the children coming to the clinic suffered from kwashiorkor. Malaria, dysentery, and worms were endemic. In the words of the poet, life was "nasty, brutish, and short!" Certainly, the development challenge was very fitting and proper to the area.

The Bedeno Wereda Governor's Office

Focusing On a Plan

As soon as we received word that we were appointed to live and work in Bedeno, I got busy and formulated a strategic plan to begin the work of promoting development in the area. The result was a project proposal and funding application for the "Wobera and Garamuleta Rural Development Project" which I sent off to "Brot Fur Die Welt" in Stuttgart, Germany for their consideration. I was somewhat surprised and elated when the proposal was accepted.

This very ambitious plan envisioned a low-cost program in agricultural extension and community development with a simple research and demonstration component. We would promote improved land use management with the introduction of fertilizers and improved seeds, erosion control, reforestation, crop rotation, and weed control. We wanted to introduce the improved breeds of livestock by distributing improved chickens and demonstrating the keeping of dairy cows and goats and wool producing sheep. We would set up breeding stations with a bull, a ram, and a male goat for use by the farmers who wanted to crossbreed. We wanted to promote the making and marketing of handicrafts. We also included a plan to introduce low-cost rainwater catchment tanks.

The plan called for a full-time expatriate to coordinate the program from Bedeno, and a half-time expatriate to manage the Deder program, and three Ethiopian secondary school graduates who would be trained to work as full-time field extension agents. Two would work at Bedeno and one at Deder.

In general, our strategy would be to introduce only those ideas which can be understood, accepted, applied, and passed on to others by the farmers themselves. When one idea was accepted in a community, the field worker would move on to another community with that idea. At the same time, he would introduce a second idea in the first community. Only those ideas that the subsistence farmer could incorporate into his economy and way of life would be introduced. We planned on the belief that it is better to help many people one step up the ladder than to help a few climb all the way to the top.

An Extra Blessing!

About this time, we heard the rumor that the dresser who was running the Bedeno clinic, Ato Assefa Haile, was going to take a wife very soon. In fact, the lovely young Miss Grace Keeport was soon returning from her home in Pennsylvania, prepared to do her part to make that a reality.

Having completed a three-year term as a missionary nurse at the Nazareth hospital, Grace had returned home for a time of rest and refreshment. But she had no intention of settling down to a mundane life in her home environment. Somehow, she found herself irresistibly drawn by the bonds of love so carefully woven by the handsome young Assefa, one of the Ethiopian dressers she worked with and learned to love. Yes, it would be a cross-cultural and interracial marriage, and there would be issues and adjustments to be made.

The call of love was stronger than the obstacles that stood in its way. A determined Grace was suddenly back, and a wedding was being planned.

At 4:00 p.m. on April 22, 1972, nuptial rituals were duly and adequately performed in the church at Nazareth, and a joyful feast followed in a Nazareth hotel to celebrate the joining of Assefa and Grace as husband and wife.

We were particularly interested, for the happy couple would soon be our next-door neighbors living in the lower house on the Bedeno mission station. They would be working together running the clinic on a private contract basis. Vera was especially elated at the prospect of having an English-speaking neighbor of the same sex and the same tribal and cultural background as herself.

Kristina Rose

The Ethiopian women were quite intrigued whenever Vera would mention her "due date" as May 16th. How can anyone know when a baby is supposed to come? They just come when they decide to.

On Monday, May 15th, Vera and I traveled all over town buying paint and supplies for repairing the Bedeno house. It seemed that the baby could hardly wait for Tuesday, the 16th, to get here. At 3:30 a.m. Vera was awakened by that special feeling, the beginning of contractions. Yes, it was May 16th, and the baby "decided" to keep her appointment!

Contractions were about twenty minutes apart, so Vera tried to relax in bed until 6:30 a.m. Then we got up, had breakfast, and sent the kids off to school. I recalled the twelve-hour ordeals of waiting for earlier births at Nazareth, so was in no hurry to get her to the hospital.

The contractions were getting more severe and frequent. By 9:00 a.m., we decided we better be going. The modern Empress Zewditu Hospital was just a mile or so from our house, so there was no hurry.

When we entered, the British midwife whisked Vera away to the examination room and closed the door in my face. For a moment, I stood there alone facing the closed door. Our intention was that I would accompany my wife into the delivery room as per the last two times.

Behind the closed door, a quick examination revealed that the baby was well on its way, so the midwife transferred Vera over to the delivery table right away.

I got tired of standing in front of the closed door, so I struck up a conversation with another prospective father who was just as miserable as me. He suggested that we go to a snack shop for a cup of coffee while we waited. I, being psychologically prepared to wait most of the day anyway, agreed. We must have been there for the better part of an hour.

When we returned the midwife scolded me: "Where have you been? We have been looking all over for you! You have a baby daughter, and your wife is crying!"

At first, I wasn't sure she was talking to the right man. It was too quick. Mine will not come till afternoon.

Finally convinced, I went in to comfort her. It wasn't altogether my fault that I was left out of the action, and I did feel a little bit cheated. On the other hand, it was a great relief to not have to agonize with my beloved the whole day. In that we rejoiced.

The baby cried a lot the first day. Born at 10:20, she was late for breakfast and wanted to eat right away, but the nurses made her wait half a day for the next mealtime. Newborns must learn to fit into adult schedules right away!

Some very excited sisters came to see her during visiting hours that evening. They had some interesting observations. Cindy thought she looked like a boy and did not like her hair style. Cindy and Karen had wanted her to be a brother, but Sheryl knew she would be a girl. She had waited so long; she thought the baby would never get here. Cindy said, "It seems our family isn't the same with adding a baby!" They wanted to call her "Rosa" or "Rosy." We wanted to call her "Kristina," but they weren't sure they liked that name, so we made a compromise and named our fourth daughter "Kristina Rose." Everybody was happy for our new baby Kristina Rose Hansen.

A Cautious Focus on Bokay Teffe

At the same time, we were going ahead with plans to develop a farm at Bokay privately. I had not forgotten about the 1000 acres we reserved there. We formed a kind of unofficial company with Alemu Checole, Alemayhu Assefa, and Girma Tsige to hold the land and develop it slowly.

185

At first, we were going to pool our money and hire people to clear the trees and hire a tractor to plow a few hundred acres. However, the pioneers who plowed and planted 200 acres in the first year suffered a complete crop failure and lost all their inputs. The second year the rainfall was inadequate again. This fact combined with the fact that no rainfall studies had ever been done made us a bit more cautious. Also, the scarcity of capital added a restraint on our ambition.

We decided to scale down the size of our beginning. We would go ahead on an experimental basis. We would just hire a few men to go there and cut down trees and begin plowing with oxen.

We began to implement our plans. First, I drove to Asella and purchased some "improved" ox-drawn farm equipment made of eucalyptus wood and metal manufactured by the CADU Project at Chilalo in Arussi Province. Five moldboard plows, three harrows, and one ox cart were delivered to the Bible Academy in Nazareth.

Then we decided to hire Ato Damti, a trusted neighbor from Nazareth, and take him to Bokay along with the equipment and supplies. We would leave him there alone to start and supervise the work of clearing, plowing, and seeding the first year. He would try a variety of crops such as teff, beans, maize, lentils, and sorghum. We would combine this trip with our move go Bedeno.

Now that our daughter was born and safely established at home and mother was recovering well, I was very anxious to get on with moving to Bedeno. We decided that I should go on ahead and supervise the reconstruction of the Bedeno mission house. I would take four-and-one-half year-old Karen along with me to reduce the load on Vera a bit. We would board at Assefa and Grace's house. Lacking basic experience in building in the back country, we thought this would take approximately three weeks to complete. Events would teach us differently.

On May 25th, 1972, Karen and I left Addis Ababa in a tan colored 1965 Toyota Landcruiser, hereafter known as the "Bedeno Toyota" as distinct from the "Deder Toyota" which was an identical twin. This powerful rugged long-bodied four-wheel-drive vehicle was to become as familiar to me as my own body, taking much of my time and sapping much of my energy, and would be valued highly as our only link with the outside world for the next three years. We carried with us considerable luggage and paint and building supplies.

Landcruiser loaded for trip to Bokay & Bedeno - May 1972

Karen was almost beside herself with excitement. She was especially privileged to go on this long trip alone with her daddy. She would be the first to see our new home. And she was the lucky one chosen to go to "help" her daddy fix it up. Little did she realize how long the journey would be nor how rough nor how big the task. Soon she was asking the standard questions: "How far is it?" "Are we almost there?" "When will we get there?" and finally in disgust, "We will never get there!" and "I wonder what Sheryl is doing now?"

We stopped for the night at Nazareth where we loaded four plows, two harrows, and the oxcart on the roof rack. Inside we added 300 lbs. of teff seed and 200 lbs. of wheat seed. At 6:00 a.m. the next morning, we added Ato Damti and all his housekeeping supplies and luggage to the load. Then with Alemayhu Assefa, we set out for our land at Bokay Teffe.

We drove steadily and arrived at Bedessa in time for Joad's new bride to feed us a tasty lunch. Joad Abdo was one of Shemsudin's brothers. We waited and waited for Mohammed Abdo, another brother, to return from a trip to Gelemso. Finally, he returned. After Mohammed ate his lunch, we added him and his cousin, Ali, into our over-stuffed vehicle and went ahead with the remaining one hundred kilometers of our journey. It was getting late.

The load was very heavy, and the road was rough. The Toyota

could only creep over the rocks and ruts and washed-out places. Karen was getting tired and hungry and thirsty. We kept on going and going. The sun sank low in the west. Still, we kept going. The road seemed to have no end. Darkness began to descend, then we had to turn on our lights, and suddenly it was night. Still, we kept going. Karen fell fast asleep. When we finally reached the little settlement of grass huts, it was close to 9:00 p.m. Those last one hundred kilometers took six hours.

When the Toyota finally came to a stop, the doors popped open, and the compressed passengers spilled out. They were still all alive and able to move about, except Karen who was lost in sleep. We left her there on the seat.

After a late but welcome supper, Alemayhu and I slept in the "guest house," the grass and cornstalk edifice we quickly dubbed the "Teffe Hilton." I had learned a lesson on my last visit when the bed bugs had left me sucked dry and incredibly itchy. This time I came prepared to wage chemical warfare. Thanks to the large can of Shelltox, we slept well. Ali slept on the back seat of the Toyota to keep Karen company.

"Guest facilities" at the Bokay Teffe settlement

Soon after I was in a deep sleep, Ali came to wake me. Karen was crying. It was as black as pitch outside, and she had no idea where she was nor where we were. After consoling her she went back to sleep and so did we all.

The next morning, after unloading the machinery, we took an exploratory trip around the settlement area. Government surveyors had slashed the bushes in straight lines one kilometer apart in squares and made their survey marks. We tried to find our 1000-acre plot. It was covered with grass and small bushes.

I fell in love with this wild place and secretly wished I could stay there and work at developing the dream settlement. It was so quiet and peaceful, so remote from the "civilized" world of noise and pollution. The nights were quiet and dark. Yet our intention was to bring man and "civilization" and "development" here to spoil the very thing I loved about this place. How ironic!

We spent a second night at the "Teffe Hilton," then set out at 5:00 a.m. on our return to "civilization." At Asebe Teferi we released our companions to return to Nazareth by bus, and Karen and I turned eastward towards Deder. There we spent the night with our friends, then loaded up some cement and other supplies and drove the one-hundred-kilometer trip to Bedeno in five hours.

CHAPTER 15

A Home at Bedeno

Assefa and Grace welcomed us into their home most warmly. They had been married for a whole month now and had settled into a routine of living together in their freshly painted house and were working every day in the clinic just across the lane.

Now we moved in with them and stayed for three weeks. Grace cooked for us and pampered us with her usual cheerful disposition. They took to Karen right away, but Karen wasn't so quick to take to them.

The main missionary house in which we were to live had a major flaw which needed to be corrected. Apparently, when it was built back in 1950, the builders had excavated the upper side of the hill to make the site level. When they dug out and laid the foundation, they did not go deep enough on the lower side. So, while the upper half of the house was resting on solid ground, the lower side was resting on ground that was less solid.

As time went on, the lower half settled a bit. Consequently, the house was splitting down the middle with the lower half beginning to move just a bit down the mountainside. At both ends of the house, there was a two-inch crack at the top of the wall through which rats gained convenient access and a crack across the full length of the floor with the lower half sloping to two and one-half inches below level.

Besides that, the roof leaked, and the kitchen sink cupboard had completely rotted out. The rest of the house was in dire need of refurbishing. At a glance I could see the restoration was not going to be a small job. Yes, it would take the full three weeks.

To make our job a little more complicated, the Gamber family had gone home on furlough a year before leaving their possessions behind, locked in one of the bedrooms. But we were going to rebuild the wall in that room. All their things would have to be moved out of that room, and eventually they would have to be moved to Deder, where they would soon be living. The Mission also owned the house furniture and a lot of other household things. With all the workers around, and the house being wide open during construction, we were nervous about theft.

To speed up the repair of this house, Robert Garber had been there before me. In his usual helpful way, he had made all the arrangements beforehand to make my three-week job of construction supervision as fast and smooth and efficient as possible. He had left detailed instructions as to how to proceed. Stones had already been brought and gravel had been made by many laborers who sat on the ground with small hammers breaking the large stones into many tiny stones (the "appropriate technology" version of a rock crusher).

We found a local mason to whom we gave the contract for the masonry work. He was to completely dismantle the two lower broken corner walls, dig down to the foundation, lay a new wider foundation with iron reinforcing rod and concrete. Then he was to rebuild the stone walls using cement in the mortar. He was to excavate the broken sagging floor in the living room, bedroom, and bathroom, and pour fresh concrete floors that were level. Then he was to plaster the walls he had built inside and outside. This involved about one third of the total outside wall of the house.

While he and his men worked on the masonry, I hauled many loads of sand with the Toyota from a mountain seven kilometers away. Some schoolboys were hired to help me fill cracks in the partition walls inside. I set about rebuilding the kitchen sink cupboard. We also laid ceramic tile on the shower walls. Then everything needed several coats of paint, but time had run out, and I had to return to Addis to meet an appointment with Hershey Leaman of EMM who was passing through.

By this time, the big rains were upon us. Early morning mist often enveloped the station in a cloud of dull, cold grey. When the clouds lifted a little, which was usually quite early, we could see clouds far below us filling the valley or floating over the hills in the far distance. We were literally "living in the clouds." The rain usually fell at night, leaving the day to the farmers to do their work in the warm, humid sunshine. With the rain came the mud, so sticky and deep red that it stuck to everything it touched and made deep stains in light colored clothes that were next to impossible to wash out. We quickly learned to love the weather at Bedeno. At 6,800 feet, it was not as harsh cold as Addis or Deder at 8,000 feet, nor as hot and dry as Nazareth at 5,000 feet.

Meanwhile, Karen had adjusted well to the climate and the situation. She loved living at Bedeno. She made many friends among the students who were very curious about this little white stranger. She even identified her first "boyfriend," the Yemeni Arab/Oromo mixed-race boy called "Abduh Fatah."

On Saturday afternoon we stuffed the Toyota with some of the Gamber things and packed as much as we could on the roof rack, tying it tightly with what I thought was good quarter-inch sisal rope. That was before I learned how to "tie" things. Then Karen and I started the long journey out to Dire Dawa.

With the rain, the road had completely changed its character. It was horrible. The vehicle lurched wildly from side to side as we slowly crept over large boulders, spinning through deep mud-holes, bouncing through sharp potholes, sliding into deep ruts and eroded places, sometimes leaning with one side up almost to the tipping point, then lurching to the other side, ever climbing, and twisting and turning up the steep incline towards Garamuleta mountain.

After an hour or so, we had made ten kilometers. There seemed to be more noise coming from the roof rack, more banging and clattering every time the vehicle lurched. We stopped to check. Sure enough, the ropes were all loose. I climbed up to tighten them. Then I noticed that a couple of items were missing. Mrs. Gamber's portable sewing machine was not there. And a small petrol drum was also missing. Apparently, they had fallen off the back when we made a hard lurch at a steep place.

We tied the things extra tight once more and retraced our steps for a kilometer or so, but the items were gone. What good fortune smiled on some Oromo peasant to provide him with a fascinating "makinah" ("machine") just on his path. He may not know what its use was, and he may not know how to fix what was likely broken in the fall, and he certainly had no electricity to run it, but it was worth taking home and hiding as a sign of Allah's generous provision.

Weeks later we sent a search party with a police officer to the area to investigate which neighbor was hiding the lost "*makinah*" in his hut. Of course, community solidarity required that no one tell the government police officer what everybody knew.

Finally, the police officer arrested their clan leader and brought him to us for questioning. Of course, he knew nothing! By this time, I was remembering that we were here to build bridges of friendship with these people. This was certainly not the right approach. It was becoming a political tug of war between the conqueror and the conquered, between the rich and the poor, between the Christian and the Muslim, between the foreigner and the national.

I changed the subject and explained our new program to help the community with agricultural development. We showed the leader some of the things we wanted to promote. We apologized for bringing him this far and sent him off proudly carrying a big white leghorn rooster under his arm. We told him to use it for seed, for crossbreeding purposes, not for eating. He went home apparently pleased and just perhaps our new friend. What they did with the sewing machine we never found out.

We left the remaining things and the car in Dire Dawa and took the Sunday morning train back to Addis. That evening we surprised Vera and the three little girls when we walked in the door. Vera was shocked, and my daughters were delighted with my three-week old beard. Karen was a celebrity among her sisters as she proudly told them all about her adventures and discoveries. Now they were all very eager to move to our new home.

The next full week was spent packing. Everything went into eight barrels, and on the following Monday everything was loaded on a train. Vera and baby Kristina flew to Dire Dawa in fifty minutes while the rest of us valiantly suffered the third class train all day. When we arrived in the evening all tuckered out, we found that Vera had already done a day's shopping. Tuesday was spent buying furniture for our new home, a large dining table, a set of chairs, and a cheap sofa set. Beds, dressers, desk, wardrobe, and buffet had remained in the house.

Wednesday, we loaded the Toyota to maximum once more and set out for Bedeno. Whatever possessions we could not bring plus the furniture would follow on top of one of those big lorries that came in once a week, bringing in goods for the merchant's shops and whatever mail there was, before returning loaded with coffee.

The Unforgettable "Bedeno Road"

As intimated earlier, the Bedeno road had been hastily built by the Italians during the war and had not seen much improvement in the thirty-five years since. It was a one-lane-wide trail made of large stones laid close together. At one time the small cracks and spaces between the stones had been filled with smaller stones and soil, making a fairly smooth road surface. But thirty-five years of rain and erosion and use had long since changed that. For three and one-half decades, heavy coffee lorries had pounded the stones down into two deep ruts, leaving a high center between the tracks and narrow, high broken ridges along the outer edges.

Small vehicles like our Landcruiser could not drive in those ruts without getting high-centered, so we had to drive with one wheel on the center and the other on the narrow and often broken edge. That is why we had to go so slow and why it was so rough. When these rocks were wet, they were slippery, and the car would slide off and get hung up on the center. Since there was no "Triple A" service or cell phones, we would have to get out our big Hallman "Do-All" jack and lift the stuck end of the vehicle up and build a road of stones under the wheels to give it the necessary clearance to drive out. Or sometimes we could jack the whole end up high until there was about eighteen inches or two feet clearance between the tires and the highest part of the road. Then we would give the car a strong sideways push and it would slide off the end of the jack, landing back on the high ground out of the ruts.

This was Vera's first trip to that long talked-about place and her first time on that legendary road. What an ideal time for it to rain! The road was wet and muddy. We had to put chains on the front wheels to pull the overloaded vehicle up the slippery mountain.

On one of the first sharp, steep hairpin turns, we got badly stuck. The right rear wheel dropped into a soft deep hole shifting the weight to the right rear corner. Reversing and trying again only made the hole even deeper and accentuated the steepness out of which the

Toyota would have to climb. Vera and the children got out. We rocked it backwards and forwards some more. Now the weight had shifted so badly that the left front wheel lifted two feet into the air spinning its chains uselessly. Vera burst into tears.

We realized that it was getting close to tipping downhill. We were not yet experienced at this sort of thing, but we knew we were alone, and there was no one else to come to our rescue. We would have to find a solution ourselves. We finally got out the big jack and lifted the right rear corner of the machine shifting some of the weight towards the front wheels and piled in enough rocks to fill the hole.

Finally, all four wheels took hold and dragged the heavy load on up towards the summit.

Karen & the Landcruiser on the notorious "Bedeno road"

Some places where the road hugged the mountainside too much, erosion had sloped the road so that the top of the load actually leaned out over the canyon a thousand feet below. Driving on this road when dry was scary enough for us greenhorns. But today it was wet and slippery. I made everybody get out. In fact, it did not take any coaxing.

Then with the chains on the front wheels hugging the mountain, engine idling in low gear, the Toyota crept cautiously forward as close to the mountain as possible, my knuckles white, as fingers dug into the steering wheel, tense body leaning hard towards the mountain, the back wheels sliding downhill sideways, now and then, coming within inches of the precipice!

Then the relief of reaching level ground, stopping, getting out to relax while the family got in, body shaking from nervous tension, calming down and continuing, it was an experience not quickly forgotten!

We got stuck eight times in that seven and one-half hour trip. We all were very thankful when we arrived safely at our new home late that afternoon. I was completely exhausted, as if I had been shoveling concrete all day. We all felt like just flopping in bed. Practically in tears, Vera confided, "I never want to leave this place, to face that horrible road again!"

With more experience, I later learned it was better to approach such slippery slopes with a modest bit of speed. The forward momentum would help keep the load from sliding downward toward the precipice.

Settling In

We six newcomers swelled the population of Assefa's house for another six days, testing their generous capacity for hospitality far beyond all reasonable limits. Vera pitched in to help me bring some order to the chaos that was to be our dwelling. The kitchen was all finished except for the formica sink top. We worked on the other rooms from early morning until late at night, filling hundreds of cracks, sanding them smooth, painting several coats until the patches became invisible, and then painting the trim to match.

Sunday was a welcome break. There was a worship service in the school. The worshipers were mostly staff and students and mission employees plus a few faithful from the community. After church, the grades five and six students put on a special welcome feast for us at the school and invited all the teachers.

We could have gotten the house finished quite quickly if we were allowed to concentrate on the task at hand, but there were so many other demands. Community people came to welcome us and to get acquainted. Station workers wanted our opinion about decisions or problems they faced. We needed to get out to meet the officials and the people. We had to take steps to start the development program. Then there were business demands that called me out to the city.

Finally, we decided we had to move into our house whether it was finished or not. On Wednesday we were able to push the rubble and plaster and dust back away from the front door so that we could find some clean place to move in.

Then on Thursday I had to leave the family and return to Addis for "urgent business." A trip out like that usually meant being away for a full week—two days to get there and two days to return, and two or three days for business.

Our children fell in love with Bedeno at once. After being cooped up in the tiny city compound for ten months, the big yard which included the whole school playground was like heaven. There were so many interesting places to explore and fun things to do. They loved the attention they got from all the older Ethiopian students. They became special friends with Zemedkun Baykada, whom they dubbed "the chicken boy."

They were fascinated with the chicken project. The white leghorns were just starting to lay eggs. The girls spent a lot of time with them feeding and watering them, "nursing" the sick ones, and patiently watching and waiting for them to lay eggs, then rushing to the house to show mom the fresh warm egg. They enjoyed it when one of the extension agents would come home from the field and give them rides on the tired old mule.

After returning home from that trip, I was able to work for ten days. Then it was time to go again with the whole family for the annual missionary retreat. This meant another ten days away from the work at hand. It seemed like we would never get our house finished. We would get up at daylight, work at painting or fixing for an hour, have breakfast, go about our development work during the day, have supper, put the children to bed, and then paint or fix again until the generator ran out of fuel or until we were about to drop with exhaustion.

It was October before we completed putting on the finishing touches and could relax and enjoy our evenings as a family.

The Romance of Travel

This trip out was sort of typical of the innumerable trips we would make in the next three years. Sunday morning, July 24th, we left Bedeno for Deder. The road was dry, so we made the run in six hours and did not even get stuck once. After sleeping that night at the Deder Mission, we left Monday morning in a smaller car for Nazareth, arriving at 3:30 p.m., and staying with Esther Becker at the Bible Academy. Tuesday, I attended a meeting of a committee reviewing the educational philosophy of our Church in Ethiopia. The next three days were spent in Addis Ababa doing shopping for our family and for the project and for all the potential friends who requested: "When you go to Addis, please bring me...!"

Friday evening found us at the Annual Missionary Conference at the SIM Guest House, which was perched on the edge of Babugaya, a beautiful crater lake near Debre Zeit or "Bishoftu" as it is called in the Oromo language. After two days of inspiration, challenge, and fellowship with all the Mennonite missionaries in Ethiopia, and refreshing swimming in the cool waters of the 800-foot-deep crater, we moved on to Nazareth to sleep Sunday night. Monday, accompanied by a German Shepherd puppy from the Academy, we made the trip back to Deder.

About one and one-half hours before reaching Deder, a tire went flat. Of course, we discovered that the spare was also flat. So, what to do? I reluctantly set about getting out all the equipment for patching the tire. There was an animal's tooth in the tire.

We put a patch on the hole, put the tube back in the tire, and both back on the rim, and pumped and pumped until the sweat ran down, but the tire would not fill up. So even more reluctantly, I took it apart again and found two more holes in the tube which I promptly patched.

Then I put it together again and pumped and pumped some more. Still the tire would not get full. So, we were compelled to take it off a third time. This time there was a good-sized gash in the tube. Was the Devil in the tire, or was I doing something wrong as an amateur tire repairman? Somehow the tube was being pinched by my clumsy use of the tools in the putting together. By now all the patches in the kit had been used up. What more could we do but wait for an equipped "Good Samaritan."

But one should never be hasty in accepting defeat. Had we exhausted all avenues? I suddenly remembered there was one other old tube in the car. I very carefully put that in the tire, cautiously put the tire on the rim and pumped and pumped and pumped. This time the tire swelled up and became hard and full. Praise the Lord! Victory at last! We quickly bolted it into place and were on our way. The whole operation took two hours.

On Tuesday we drove on to Harar City to care for some business, then backtracked to Dire Dawa for the night. Finally, Wednesday evening found us dragging our weary bones into our half-finished home in Bedeno, ten full days after we had left.

This time we were able to stay home and work for about a month before we had to take another two-week trip in September. I had to attend and give some input into a week-long evangelism seminar at Nazareth for about seventy church leaders. Vera spent that time in the Nazareth hospital where she had some minor surgery. These kinds of journeys did not help make "home schooling" any more effective or satisfying.

On our return trip about one hour after leaving Dire Dawa, a tire went flat. We changed tires. Then we came to the place where we always got stuck on that first steep hair-pin curve. Sure enough, though it was generally dry, this place was a bit boggy.

The passengers all got out to reduce weight and to lend a few pounds of gravity defying force to the rear end. Vera heard the air hissing out of another tire. We all listened. Sure enough, the air was coming out. What shall we do now? The other tire was already flat, and we had not brought any patches nor patching equipment. And it was getting towards mid-afternoon. No "Good Samaritans" would be by for a week at least. What should we do?

If you don't know how to solve a whole problem, it is good to break it down into its parts, to look for the small first step that you can do. I decided that at least we should drive the Toyota up to a more level place more suitable to tire repairing or sleeping before the tire lost all its air. Upon reaching the first level place, we stopped. The air was hissing out, but the tire was still hard. I said, "Let's go on until it goes flat!" Everybody crawled back in, and we went on. Grace, who had joined us in Dire Dawa, said, "I am praying!" We went on a bit, then stopped again to check the tire. It was still up. So, we went on again.

Darkness was settling over Bedeno four hours later when we drove into our yard. We thanked God for this "miracle." The next morning the tire was flat!

Homemaking

Slowly, our house was getting into a shape that met our minimum standards for aesthetic comfort and physical wellbeing. We whitewashed the outside walls and painted all the doors, door frames, window frames and shutters black. It was a very attractive bungalow.

Inside, the walls in each room were painted in very pale pastel colors, and the hardboard ceilings were white. The thin slats that covered all the joints between the sheets of hardboard on the ceiling, the window frames, and a six inch "baseboard" strip were all painted a darker shade of enamel, beautifully matching the color of the walls. Vera sewed curtains for each room that also matched. Then we put down our original patched-together carpets of many colors in each room. Everything was so nice and attractive and clean in each room, a nest worthy of the five beautiful ladies that made our home complete.

The kitchen had a full-sized, wood-burning black cast-iron and chrome "kitchen range" that was "just like Grandma used to have." It kept the kitchen warm on those chilly mornings and cool evenings during the rainy season. It also kept Mohammed Umer warmed and fed, chopping down huge eucalyptus trees, and splitting them into stove-sized pieces of firewood once every three months or so. When the heat was not needed, and if bottled gas was available, Vera used a two-burner gas hotplate for cooking.

One convenience we did not have was a refrigerator. We learned to eat the leftovers quickly. Vera bought meat twice a week in the market and stored it on the open shelves in the screened-in pantry. By the end of the third day, the smell of it had a definite dampening effect on one's appetite.

Around Christmas time, Vera's mother sent money she had

collected from church friends for us to buy a fridge. When we were in Addis, we bought a nice, little propane model. We had it shipped by train to Dire Dawa, then brought it on the roof of the Toyota. It served us well for a few months; then the cooling unit refused to work anymore.

So, we had to pack it up again and take it all the way back to Addis to be repaired. The importer had to send to Sweden for a new cooling unit. This took months and cost almost as much as another fridge. Finally, we were able to bring the repaired convenience home again and enjoyed its service for a few more months. Again, it stopped functioning. This time we gave up on it and got along fine without its services. But it continued to stand in its proper place, giving our cozy home a deceitful aura of modernity beyond its just deserts.

The station had a little Lister Diesel generator unit in the garage which stood some fifty feet from our door between our house and the school. It supplied 1200-1500 amps of 220 volts current to the two mission houses and the clinic. The generator was reserved for night use only except when certain medical procedures required electricity at the clinic during the day, or when Vera needed to use the electric-powered washing machine. She did her ironing and sewing at night. The Lister would be hand-cranked into action around 6:30 p.m. and would run until we were exhausted enough to call it a day, or until the fuel tank ran dry sometime past 10:30.

Clever Mr. Henry Gamber had installed a wire attached from our bedroom window frame that traversed the fifty feet of yard separating the house from the garage and ran it through the garage window and connected it to the "off" switch of the generator engine. When we got skilled at using this wire, we could pull it until the motor slowed down almost to a stop and quickly scramble into bed before the lights went out. However, sometimes our timing was a hair off, and the dying motor would resurrect along with the light in the room.

Assefa Haile and Mohammed Musa, our local technicians, both became adept "electricians." A dilapidated wire sometimes could be persuaded to carry the current to the school as well for special meetings. Somehow it could more easily do so if there was going to be a movie projected onto the white back wall of the school on a moonless night, a rare treat that drew large crowds from the community and was talked about for days after in the marketplace.

There were a lot of conveniences this town did not have, but one thing it did have was a telephone line connection with the outside world. Yes, there was a row of green-stained wooden poles, some of them leaning dangerously, stretching all the thirty-five kilometers from Grawa to Bedeno. There was also a continuous stretch of copper wire hanging on them, most of the time, connecting our house and seven other houses in Bedeno with most of the houses in the western world. Our number was easy to remember. Just ask for "Bedeno #1." We were number one in that town in at least one way. These eight phones required the full-time services of an operator at the governor's office.

To call anyone we had to turn the crank on our set to activate a little generator that sent a little current that activated a bell at the other end that caught the attention of the operator—if we were lucky enough to find the operator on duty. We would then give the operator the number we wished to call. The operator would connect us to that number's house. If the line was working that day and we got connected, we usually had to shout so loud that they could almost hear us at the other end without the assistance of the line. Sometimes the line was so noisy that it was impossible to hear. Sometimes one could only hear one way.

No matter how difficult it was to decipher what the message was, the operator would keep butting in every minute asking if we were finished. We often wondered if he couldn't tell by our shouting that we were indeed not only not finished but not able to finish, thanks to all the interference. Maybe if he took his headphones off his ears, he would be able to hear us better by opening the window of his office only a kilometer away.

While we were there, the progressive town of Bedeno opened its very own post office. They found a special corner in the governor's office near the telephone operator out of which the postmaster could serve the people. Now we would not have to have our mail sent through our office in Dire Dawa. Only the mail was still brought in the same lorry that we always depended upon before. So, the much-touted symbol of progress was to us largely just that, a symbol.

That became more obvious to us when we discovered that we had a bad postman who opened people's mail. He passed out my *Newsweeks* to his friends to read before I got to see them. He even threw away letters written by people he did not like. When complaints got too many, he was finally replaced by another relative of an official of dubious character.

Fruit was grown in abundance, especially in the Ramis Valley. Since there was no good transport out to the city, and since the people were very poor and did not consider fruit as a basic food, it sold on the market for a very cheap price. We could buy a dozen good oranges for about five cents. Needless to say, we enjoyed a lot of orange juice and lemonade. Bananas were six for two cents and guavas were almost free. Vera made guava jam and guava sauce and guava pie which in such desperate circumstances became a fair substitute for apple pie. Eggs were one cent each.

Milk was not generally available in the market. We were drinking powdered milk imported from Denmark or Holland. Obviously, it was a lot cheaper to drink orange juice than milk. It seemed rather ironic when Ethiopia could boast of having 25,000,000 cows, more than any other country in the world except India. We bought a Zebu cow for fifty dollars to produce milk for our family. When it calved it gave us about two liters a day for a few months; that is when the calf did not steal more than its share!

Hired Help

Did Vera need house help? She only had a newborn baby and three little girls plus a husband to care for, a house to keep in shape without conveniences, Cindy to teach, a garden to look after, and she was supposed to maintain the open-to-interruptions, friendly, hospitable attitude of a missionary at all times! We thought it might be justifiable to hire a maid to help her with some of the drudgery.

We hired a twenty-three-year-old girl who had been married once or twice and had two children but was living with her parents. She worked for one month and was doing well. Vera was teaching her to bake bread and pastries and many other things. Then she came one day and informed us that she wanted to go back and work for several male teachers that she had worked for last year. This was common practice here. Government schoolteachers were assigned from distant places. They came without wives, hired housekeeper-mistresses, and left children behind when they were transferred out. Often it was their own female students who were their victims.

Finally, we found Belaynesh, a young girl in her early twenties who could read and write. She had worked for the Gamber family some years back, so knew how the washing machine worked and how we "ferinjoch" wanted things done. What she did not know, she was willing and able to learn. Now Vera had some "help."

A central feature on the Bedeno mission station which no one could miss noticing was its unique watchman, namely, Ato Wolde Giorgis. Wolde Giorgis was a short black fellow of middle age. Though his body was quite thin due to poverty and his habit of substituting drink for food, he had a well-fleshed round face drawn into a perpetual broad smile, revealing a row of small, widely spaced, tartar-covered teeth and adding a pleasant puffy squint almost hiding his small friendly eyes.

Wolde Giorgis dressed in black from the top of his tam tassel to his shoe soles. Perhaps it was in deep respect and mourning for his deceased wife, or because he liked black to match his black skin? Maybe it was simply because he had nothing else to wear? Whatever the reason, he must have been wearing them for a long time because his clothes hung in rags. His jacket and trousers were well-ventilated with holes next to the multi-colored hand-stitched patches of purple and pink and green.

Wolde Giorgis was a Shankalla, a dark skinned Nilotic ethnic group from western Ethiopia. He was somewhat Amharized and claimed to be Orthodox in faith but attended the mission services. Perhaps he considered that a part of his unwritten job description? His daughter had married and become a Muslim. His wife had died some time ago, and Wolde Giorgis sought solace mostly from the bottle. Many times, he came to work half-incoherent and reeking of alcohol, and almost as many times he had been warned that with the next offense he would lose his job for sure. But somehow, he had staying power. He seemed to be a permanent feature of the mission compound, an indolent "grandfather" figure to be tolerated, or irresponsible "uncle" that the young station manager, Assefa, couldn't very well remove from the "family."

This man's job was to be a night watchman, but he hung around the compound most of the day as well. This meant several things:

first, he did not really have a home to spend time in, only a dirty, little rented room in town for which he paid three or four birr per month. He had no family to take care of or to care for him, so he might just as well hang around the spacious mission compound with the people he knew best. It also meant that he found ample opportunity to sleep well during the night while he was on duty "watching," tending the security of the Mission.

The Mission Compound

The location was carefully chosen by the first missionaries because there was a flowing spring at the base of a limestone cliff, directly about 400 meters up the steep hill from the house. They had put in a galvanized iron pipe, connecting the spring with the mission buildings. Water coming down the hill in the pipe had plenty of pressure to run flush toilets, showers, and a sprinkler for irrigation.

However, we could only irrigate our garden at night because the water pressure was too low during the day. We had built a watering place for the public below our yard near the road. It saved the community women half a kilometer of climbing up the hill to the spring. In the early morning, the spigot was opened for the down-country ladies who would be there with their gourds or buckets. In the dry season from dawn to dusk, a steady stream of people would come for that clear, fresh, cool water, sometimes standing in a long line to await their turn, sometimes quarreling, and even pushing and shoving to gain their "rights," and almost always noisy with the gossip of the day.

There was a small garden on the hill above our house. It had been neatly terraced by Mr. Gamber and was a nice place to grow vegetables. This garden could be irrigated at night with a sprinkler. During the dry season, this spot of green on a barren brown hillside attracted the "dik-dik," a small deer about the size of a half-grown goat. Their regular nocturnal visits made it almost impossible to grow much for us. So, we did the less hospitable thing and built a bamboo fence around the plot. But their aviatorial skills made a mockery of the fence.

Missionary Kids

We soon found that "home schooling" was not going to be easy. Cindy needed the incentive of the group situation and the discipline of a less personal learning institution. Karen wanted to be "in school" too, so Vera would find things for her to do. Sheryl couldn't understand why she had to keep away from her sister in her own house at certain times of the day. The baby and training house workers who did not stay interfered with Vera's teaching program as well. Reluctantly, we soon decided that Cindy and Karen would both be going to boarding school in Addis the next year, a heavy burden we parents did not want to think about.

The children made friends with two of the neighbor boys. Zemedkun and Joseph lived on the hill just about 400 meters up and over from our house. Zemedkun, they called "the chicken boy," and Joseph was "the grass cutter" because of the kinds of jobs they first noticed them doing.

Because Zemedkun Baykada was from a very poor family, the headmaster, Ato Seyoum, had given him the job of poultry attendant. His duties included feeding and watering the chickens during the day and guarding them at night by sleeping with them. He was paid four birr a month which was kept back to cover his school fees.

We confirmed Zemedkun in his role as chicken attendant, although we did not require him to sleep in the dusty smelly chicken house anymore. He was such a sensitive, caring person. He took his responsibilities very seriously. His heart ached when a chicken got sick, or when he saw injustice done at school. Our girls got quite attached to him, dubbing him "our big brother"!

*Our neighbors - Zemedkun's family – l. to r. his
father Baykada, Zemedkun, his grandparents, his
sisters, and mother holding the baby*

Someone found a baby deer in the forest and brought it to the girls who immediately adopted it as a pet. They kept it with the calf in the chicken pen at night. It grew well and was soon taking most of the milk the calf did not get. Some months later when it was quite big, a neighbor spied it grazing in the school yard. He thought this was his lucky day and ran to fetch his gun and shot it!

Later, he came rather subdued and shame-faced and apologized profusely when he found out it was our children's pet. We could hardly believe he did not know as he was our next-door neighbor, came by almost every day, and besides, nothing the *ferinjoch* did out of the ordinary remained a secret in that town.

Somebody else brought the girls a baby baboon for which I was compelled to invest twenty-five cents. It was too young to be afraid and climbed up on Cindy right away and clung to her as if she was its mother. When she put it down, it squealed in protest just like a spoiled child. Cindy adopted it as her baby. They had fun dressing it in their doll clothes and carrying it around on their backs. Kristina, who was learning to walk by this time became attached to it. She would sit down beside the baboon and put her arm around it and hug it.

Because the baboon had rather dirty toilet habits, we kept it outside. We placed a box for it in a tree and tied it to the tree branch.

But then the baboon hung himself one dreary morning when we were gone. The workers found it hanging dead from the tree. Perhaps it felt abandoned and hopeless and depressed? We were not aware of its suicidal tendencies, so suspected that the cause of death was accidental, possibly it got tangled and slipped off the tree and couldn't climb back on and eventually strangled. Whatever the cause, it was sad that Kristina had lost a friend! So, we got another puppy for the girls as a replacement.

We could have started a zoo if we could have kept our pets alive. A baby wild pig was brought to us for which I paid thirty cents, but it was sick and died the next day. Baby wild cats were brought to us as well, but I thought it was best to refuse them. One has to draw the line somewhere!

Kindred Spirits

We were very isolated from the outside world because of the very challenging road. Yet, we were surprised at how many visitors from the outside world put Bedeno on their "must visit" list and ventured out of their comfort zones to find us. They were always welcomed warmly and usually left too soon. Vera, who did not go out as often as I, especially felt loneliness and isolation from people of her own kind. Many of the visitors may have forgotten our meager hospitality but few of them will ever forget the infamous Bedeno road.

Every two months a medical team from Deder, including a missionary doctor, made a supervisory visit to our clinic for a few days and took care of some of the difficult cases. Since we were there, the doctor often brought his wife and children along. Dr. Harold and Esther Kraybill had gone home and a new couple, Dr. and Mrs. Ray and Eleanor Martens from Manitoba took their place at the Deder Hospital.

In early October, Henry and Pearl Gamber, who now lived in Deder, brought this new couple for their first visit to Bedeno with their first baby boy. This little blond-haired Jon-Jon was two days younger than Kristina. Later, when they were a few months older, they became the best of friends.

As a fitting introduction for the new doctor and family, a heavy rain obligingly soaked the road, especially for their trip! Although they were not doing the driving, they arrived in a state of nervous exhaustion. They were horrified by the way the vehicle had almost tipped over in one of the many places in which they were stuck.

Among those coming to visit from our mission were the director and his wife, Nathan and Arlene Hege, from Addis Ababa. They had been the first pioneer missionaries at Bedeno back in 1950. Shortly thereafter, Dr. Paul T. and Daisy Yoder came from Nazareth. They were starting a mobile medical work among the Danakil in the desert east of Awash.

One of these unforgettable guests was Peter Batchelor, the famous British Presbyterian missionary who lived many years in Jos, Nigeria, where he pioneered in agricultural missions. He had started "Faith and Farm," an organization that integrated agricultural development with the program of the church. After the success of that organization, he founded "Rurcon," a consultancy organization that also published a newsletter available to rural development workers. In later years he had been traveling extensively throughout Africa as a consultant to Christian organizations and churches involved in rural development, such as ours.

Peter Batchelor was coming at our invitation, which meant that we would provide transportation both ways. Conveniently for us, I had to take a sick man to the hospital at Deder on Sunday afternoon. Then I could just drive to Dire Dawa to pick Peter up on Monday. He flew in to Dire Dawa with Gordon Hoskings, another British gentleman, a recently retired actuary. The two were touring Ethiopian projects together. We had an exciting visit the full five and one-half hours into Bedeno. Fortunately, the road was dry.

At the end of the journey, I asked Peter if in all his travels in Africa he had seen many roads as awful as this one to Bedeno. He replied that he had been on many terrible roads in his many years in Africa, but he did not think he had ever been on a road that was so consistently terrible for so great a distance as this one!

The guests spent a day with us examining all aspects of the project, giving us suggestions here and there, and approving most of what we were trying to do. Then it was time to take them on to visit Deder. Our family enjoyed having these two jolly gentlemen as our guests and went with them on the trip out. With their British humor they were a riot, joking with us and especially with our children.

Before Christmas of that same year, Ralph Borgeson came with his family and a few other guests. The Borgesons were Presbyterian missionaries with the most interesting stories to tell of their many experiences in the Sudan and in western Ethiopia. Ralph was a civil engineer and was doing a special ministry in water exploration and drilling. They set up camp in our yard and stayed for four days.

Ralph went out with me to investigate the water situation in the lower areas around Genemie and Burka. We did electro-resistivity tests at several locations but did not find any results that were encouraging.

One of the guests that came with the Borgesons was Dr. Esther Lehman, one of my former teachers, a professor of Christian education from Eastern Mennonite College. In fact, there was a long-standing relationship between Vera and her family since Vera and her friend, Grace Neer, shared a small apartment in Dr. Lehman's father's home for a year following college days.

Now Esther was devoting her sabbatical year to teaching at the Good Shepherd School in Addis. She was also there as an advisor to four young female EMC students who were taking one semester at the Haile Selassie I University as a part of their cultural exchange program. They would be doing their student teaching practicum at the Good Shepherd School under Dr. Lehman's supervision during the second semester. It was a pleasure to have this distinguished professor and family friend to visit us at "the ends of the earth" and to show her around the community we had come to love as "home."

Shortly after these guests had gone, the Calvin and Marie Shenk and Harold and Pat Leaman families, from the Nazareth Bible Academy, paid us a friendly visit. As soon as they left, Shemsudin Abdo stopped in for a few days. He was a member of the Meserete Kristos Church Development Board, so in a sense was our "boss." He also reported on progress or the lack of it at our Bokay project.

Then the four tender, young American female students also got the urge to visit our remote specimen of an authentic "mission station" during their January break. Only they decided to use the older, more proven, though currently less fashionable, mode of transport, namely mules! They persuaded a single male volunteer, Nelson Kling, to accompany them. They would take the bus to Deder, rent some mules, and come across country the short way. This was only about thirty kilometers instead of the one hundred kilometers by road. It sounded like a great idea, and they managed to pull it off.

At Deder they hired mules and two guides to escort them. The route was short, but not easy. It involved crossing two rivers situated far down in deep gorges and separated by a high plateau between them. They started the journey at the first streak of dawn, fresh and excited and soft from a university lifestyle. The mules soon sensed that these were not conventional mule-riders, and quickly became obstinate and uncooperative. The cool of the dawn quickly turned into scorching sun and intense heat, as they descended the steep slopes into the lowlands of the river valley floor.

It did not take long for the posterior dorsal side of the riders to develop tender spots which, under the constant massaging of the wooden saddle, soon developed into sore spots that quickly swelled into something unbearable to sit upon. This meant the only alternative was to dismount and continue on foot, sweating and panting up the canyon wall on the far side and pushing on through the next valley beyond, leading the useless mules all the way.

To make a long tedious story short, the guests whom we expected to arrive at 5:00 p.m. arrived one hour before noon the next day, covered with dried dust-encrusted sweat, sun blistered, sore, exhausted, dehydrated, hungry, and very satisfied that they had just finished their last mule ride ever! Night and exhaustion had overtaken them in the Ramis Valley, and they had found refuge in the home of acquaintances of the guides, experiencing true Ethiopian hospitality. They were happy to take the "long scenic route" back by Toyota a few days later.

One of those plucky young ladies, Christine Yoder, must have recovered. She later spent several terms as a missionary with her husband and children on the back side of the Serengeti in western Tanzania.

CHAPTER 16

The Development Program

We hired two young men, Tsegaye Dubale and Mesfin Lemma, both fresh graduates from the Bible Academy, as extension agents-in-training. Both men were born and raised in the Bedeno-Genemie area and knew the people and their languages and culture. Tsegaye was the older of the two and had experience working with malaria eradication which involved a lot of field work. He could be counted upon to go ahead with assignments and to bring helpful suggestions. Mesfin was younger and less experienced and less sure of himself.

For their transport we would need some mules and saddles to extend their range in visiting farmers up and down the mountain sides and in the distant valleys. I hardly knew the front end of a mule from its rear, and I certainly was inexperienced in the ritual of negotiating their purchase. So, I instructed the two agents-in-training to find two good specimens of mules, that they would be happy to spend many hours riding each day and negotiate a good price and bring them to me for final decision.

In this assignment, both boys let me down quite badly. Mesfin brought a mule trader with two scruffy specimens from his hometown that he recommended we buy. Mesfin vouched for the fine character of the seller who promptly extolled the virtues of the scraggly beasts. They came complete with harness and saddles for a "very low" price "especially for you" since he realized we were "here to help the community." It was "one small way" he "could help with the project"! Both agents thought the mules were okay and the price to be fair, so we bought them.

The first use of the brutes convinced us that one was completely bad—old, ill tempered, slow, and worn out. The other had a few redeeming qualities and was marginally usable. Likewise, the saddles were ill-fitting and worn out, and the straps were rotten and unusable.

We fully realized how badly we had been cheated when Assefa came home with a young mule colt, for half the price, which could run a trip in half the time that our plodders took. We soon had to sell the useless one and buy a better one. A few months later, the police took it from the unlucky buyer because someone from Burka claimed it as his mule that was stolen in the Somali war that took place seven years previously!

Some members of our team – Mohammed Umer, Abebe Aseged, Mohammed, Hassen, Solomon Kebede, Belayneh Kassai, Ahmed, Mohammed Musa, and Eromo Shirango - 1975

It was seeding time when we started the program. The two recruits were sent out with string and pegs and five-kilogram samples of the most recommended type of fertilizer. They were to choose a representative farmer in each locality who was seeding, introduce themselves to him, introduce our program, and offer him, free of charge, a sample of fertilizer to test. If the farmer was agreeable, the agent would lay out a given size of rectangle with the string and pegs. The farmer was given the five-kilogram packet to spread within that designated rectangle. When the fertilizer was evenly spread, the agent collected the string and pegs, and the farmer would continue seeding his crop over the whole field. The agent would then move on to find the next "research collaborator."

Within three weeks reports began filtering in. The farmers were very excited with the new "medicine" that made the crop grow darker green and taller than the crop outside of the rectangle. The agents made periodic visits back throughout the growing season, and again at harvest, to check the progress, the results, and the farmer's attitude towards this new miracle "medicine."

Ato Seyoum Zelellow, the mission school principal, had a mind for development before we arrived. He made every student keep a small school garden. He had annoyed Mr. Garber by using precious school funds to build a strong poultry house and brought one hundred one-day-old chicks from the Agricultural College in Alemaya to teach the students modern agriculture. Several students were assigned to care for the little leghorn peepers in lieu of school fees. When we arrived, they were almost ready to lay eggs.

Our plan was to sell the cocks to farmers for cross breeding with the local hens, and to sell fertilized eggs to be placed under local setting hens for hatching. Thus, we hoped to upgrade the general quality and productivity of the local poultry population. Farmers did take an interest in the eggs but were slow to purchase the cocks. According to their tradition, farmers did not buy chickens, they raised them and sold their surplus!

Some of the farmers were asking for vegetable seeds. There was no supplier in the area. We decided to continue a practice that Mr. Gamber had started by bringing in seeds in bulk and repackaging them in small pill envelopes and selling them for ten cents apiece. This made the farmers very happy. It also made me realize that there was a need for an agricultural supply store. Improving their agriculture would require input from outside.

To facilitate evangelism, the Church sent an evangelist to Bedeno. Ato Shimeles was a nineteen-year-old Pentecostal boy from Dire Dawa. He had very limited training but was willing to do what he could. He was to begin by opening a reading room on the main street in the town of Bedeno. He made it nice with tables and chairs and a shelf with good books. During opening hours, idle people who could read were free to wander in and read. The evangelist was there to answer questions or counsel anyone with a problem. He organized young people into a singing group and evangelized among the youth.

Scratch Where It Itches

Perhaps our most important development activity happened by chance without forethought or public opinion poll or baseline survey. A neighbor farmer came to us asking if we had any remedy to kill the ants that were attacking his coffee trees? Well, I did not think black ants would destroy living trees. He wanted us to come and see for ourselves.

What we found was that tiny scaly green insects (which the farmer had not noticed) were sucking the sap out of the tender coffee leaves and stems, and the ants were deriving some benefit from secretions from the scaly insects. A simple insecticide like Malathion would rid the bushes of the scales.

When we brought the knapsack sprayer and the Malathion and began to spray the coffee trees, someone casually asked if this "medicine" would kill bedbugs? Well, we hadn't thought of it or even heard of it, but Malathion was an insecticide, and bedbugs were insects, so we supposed it probably would. Why was he asking? Were bedbugs really a problem here? A "problem?" They assured us that they were more than a "problem," they were a plague that drove them out of their houses at night. One man said he had not slept in his house for over two years. Others agreed. They said the only way to get away from them was to build a new house. And if they did, it would be infested in a few weeks anyway.

We heard their testimony and agreed to do a test on a few houses right away. The next morning the owners came singing our praises. There were no bugs left in their houses and they slept better than they had slept in many years. Their neighbors demanded to have their houses sprayed as well. The "Gospel" of Malathion spread like wildfire throughout the countryside. This was real development. Literally "scratching where it itches"!

The demand for Malathion was almost instantaneous. First, the people wanted us to come with our knapsack sprayer and spray all their houses. We made a special trip to Addis to buy another sprayer and some five-gallon containers of the poison. We couldn't possibly spray all the houses ourselves. There were hundreds of thousands of them. Finally, we encouraged them to use the little hand-held fly sprayers and do the job themselves. They would bring their beer or coke bottles and we sold them the Malathion at ten cents a spoonful. Two spoonsful mixed with a liter of water was plenty to spray an average hut.

Even while they were still in the act of spraying, the bugs would start falling like so many drops of rain from their hiding places in the sticks and grass in the ceilings. After spraying, they would shut the door for a few hours allowing the deadly fumes to do their deadly work, then open it to air it out before the family moved back in. All marveled at this new "medicine." It was simple, fast, effective, and deadly!

The five-gallon containers were soon empty, and we started bringing Malathion in from Addis by the barrel and selling it by the spoonful. Some enterprising people bought sprayers and a gallon of the insecticide and went far away spraying people's houses for a handsome profit. People came from as far as 130 kilometers away to buy a few gallons to take home and spray in their communities.

In reflecting back on this trade in deadly poison, I realize that it wasn't an unmixed blessing to the people as a whole. We will never know how many young girls might have used the drink to commit suicide after discovering they were pregnant while yet unmarried or jilted by their lover. We don't know the long-range effects it may have had on those who became "professional" sprayers without using any protective gear. But we do know that there was a lot less itching and a lot less scratching going on and a lot better resting and sleeping in those thousands of homes!

South To Burka

With the end of the rainy season in early October, the weather at Bedeno is simply gorgeous. The nights are pleasantly cool. With the direct sun beating down at high noon, it does get a bit hot, but under shade it is cool, and the mornings and evenings are just right. The sky is so clear that, from our perch on the mountainside, we could look down over the valleys and gorges and successive ranges of hills and plains sloping to the south and south-east towards the distant Ogaden wilderness where the nomadic Somali camel-keepers dwell.

Since the rains were over and the roads had dried up a bit, we were eager to explore the community in which we would be working. Vera and I, with our children and Tsegaye and Mesfin, took a trip south to visit the little market town of Burka about forty kilometers away. The road from Bedeno to Burka was very different from the Bedeno road. It was not built of stones but was a more natural trail worn deep in the red clay earth by traffic and erosion. Some places there were deep gullies, other places large rocks to avoid. But most of it was rather smooth, and we could drive much faster.

Burka market is the meeting place of the sedentary Oromo and nomadic Somali peoples. Everything south and east of Burka is Somali territory, "the Ogaden" where the nomads herd their camels and goats among the thorn bushes. Everything before Burka is Oromo territory with a lot of good agricultural land.

Burka was a tiny town with a large open marketplace, two shops, a police barracks, some huts, a new school building, and a governor's house and office. It had no clinic or health facility whatsoever. It was a dry, hot place with few shade trees. The town was located just up from a very strong spring from which up to 9,000 people and their cattle and camels drank during the dry season.

The town of Burka had been the scene of a massacre about eight years previously, when relations between Ethiopia and Somalia had heated up to a low-grade war. The larger context was the claim that Somalia laid to the Ogaden as a part of "Greater Somalia." The claim made sense when one considered the fact that between one and two million Somali people lived in the Ogaden and would have preferred to be ruled by the Somali government in Mogadishu rather than by the Habesha government in Addis Ababa if they would have been consulted. The propaganda from Radio Mogadishu stirred their emotions to this end. On one market day, a group of Somalis came with guns and pulled out grenades and threw them into the Oromo and Amhara crowd. A lot of blood flowed that day.

But on this day the two peoples were trading peacefully enough. Of course, they were trading under the ever-watchful eyes of the Ethiopian police garrisoned one hundred meters away. We bought some honey and maize in the market to take home.

We stopped in to meet the governor at his clapboard office. He was a younger man, better educated, and more progressive than the ones at Bedeno or Genemie. He urged us to come and set up a clinic in the town, at least on a part-time basis. He also invited us to extend our development activities to the area. He wanted us to help him clean up the water hole and make it sanitary. We took note of the needs he expressed and promised to do all we could according to the limits of our resources.

Though it was now the dry season officially, some contrary wind discovered that we took advantage to visit Burka, so it sent a very substantial rain just ahead of us as we returned. The dry dusty red clay turned into a wet slippery red clay, and we had to fasten the chains on the front wheels for the slow slippery climb up the long hill to Bedeno.

Some weeks later we ventured down south once again. Only this time we went to visit the community in the town of Genemie, twenty-six kilometers from Bedeno. This was a largely Amhara town built on a hill overlooking the long valley that stretched from Bedeno to Burka. It was the seat of a Wereda government and had a police post, an Orthodox Church, a school that had been founded by our mission years before, and a clinic as well as a number of small shops. The resident Amharas were mostly farmers and landlords in control of the lands lying in the valley below. The resident officials made up the rest of this tightly knit Amhara community. This was Mesfin's home.

This time we came with our tent, intending to spend the night, but someone extended their hospitality, inviting us to spend the night in an empty room in the clinic instead. They brought in several mattresses and laid them nicely on the floor for our comfort and convenience. It was easier than erecting our tent, and it would have been rude to turn down such generous hospitality.

Before going to bed, we decided to go on a wild pig hunt with a young police officer who had a gun and a flashlight. The wild pigs creep out of the forests at night and feed on the farmers maize crops. When their numbers increase, they become a serious problem for the farmer who must vigilantly guard his crops against these herbivores all night long. Then during the day, the baboons creep out of the forest determined to eat whatever leftovers of his crop the vigilant farmer managed to rescue from the pigs. So, the harassed farmer must be vigilant both night and day in order to save a portion of his hard-earned crop for himself and his family (and his landlord).

That night we did not see any wild pigs or wart hogs, but we did see a small deer. With a flashlight, all one can see is the two eyes reflecting the light. The police officer took aim between the two eyes, and the deer fell dead. I shuddered to think, would he really be able to tell the difference if those had been human eyes?

Anyway, though hunting was illegal, this "defender of the law" and we took that small deer home to the camp. Our friendly police officer joked and told stories while cutting it up and cooking it. By 10:00 p.m., we were all feasting on "the King's" venison. After the feast, still hoping to surprise a guilty pig, we went back to the hunt, stealthily combing the narrow paths between the dark silent fields. In vain. Two hours later, we gave up and returned to our base and went to bed.

We laid out our sleeping bags on the mattresses and slid our weary bodies in and shut our eyes.

But just before going off to dreamland, I felt the first little hot spot, a burning sensation that indicates a bedbug bite. Well, we had company! I slapped at the imagined spot where the bug must be, but in the dark found nothing. Soon there was another one, then another, and another.

How I wished we had put up our tent. Here we were dying of bites when we had all the paraphernalia to wage chemical warfare just outside in the vehicle. It did not make sense. But somehow it did not seem right either to the laws of hospitality to get up at 1:30 a.m., to light the lamp, mix a concoction of Malathion and water, put it in a knapsack sprayer and spray one's room when the host and everyone else was pretending to be sound asleep! I must have gotten 150 bedbug bites that night, and, as tired as I was, did not sleep even two hours.

We had sweet revenge the next day when we sprayed eighteen houses with Malathion to rid them of the nasty pests. Bedbugs were present in epidemic proportions in that town. Many people had evacuated their houses to sleep outside because of the infestation. The results of that spraying were so positive that we sent two men back the next day with more insecticide to spray every house in that town. We only charged them thirty-five cents per house for that cleansing. This was a very effective way to make friends.

While at Genemie, we surveyed the water situation and found it appalling. The town had a spring-fed water hole, which in this dry season seemed to be the sole source of life for all living creatures in the community. The water trickled out from under some hillside rocks and collected in a small pool. It was an open place where birds and wild animals could come and drink and bathe at will; where the wind-born dust and leaves and debris collected; where zillions of bees and wasps and butterflies and every kind of flying insect came to suck moisture out of the soft muck that lined the edges of the pool; where myriads of people dipped their dirty gourds and washed their dirty faces and dusty legs and feet, where they left their broken gourds floating in the stinking green scum. The pool had its own eco-sub-system complete with algae, water plants, and moss-covered rocks along the edges; and frogs, tadpoles, and an infinite variety of visible and invisible protozoa and metazoa swimming happily under the surface; and water spiders skimming above among the floating decomposing debris.

This was the source, the water supply from which everybody dipped the life-sustaining liquid to quench their own thirst, to give to their cattle and goats which were kept out by a crude fence, and to fill their buckets or gourds to carry to their families at home. We were glad the morning tea we had been served was boiled well.

The town elders eagerly showed us this revolting situation and told us how difficult the water problem was during the peak of the dry season. They matter-of-factly told us that when the water sources dried up in the valley below, the Oromo women came up to get water from this spring. They openly told us that they had to place police guards to enforce the unwritten but well understood community rule that no Oromo should be allowed to take water until all the Amhara had first taken all they wanted.

At that moment I felt the first tinge of disgust and dislike for these arrogant feudalist elders of Genemie. This was a manifestation of the same disgusting human phenomena experienced in our country in the Jim Crow era or under South Africa's apartheid regime.

They wanted us to help them improve their town water supply. They thought that if we dug deeper into the rock we would find the source, an imagined "underground lake" of which the spring was just a small leak.

We could not promise them any such miracle, but we suggested that if they cleaned out their water hole, they might find a richer flow.

If they were willing, perhaps we could help them box the spring and protect it from all the unsanitary filth.

Yes, they would be willing to start if we would pay them to clean the spring. But it is their own spring! I lost interest at once. Let these selfish exploiters drink their own filth! I wanted to go down the hill to see what the water situation was like for the Oromo population in the valley below.

Some Oromo elders volunteered to show us around. Here in the valley, the people were drinking chocolate-colored water out of stagnant stock ponds which they had dug to collect the rainwater runoff. They told us that this supply would dry up in about one month. Then they would have to climb over Genemie hill and descend down into the Ramis River gorge 2000 feet below.

They said it takes three hours for a strong woman to climb that distance down to the river, and then of course there is the return trip up the cliff-path again loaded with a gourd of water on her head, one under each arm, and one or two tied on her back. And all of this under the blazing sun. How dare anyone call these African women "lazy," or "the weaker sex"! Now I understood why their clothes were not always "ivory white," and why their bodies often exuded that particular "unwashed" odor!

We suggested that maybe they should dig a well for water. They did not think that was a sane suggestion at all. Any fool knows you can't get water out of dry ground or rocks. New ideas do not always catch on with the first suggestion.

We went to Gerbie, another community about seven kilometers further south towards Burka. There they had a dirty pond in which the cattle walked and defecated and urinated while drinking. About 1000 people carried their drinking water home from this same pond. They told us there was a spring at the bottom, but it silted shut every rainy season. After the pond dried up in another month or so they would dig down about twelve meters to the spring. Then the next rainy season it would be silted shut again.

They begged us to help them fix the spring so that it did not silt shut and so they could get clean water from it. They promised to pay the expenses if we supplied the expertise. It sounded like a reasonable request. We would just build a stone and cement curb and install a pump. A diversion ditch and a dike would keep the surface

221

water out. We thought we could come back in a month or two and do that. Quite simple. Little did we realize how complicated and difficult this undertaking would prove to be. We still did not know how much there was to learn about implementing development in a new community.

All along this valley we wrongly suspected that, if the people would dig, they would find ground water in plenty. But digging is hard work, and how do you persuade them to give it an honest try, to get that first experimental well dug? If it produced water, it would not take long for every village to have its own sanitary water supply. And if it did not...?

We were willing to put our credibility on the line, but we were not about to resort to the monetary incentive, to do as so many first world development agencies do: pay them to dig their own wells. This was a community problem, and it must be solved by the community in proper ways that could be replicated by the community.

At another spot there appeared to be a sink hole out of which it was said that abundant water bubbled in the rainy season. We thought if we could dig down into it, there might be an underground river or stream. There was only one way to find out. That is to dig.

The people were excited about the prospect of digging here except for one serious problem. They were reasonably sure that the "fairies" down there would get angry if men dug into their private domain. They might even pull the invading diggers down into the cave or at least grab and pull their tools down! This well digging was getting a lot more complicated than we thought.

We finally persuaded them that, while the danger posed by the naughty spirits is always there, the prospect of finding a good supply of water would far outweigh the risks. They agreed to start digging next Wednesday if we would be present to lend them moral support, i.e., keep the fairies at bay! We thought we could manage that responsibility.

The outcome of this exchange was that the community people did get organized and dug a huge odd-shaped hole in a level field. At first, they dug with great enthusiasm. As it got deeper and deeper, the work got harder and harder. Besides giving them advice and encouragement, we supplied them with buckets and ropes. We also managed to keep the "fairies" at bay!

"And the location of her phone was also a clue," Daniel said. "Which means we know where we need to continue working."

We found a hotel closer to North Potomac and moved our base closer to Rebecca's location. Like the last one, we had two hotel rooms, one for Daniel and me and one for Sarah, connected by a central living and kitchenette space. The living space had a mini kitchen, dining table, and couch, plus a window facing the street. It was the perfect setup for our HQ.

We filled Mr. Truth in on the status of the mission, then made a plan for our next move. After watching the tracker for most of the day, we found that Rebecca came and went from one location, and after sundown the tracker stayed put there.

"This is either where she's staying, or where she's working, or both," Daniel said, tapping the location on the screen. "Let's find out what's here." The map zoomed in to show a large piece of land enclosed with a fence. Several small buildings dotted the area, and one larger, Y-shaped building sat in the middle of the complex. "Must be some sort of business," Daniel said, searching the location for more information.

"Wanna bet it's related to power companies?" I joked.

The information loaded and I was proven wrong. The complex belonged to millionaire J. Xavier who owned the JX clothing brand. "Looks like the JX clothing headquarters," Sarah said, scanning the information.

"Explains the nice suit the guy with Rebecca was wearing," I said.

"What does a clothing company have to do with all of this?" Daniel wondered, ignoring my comment.

"Maybe the location is a front, or they need the complex for some reason," Sarah suggested. "Or maybe MAX works for or with the company."

"Is this complex open to visitors? Like, does it have a store or anything?" I asked.

Sarah pulled up the website for the location. "Yes, there's a shop at the front of the big building."

"So, should we go visit then?" I said, raising an eyebrow. "I could use a new suit."

Daniel winked. "I'm sure you could."

I rolled my eyes, knowing Daniel was referring to my plan to propose to Rebecca. *Stay focused,* I warned myself. "What time does the store open tomorrow?"

"9 a.m.," Sarah read.

"Let's plan to be there, then."

"And do what?" Daniel asked, crossing his arms.

"Buy a suit, of course," I replied, grinning.

Daniel rolled his eyes. "That doesn't help our mission at all."

I shrugged. "We could also follow Rebecca's tracker while we're there, possibly wander around the place and see what there is to see. You know, more scouting than anything."

Daniel looked skeptical, but he nodded. "I guess we could. We'd better keep it low-key though."

"Well, if Luke actually buys a suit, it might help us fit in better," Sarah said.

"Should Sarah stay here and keep an eye on things? We don't want to cause problems with her resemblance to Rebecca," Daniel suggested.

I nodded. "I think that's the best course of action. Sarah will lead us to where Rebecca's tracker is, and then we'll scout

The first fifty feet went easily enough as the medium was soft rich soil. Then the soil gave way to hard clay. By the time the men reached sixty feet, our credibility was slipping badly. They were sure we had "promised" them that there would be an abundance of water by now. But the dry clay just got harder and drier.

When the men finally reached seventy-five feet, they all agreed that, although the fairies did not get them, this strange white man had deceived them. They abandoned the project. From our point of view, one positive outcome was the research factor. Now we knew one thing that would not work. We now knew that finding abundant ground water in that valley was no longer a possibility.

It was only later that we learned from a geologist that the whole vast dry plateau was underlaid with a 500 meters thick layer of porous limestone bedrock which rendered a water table above the rock impossible. This meant that all rainfall that percolated down into the ground continued down through this porous rock layer until it came to a hard sandstone and clay layer at the bottom that held it. At that level it came out in innumerable springs along the base of the canyon walls in the adjacent river valleys.

We realized that there was no use in digging hand-dug wells on the plateau, and the cost of drilling through those 500 meters to get water and the equipment and energy required to pump it up to the surface of that dry plateau was completely prohibitive. The people would have to resort to other means to meet this water challenge, like water harvesting and storage during the rainy season.

Research And Demonstration

Research, demonstration, and extension were the three components of our approach to doing development. We created some demonstration and research plots on the compound and in a nearby field that we rented. Most of our research had an element of demonstration in it, and our demonstration had an element of research in it, as we were proving things that had never been tried in the area before.

We tried all the varieties of cereal grains and vegetables that for which we could find seeds. We tried different kinds and applications of fertilizers. Students were given part-time jobs working on the plots after school and on Saturdays that also helped them with school fees. Results from our first-year trials showed in general that if the farmer used improved seeds and a modest application of fertilizer, he could increase his yield four times what he was used to getting.

Crop variety test and demonstration plots

Extension worker, Abebe Aseged in wheat field

We were promised a seven-acre plot of land at Burka for research and demonstration purposes. By the time we were ready to start the work, political wrangling and jealousy among the town's elite had reduced the plot to about two acres. We planted it to hybrid maize. Production was badly affected by the prevailing drought conditions, yet we caught the eye of the public because our crop was the only maize in all the Burka community that reached maturity. As a result, most of it was stolen by neighbors who needed a few roasting ears for their families. The next year we planted cotton, maize, beans, and peanuts. All of them did very well in that climate.

A major part of our demonstration and research plan was to introduce exotic breeds of livestock and modern animal husbandry techniques to the development area.

After one year I built a barn out of eucalyptus poles and corrugated iron sheets with a concrete floor big enough to keep ten cows, a bull, a few calves and some twenty sheep. It was situated beside the road and attracted a lot of curious onlookers.

I was young and foolish and arrogant enough to think that I could do anything. I decided to build the barn myself. I drew the plans and knew what I wanted, so why mess with local "contractors" who did not know or understand what I wanted. I stuck to my local helpers, sons of peasants, young men who did not know how to measure straight, saw a board straight, or hammer a nail, in other words, technologically inexperienced.

It got done alright. The concrete floor was something to be proud of. But the cause for pride stopped there. I had no experience with tin and eucalyptus poles. My roofline was exceedingly ugly and crooked and shabby. It was the roofline, not the concrete, which could be first noticed from the road. I was very ashamed when I had to admit to visitors that I had built it. When we built an identical building at Deder, we made sure that we contracted the pole and tin work out to a local contractor. The result was beautiful, a professional work of art, something of which to be proud.

Project buildings l. to r. clinic, agriculture shop,
and barn - Bedeno town in background

Extension

As a part of our extension service, we built a small building to serve as a retail outlet for agricultural supplies. Eromo Shirango, a young Christian man from Kambata, was hired to be storekeeper. He worked, lived, ate, and slept in that little tin building, about froze at night, and cooked all day. We stocked that little shop with vegetable seeds, fertilizers, simple tools, and most of all, malathion for the bedbugs.

Jimel Abdullahi was a bright boy in grade seven who seemed to have an aptitude for teaching. We hired him to start an evening adult literacy class in our school. We paid him two birr and fifty cents per week for teaching two hours of reading and arithmetic every evening. This eighteen-year-old youth managed the sixty adults who came like a master teacher, happily and faithfully teaching even when there was no electricity or lanterns, using two candles. It is no accident that Jimel went on to eventually become a professor at Alemaya University.

Vera and Grace started a home economics club for the girl students that met once a week. They taught various handicrafts like embroidery, sewing, and knitting, as well as cooking and baking.

They also taught the girls about basic hygiene. The girls put on a tea party for their mothers and felt very proud of themselves.

One of our more promising approaches was starting a "model farmer" program. The area was divided into districts. The farmers in each area were invited to choose one farmer from among them to be their model farmer. Our extension agent then related to that farmer as an adviser and teacher. The farmer in turn served as a model in his community.

To promote understanding and cooperation with government officials and community leaders as well as interested farmers, we organized a field day at the Mission compound. We invited the Governor to officiate and address the people. Our field workers gave explanations of our intentions and encouragement to cooperate and try the innovations we recommended.

Field day – The Governor addressing the community leaders – Abebe Aseged translating.

Obstacles

As mentioned before, the major obstacle to grass roots development of small-scale peasant agriculture was the oppressive feudal landholding system. The peasant had no security and was robbed of any incentive to improve his way of living or to increase his production. If he planted trees or built a better house, he risked the wrath or suspicion of the landlord. He feared the property owner would come and say,

"So you think this land is yours that you can stay here forever? Now, get out! I am going to rent it to someone else!" The peasant had no recourse, no legal protection, and would receive no compensation for improvements he had made. He would only have a few days to gather his things and leave, and it wasn't easy with a family to move, especially when it was very difficult to find another small plot to rent.

If the innovative peasant was not evicted, he could be sure that any sign of prosperity or improvement would automatically result in an increase in next year's rent. Landlords were notorious for sucking every ounce of prosperity out of their peasants that they could. Peasants should just survive so they could plant again next season—nothing more, and there couldn't be anything less.

The Sheep Project

We wanted to introduce exotic wool-producing sheep into the area. Local sheep had soft hair but no wool. They also were quite slow growing and did not get very big. We were hoping that the large dual purpose exotic sheep would be a significant improvement over local stock. We prepared our sheep barn.

In early September of 1973, after putting Cindy and Karen into boarding school in Addis Ababa, we got permission from the Ministry of Agriculture to buy forty-four of the Corriedale-Marino cross sheep, forty females and four males, from the breeding station at Debre Berhan. On Monday morning I rushed the 130 kilometers east to Debre Berhan to purchase the sheep. Buying them was one thing; getting them the 700 plus kilometers home was a different challenge.

As a visionary leader, it has been one of my strengths to plan in general broad sweeping visions, and one of my weaknesses is to fail to plan well ahead in details. I tend to trust that somehow the details will take care of themselves when we get to them. This combination of strength and weakness at times gets me into a lot of embarrassing, hot situations.

This was another of those times. My plan was to get those sheep onto the evening train from Addis to Dire Dawa, but I had made no arrangements as to how and in what time frame we were to move them from Debre Berhan to the railroad station in Addis.

Now, after buying the sheep, we spent five hours searching and negotiating for a truck to take the sheep to Addis Ababa. By the time we agreed to hire a truck, loaded the sheep, and drove with them back to Addis, it was evening, and the train had already left!

Now we had a problem. The truck was hired and had completed its obligation. The driver wanted to unload and get going. But where could we unload? What can a stranger in a big city without a home do with forty-four sheep on his hands? What hotel would take us in? The railroad people refused to give us space. I brought the problem to Mr. Hege, the mission director. He tried to be helpful and contacted several other "wise men." Our mission office did not have a "sheep fold," and neither did our guest house nor any of our other houses.

Nathan Hege came to our rescue, using his influence, we were given permission to unload the sheep at the Good Shepherd School into an empty horse barn for the night and keep them there until it was time to load them on the train the next day. I was greatly relieved, and so was the driver. He grumbled a lot in hopes of getting some small gift in compensation for his extra bother.

In unloading the sheep, one of them broke its leg and had to be slaughtered. The night security guards at the school were glad to do that and enjoyed a sheep roast while they watched over the survivors that night. The next morning, they let them have a good breakfast of lawn grass before they were loaded on another truck and taken to the train station.

They arrived in Dire Dawa twenty-four hours later where Henry Gamber had a truck ready to hustle them off to Deder. Having spent the night at Nazareth, we arrived in Deder one hour after the sheep arrived. These exotic sheep attracted wide attention from the local community, most of whom had never seen such strange animals. It took some time to persuade some of them that these were actually real "sheep"!

Some weeks later we took fourteen of the sheep to Bedeno. Within a few weeks, they started to get sick, one by one. We were not veterinarians. I used to keep sheep in Alberta when I was a teenager. In fact, I was the owner of sixty of them and never had any serious problem with sickness.

How different it was here in Bedeno. I studied literature on sheep rearing in the tropics. There were so many kinds of diseases and parasites. There were all kinds of worms in the intestines, worms in the liver, worms that preferred the lungs, worms that lived in the sinuses, worms that infected the eyes. So, a general de-wormer was a must.

We de-wormed the sheep. Still the sick sheep got sicker, and one by one they died. There were tick-borne diseases like east coast fever and heart water. We sprayed the sheep for ticks and treated them for possible diseases that might have been brought by ticks. Still, they died, one by one.

By the time I got around to demonstrating to the people how to shear the wool from the sheep, there were not very many left to shear. We wanted to crossbreed with local sheep. By the time we were ready to start that, the males had died.

Obviously, this was not the best way to go about doing development. In the first place, the people had not felt a need for these sheep; in fact, they did not even know such animals existed. In the second place, these animals obviously were not so well suited to the conditions of this environment. Perhaps they would do better at 3,000 meters than at 2,000 meters altitude. In the third place, one could not have devised a more perfect way to make us look foolish in the eyes of the local population.

I decided that the sooner they all died and got it over with, the better for us all. I took the remaining few back to Deder to let them die there. But Deder, being 2,700 meters, was better suited for sheep raising. They died there much more slowly!

The Dairy Cattle Project

Shortly after finishing the barns and getting the sheep, we began to prepare for the coming of the cows we had ordered from Alemaya Agricultural College. First, we had to get some feed stored for them.

At Bedeno we prepared a pit silo as a part of demonstration and research. We dug out a pit into the side of the hill near the barn eight meters long and two and one-half meters wide and two meters deep. Then we filled it with chopped maize. All the work was done by hand. Two men cut the maize stocks in the field. Eight others carried it on their shoulders in bundles for five hundred meters to the yard. Twenty-eight men sat in the silo chopping maize stocks with machetes or homemade hatchets into little chewable chunks. It took this crew of almost forty men six days of continuous labor to finish the field and fill the pit. Then we covered it with a plastic sheet and soil.

The men who filled the silo were all the while wondering if we were normal in our heads. It was a big outlay of money just for the wages, not to mention the value of the crop itself. They protested:

"Imagine storing green maize fodder in a hole in the ground! Of course, it will just rot like manure! What a waste of energy and money! You must be out of your mind!"

"We'll wait and see!" I tell them evasively, not quite certain that they are not right.

The men who filled the silo were all farmers, so they had real interest in the outcomes of our grand experiments.

Some months later when the cows were in place, we opened the pit and fed the silage to the cows. The farmers came around to witness this amazing spectacle and to savor the smell of this strange "manure." But it seemed to be a technology inappropriate for this setting. It was too labor intensive, and there was a lot of spoilage due to the smallness of the pit and the slowness with which it was filled. Perhaps given time we could have figured out ways to make it more efficient, but other factors imposed themselves upon us, and we were not able to repeat the demonstration the following season.

We also bought and cut a field of hay about one and one-half kilometers away. Then came the challenge of hauling it home. We tried using the car at first. We laid the back seat down and jammed in as much hay as we could. Then we piled as much on the roof rack as we were able and tied it with ropes. Then the driver crawled in and drove it home with chaff falling down his neck. Progress was not satisfactory. There had to be a better way.

The next day we offered the women of the community twenty-five cents for each load they could carry by foot to our place. At first it was slow as only a few women came, but by the afternoon the news had spread, and there was a multitude of women rushing back and forth.

It was an excellent example of capitalism at work. Driven by the profit motive, those women came staggering under their heavy load of hay, sweat running down their faces and soaking their clothes. Dropping their bundles, they took their twenty-five cents, and literally ran the one and one-half kilometers back to the field to grab another load.

One woman made ten trips in one day, earning two birr and fifty cents, the equivalent of two-and one-half days wages! She must have traveled at least thirty kilometers that day, fifteen under a heavy load and all thirty of them with bare feet on a rough, rocky road under a blazing hot sun. I would take my hat off in deep respect when challenged by any of the Oromo ladies of Bedeno! By the end of the day, the field was bare, and our yard was full of hay waiting to be stacked by the less motivated men.

Finally, the time came when everything was ready to bring the cows. We had made arrangements with Alemaya College to purchase eleven cows that were Holstein-Zebu crosses and two young Holstein bulls. A trucker in Dire Dawa had agreed to transport a load of them to Deder. On Wednesday we went to Alemaya College to get them. The truck took six cows and one bull to Deder. I had to wait until the next day to send the remaining five cows and one bull to Bedeno by foot.

After getting the guides and the cows on the road, I drove back home, arriving that Thursday evening. Friday morning while I was still in bed, there was a knock at the door. Would I please take a wounded boy to the hospital in Harar right away? The sixteen-year-old boy had gotten a bullet through the back of the head. So that was another full day on the road. When I got back home it was dark. No cows in sight yet. The cows finally arrived in good condition at 11:00 p.m. Saturday night.

CHAPTER 17

Community Relationships

Of Governors, Grawa, and Grievances

It was nearing the end of the Ethiopian year and hence the government's fiscal year as well. The Wereda (township) governor and the mayor of Bedeno came to inform me that I would be taking them to the Awraja (county) capital, the small town of Grawa "only twenty-five kilometers" away on the east side of Garamuleta mountain. They were required to be there to bring their annual reports.

I foolishly objected saying, "This is impossible! I have my work to do, and my work doesn't include driving Ethiopian government officials around!"

"Well, if you are too busy, we understand. But that is no problem!" they politely insisted, "Just let us use your car. Ahmed can drive us there!" referring to Mohammed Ishmael's driver, a Somali fellow notorious for his wild and reckless abuse of vehicles.

"That would be impossible!" I replied, "My organization has strictly forbidden me to let others borrow their vehicle!"

"But the former missionary, Mr. Gamber always took us on this annual trip to headquarters!" they pleaded.

"Yes, Mr. Gamber was a very kind man, but I am not Mr. Gamber!" I informed them, "The government has its own means. Why don't you use the police Land Rover? Or the Malaria Control Jeep?"

"No, that would be impossible. Those departments could not drive for other departments!"

"Perhaps you should take mules then!" I desperately suggested.

"No, we are big old men and Grawa is very far. We couldn't ride that great distance by mule!" they objected.

They made it very clear to me that there was only one solution left to their problem. And that solution lay solely within my powers to grant. I was their only hope. They insisted that on August 31, they would be coming in the morning at 7:00 a.m. to ride with me to Grawa.

"But" I protested, trying the one last devastating weapon remaining in my arsenal of arguments, "We do not have enough fuel in our tank nor in our barrel nor in our jerrycans to reach Grawa and return!"

"Well, that is no real problem!" they triumphantly replied. "There is a merchant in Grawa who sells benzine (gasoline). We will see to it that you get enough fuel to return to Bedeno!"

Now, as I suspected from the beginning, I was totally defeated. After all, I was the newcomer in this community. One cannot fight the community and still win it over. There must be give-and-take. One must carefully choose his battles. I smiled and shook hands all around. They smiled back, shook my hand, thanking me profusely as they bid farewell, turned, and went away happy. I could almost hear them say, "You know, sometimes it is good to have that foreigner among us. Otherwise, we would have to go by mule like we did last year!"

On the appointed day at the appointed time, eight government men showed up at our doorstep at 7:00 a.m. eager to go. Yes, Africans can be on time when it is in their best interest to do so. The august group included the three governors of the three Weredas of Bedeno, Genemie, and Burka and their corresponding retinue of tax collectors and assistants. The governor of Burka had already traveled forty kilometers by mule to reach Bedeno. They all packed into the Landcruiser, eight robust officials plus me in our six-seat capacity vehicle.

Interestingly, I had also promised the three friends, Kalifa, Tsegaye, and Mesfin that they could escort me. They could have squeezed in the luggage space at the back except that each official brought luggage for staying overnight plus some "small gifts" for friends in Grawa such as a few small sacks of maize, a few bunches of bananas, a can of honey, a few live chickens tied by the feet, and so on. Gifts and luggage and fat officials together made a very full load. Tsegaye and Kalifa opted for sitting on the roof rack, something I never allowed before—nor since.

Like the camels of the three wise men, we got off to a groaning start. With the fuel gauge at the half-way mark, I felt a bit uneasy starting out on this unknown journey, not unlike following a strange star. How far is Grawa really? Can we make it on half a tank? Is there really a merchant there with abundant stocks of this precious liquid? What else can we do but go and find out!

The three governors told stories and joked and laughed with their companions as we crept up and down the steep slopes, forded trickling streams, eased over all the holes and rocks, and turned back and forth, following the curves around the gullies and ridges until we passed Garamuleta mountain and joined the road east to another sharp range of distinct but smaller mountains.

Across the deep canyon between, they pointed out the site of Grawa. What a magnificent view! They assured me it was "only ten more kilometers." We had already driven twenty-five. While enjoying the scenery, my eyes were silently glancing at the swiftly sinking fuel gauge in growing apprehension.

"Wonders never cease!" And one never ceases to wonder at the paradoxes that turn up in the oddest places! Here on this torturous road where one cannot exceed ten miles per hour even if he hated his vehicle and his own aching back; here on this desolate road where one might wait three or four days without seeing a single vehicle; here, of all the places in this "best of all possible worlds," one would have to snag a cop!

It was incredible, but there he stood in our path with his forbidding hand raised high. Yes, this was his lucky day, not only to see a vehicle at all, but to find one coming grossly overloaded and with two passengers riding on the roof to boot! Triumph shone in his eyes as he approached my rolled-down window with that most accusing look of supreme authority!

But the moment of triumph was just that, only for a moment. For as he started counting passengers, he counted three governors with deep scorn written all over their fat faces. He knew only too well that their presence far exceeded any rule of law to which he could appeal. His countenance changed completely as he welcomed us profusely and wished us a successful journey. What a lousy, rotten day after all! How many more days would he have to wait to get that much coveted "baksheesh," that "something little for tea"?

We drove around the end of the canyon and reached the main

body of that Grawa mountain range when the Toyota sputtered a few times, continued a few hundred meters, then sputtered some more, slowed down sputtering, then coughed twice, jerked to a halt, twitched, and died. Now all eight official voices stopped their joking, and all sixteen official eyes focused on the back of my head silently demanding a proper explanation.

"Out of benzine!" I announced almost gleefully, a trace of sadistic joy soothing the submerged burning bitterness at being compelled by officialdom to abandon my own agenda for today to cater to their official convenience. To make the governors walk in the end was a bitter-sweet revenge of sorts. After all, I had told them there was not enough fuel, hadn't I! It felt good to be found right, to show all the "doubting Thomases" that my word is as good as gold! If I say, "There is not enough fuel!" I mean, "There is not enough fuel!" I am not to be taken as one of the regular liars who say such things only as a flimsy excuse. In fact, I felt deep satisfaction in walking the next seven kilometers with the fat governors, happily conversing with them as we sweated along together under the broiling noonday sun. Of course, I knew that they would just walk the seven kilometers, while I would have to walk another seven kilometers back with the benzine, if in fact there really was a merchant selling it. And, if not...??

Upon reaching the town, the governors walked up the hill to their meeting in the Awraja Office. One of the lesser souls took us to the shop of the merchant, Yusuf Mohammed, who it turned out was a short middle-aged Arab. He was a strikingly active little fellow, talking fast and excitedly with animated face, gesturing dramatically with his short arms and hands, and indeed his whole body. He reminded me intensely of the typical stereotype of one of the sons of Abraham, maybe a descendant of Zacchaeus!

Now it seemed to be illegal for this particular merchant to be selling benzine, for the nature of our need was disclosed to him in his own language behind closed doors. He acknowledged sympathy for our predicament and gestured secretively to us that in due course he would attend to our request. But first we must have something to eat and a soda for refreshment. And we must pretend that we have no further business with him. At least, not the unmentionable.

After we were refreshed, Yusuf gave orders to his shop attendants to divert their attention while he took out a set of keys, glanced furtively up and down the street making sure no police were in sight, turned toward us dramatically sucking his neck down into his chest while putting his finger across his lips and moving his eyes both ways, he beckoned for us to silently follow him.

We set out following him down the street, turned into a back alley and entered through a gate which he unlocked. Inside was a rusty old shed with a big padlock on its door. Unlocking the door, he showed us a dozen barrels standing in the gloomy interior. He poured us a jerrycan of fuel and sent us on our way. Apparently, he was allowed to have benzine for his own vehicle, but not for sale. I really was amazed at all this pretense at secrecy when even the governors as far away as Bedeno and Burka knew that he sold benzine!

By late afternoon we had the Toyota with us in Grawa, filled its tank with the "secret" fluid, and found a hotel for the night. This was a cute little two-story wooden structure with a little balcony hanging out over the front street. Facilities were very basic since there was as no "water system," let alone "sewer system," as we normally know it. The governor of Bedeno took a room in this "Grawa Sheraton" as well.

The next morning, we woke up early and refreshed ourselves over the "Sheraton's" pit latrine and washed our faces at the communal washstand with the five-gallon can having a small tap soldered at the bottom. Then we strolled around outside watching the town come to life while our breakfast was being prepared.

It was Friday, the Muslim day of worship and alms giving. We watched the beggars gather en mass before the door of Yusuf Mohammed's shop. Sure enough, at the expected time, the door opened, and our "Zacchaeus" appeared with large trays of food carried by his servants. With an expression on his face approaching glee, he personally scooped up large portions with his hands and placed them in the diverse baskets and containers held in the outstretched hands of the town's destitute. Thanks to this "son of Abraham" and his reverence for God, they enjoyed at least one "good" meal each week!

After breakfast, the meeting at headquarters on the hill continued. We decided to visit the site. The building that housed the Garamuleta Awraja Office was of some historical importance. It had been built especially as a royal prison by His Imperial Majesty Haile Selassie I for his cousin, Lej Iyasu, who had been Menelik II's grandson and chosen heir to the throne.

Lej Iyasu had the misfortune of being given adult responsibility before his years. His ageing and sickly grandfather appointed him Crown Prince and regent in 1909 at the ripe age of thirteen within the same month that he married the royal Romanawarq Mangasha. When Menelik II was incapacitated in 1911, Lej Iyasu assumed full responsibility for both. To manage an empire and a royal wife would be a major challenge for any of us men. But this unfortunate lad was not an ordinary man!

Apparently, the challenge did not meet the full requirements of his amazing capacity, for he courted several other women on the side including Muslims. This did not endear him to the Orthodox Church establishment. He was also accused of being too friendly to the Muslims and favoring German and Turkish elements during the Great War. So, in 1916, he was deposed by those who favored Ras Tafari, son of Makonnen, a cousin of the emperor. Tafari assisted as regent under the Empress Zewditu until she died in 1930 when he assumed the crown as Haile Selassie I.

Being a good "Christian" and following the tradition of the Christian kings of Ethiopia, Ras Tafari kept the royal competitor and cousin locked in this royal prison on this isolated Grawa mountain for life rather than executing him as many less principled tyrants would have done.

The prison consisted of an outer stone wall about twelve feet high surrounding an equally high inner wall separated from it by about twenty feet of "no-man's land" space. The inner wall surrounded a small yard holding a well-built four-room stone house which served as the permanent residence of the royal prisoner. Within these walls he had freedom to entertain women and banquet his friends as he pleased. But he was not allowed to go outside.

His life was terminated in 1935 under questionable circumstances when the Italian invasion was threatening. A rival to the throne could not be allowed to fall into Italian hands.

As for our "Zacchaeus" look-alike, it was our privilege to meet him again on several occasions. About a year after this first encounter, business brought us to Yusuf Mohammed's home again, this time as overnight guests. He extended true Arab hospitality to Mesfin and Tsegaye and me, welcoming us into his house in late afternoon. I was treated with special honor. They put me at a special table, in a large room, all by myself, and soon a lovely young woman quietly entered and gracefully placed a huge platter of the finest spiced meat and rice blended to a standard of perfection that would make any other Arab merchant envious. Yusuf proudly introduced her to me as "Fatuma," his daughter!

She was a beauty, a model of perfection! I almost gasped in amazement, trying hard to remember that I am a married man. How could such a short squat homely old man possibly be the progenitor of such a marvelous epitome of feminine perfection? She must have had some mother! To me one of the unfathomable mysteries of God's complicated creation is how even the ugliest specimen of masculinity can often manage to father the most beautiful of daughters!

They left me to eat alone puzzling over this mystery. Tsegaye and Mesfin shared food at another table off to the side and visited with members of the household. I felt terribly embarrassed eating all alone. I love eating, especially when the cuisine is of such exotic and superb quality, but it spoils the fun and makes me feel uneasy to be watched as I eat. I assumed it was meant to be an honor, but I felt isolated. Some things in other cultures are hard to appreciate.

Later in the evening, a very rough, homely-looking Arab man of about my age came in to meet the guests. He seemed to be a most unremarkable man in every respect. Yusuf introduced him as his "son-in-law," the recently married husband of the beautiful Fatuma! Again, I was made to ponder the mysteries of human behavior. Why would the rich merchant give his marvelous Fatuma in marriage to this nondescript nobody? And why would the young princess consent to be so given? I did not deem it polite to ask this intriguing question. But the answer could be the basis for a very fascinating romance novel.

Upon later reflection, of course my preliminary evaluation was extremely superficial and unfair. Never judge a person by his or her appearance! It is better to presume that the wise Yusuf saw in the son-in-law a man of impeccable character, complete with all the desirable qualities that a woman would want in a husband and a father of her children, as well as a valued member of the family and a fitting partner in the family business. And as for Fatuma, "beauty is only skin deep" and is also subjective to the eye of the beholder. It says little about the inner beauty or ugliness of a person's personality and character. Let us not judge by preliminary appearances.

When the hour of repose arrived, Tsegaye and Mesfin were led away with the young men of the house to find a place to sleep. Yusuf led me out to his shop. There the servants set up a single cot in front of the counter where the customers stand during the day. On it they placed a foam mattress and some blankets. This was to be the "guest bed." Then they pulled down some bolts of cotton material from the shelves and unrolled a thick layer on the counter. This became the bed of the master of the house. Their work completed; the servants left us alone to accommodate themselves elsewhere.

Then Yusuf put out the lamp and hoisted his short body up onto his high, narrow counter-bed and made himself comfortable under a blanket, and I tucked myself into my guest bed. As I lay there in thought, it struck me that this was a rather interesting and unusual situation. Here we were, an Arab Muslim and a Canadian Christian sleeping together in an Amhara Orthodox Christian town in an Oromo Muslim community in Ethiopia, Africa. He, sleeping on that narrow counter, the symbol of his occupation, and I sleeping in his bed, a symbol of the finest Arab hospitality, in front of the barred and locked door of his shop, a symbol of his relationship with the larger community.

"Zacchaeus" slept like he lived and worked, intensely! He snored loudly. Throughout the night he turned and tossed restlessly, mumbling, and grinding his teeth, and exploding loud short fragments of commands, while repeatedly clearing his throat and sucking in forcefully to clear his nasal passages and spitting the offending materials into the darkness. I could only hope his aim was in the direction of the floor rather than down on my cot!

I was glad to hear the rooster crow behind the counter and see the first streaks of dawn through the cracks in the door. My friend woke up fully refreshed and full of vigor to approach another busy day of business. I, too, arose refreshed and eager to be moving on with another day's challenges, but not with the same vigor as the mighty little Yusuf!

Ramadan

It was the holy month of Ramadan, the ninth month of the Muslim year, the month of fasting. The good Muslim will eat nothing from sunup to sun set. The real good Muslim will not even swallow his own saliva during those off hours. But after sunset the night is devoted to feasting, fellowship, worship, smoking, and chewing "chat." They may stay awake the whole night. Since it is hard to work long in the hot sun without food and water, especially if one has been up most of the night, most Muslims sleep a good part of the day during Ramadan. Of course, they can't work at night, so they use the time to socialize.

One evening I was invited to go with Tsegaye to visit an Arab merchant's home in Bedeno during Ramadan. We took our shoes off at the door and were ushered into the little living room behind the shop where we sat on some cushions and blankets on a raised platform-like part of the floor. Some of the best-tasting spicy rice and goat meat that one could ever wish for was brought to us. The sweet aroma of burning incense filled the room and left a smoky haze in the lamp light. People from different levels and walks of life came in, sat down awhile and chatted. Some left again while others stayed and chewed "chat" and sipped tea. Finally, a sheikh came in and led the group in religious exercises. We left about 1:00 a.m.

A day later I learned that I had a new name, "Kabier Hassen." "Kabier" means "teacher" or "religious teacher." Someone told me it can also mean "witch doctor." Should I be flattered, or not? I chose to be flattered.

One day Tsegaye, Mesfin, and I went by mule and on foot for about an hour's journey to "Eliko" where we treated a man's coffee plantation that was suffering from scaly insects. It was Friday, the Muslim "sabbath." They do work on that day but take time out to pray. After spraying the coffee plants for a time, the call to prayer came from a nearby mosque. We "infidels" went and waited outside from 12:00 to 1:15 p.m. When the worshipers came out of the mosque, their leaders invited everybody to sit down on the grass while we introduced ourselves and our program. There were about 130 adult men there. They showed real delight with our program and invited us to come again and teach them better ways.

Danger of Gossip and Lies

Later, I learned that it was somewhere near the same spot in Eliko only two years previously that Mr. and Mrs. Gamber had narrowly escaped death at the hands of an enraged mob of peasants. The rumor had been circulating that the missionaries were catching small children and draining their blood to be used in the cure of a rich merchant's wife's skin disease. When the peasants saw this couple coming, they assumed this couple were out looking for more children for their strange medicinal purposes. They must end this terrible threat to their children once and for all!

Providentially, an Amhara farmer, who knew better, came by and rescued the couple from probable death. Obviously, the Mission, having been in this community for more than twenty years, had been less than successful in public relations. Just as obvious was the fact that this community was still on the far side of some major changes it would have to go through before it could be called "developed."

Friendly community relationships should not be automatically assumed, even if one's intentions are blameless. One day the public health officer came to Bedeno and closed an illegal clinic in town and confiscated about 2000 birr-worth of medicines. The "doctor" had been running that clinic without a license for many years. He treated certain influential people for free and had a lot of friends among them, so he did not need a license.

This "doctor" had a longstanding quarrel with our clinic, having at one time been dismissed from its employment for unsatisfactory conduct. Since then, he was determined to destroy our clinic by stealing as much business from it as possible. He had almost succeeded until Assefa and Grace accepted the challenge of providing the best medicine at the most reasonable prices.

The "doctor" was frustrated by the new competition, so he began to pay certain friends to post themselves on the different roads coming into Bedeno to watch for any sick person being brought to our clinic. They would tell them, "That clinic is closed today. Take your patient to the clinic in town!" or they would say, "The Mission's medicine is old and bad, it won't help you! Go to the clinic in town. Its medicine is much better!"

Assefa and Grace were not the fighting kind, but this kind of smear campaign really hurt. They had to have a certain amount of business to earn their living. Therefore, Assefa began traveling by mule or bicycle to Burka and Furda once a week to hold clinics in those places on market days to supplement their income. They did not want to quarrel with the Bedeno "doctor."

When the public health officer closed this chap's clinic that day, he became livid with rage. He blamed Assefa for bribing the officer to close his clinic so that he could get all the business. He threatened to kill Assefa. He roused the people of the town on his behalf. The crowd gathered stones to stone the health officer as he passed back through the south end of town the following day.

The governor had to call out the detachment of soldiers to pacify the people and protect the life of the health officer. The crowd even insulted the governor to his face, but they had to give way to the army. Then they tried to march north against the Mission en mass, but once again were thwarted by the soldiers who got wind of it and out flanked them and cut them off. Finally, they wrote up a petition demanding that the whole Mission—school, clinic, and development project—be expelled from the community. Many people signed it.

The petition divided the community into pro-Mission and anti-Mission parties. It looked like the beginning of a civil war. The authorities were on the side of the pro-Mission party with many of the leading citizens who knew right from wrong. At one point Haji Adam, a leading Oromo official, challenged the anti-Mission town people: "For every one-hundred people you can raise to oppose the Mission, I can raise ten thousand from the countryside to support the Mission!" The anti-Mission party included the rabble rousers and the urban masses who were easily swayed by the most amazing lies that the "doctor" could fabricate.

The author with Haji Adam and Belayneh
Kassai and some students

Law and order finally won the day. Or did it? After about three days of unrest, the illegal clinic miraculously began operating again. Supposedly, he had a reserve supply of medicines in his house. But why was the public health officer so quick to drop the charges and restore his friendship? As suddenly as trouble had flared up, things returned to their normal level of peace and tranquility. We never ceased to be amazed at how resourceful and clever Ethiopians are in inventing ways to resolve conflicts and preserve or restore relationships in the most face-saving ways.

One Sunday afternoon, a beggar, a gentle simple old man who had lost his mind and who wandered around town, came to our door. He kissed my hand and talked to me in Oromo, which I did not understand. A couple of coins made him go away peacefully. This too was a son of Adam.

Another old Amhara man, who still possessed good mental faculties, came to complain that he was hungry. He was so polite and such a dignified elderly white-haired gentleman; I couldn't say no to him. Some weeks later he returned for another handout. Then he came more often. Finally, he became our regular "customer" coming weekly for his birr. One day I asked him if he did not have any children that could take care of his needs? "Yes," he replied. "I have one son who works in town, but he has many children to feed, and has nothing extra for me!" It is so sad. Poverty can be so dehumanizing!

The Wedding

"How can such a corrupt and mean judge have such a beautiful daughter?" I asked when the sixteen-year-old beauty was first pointed out to me from among the other students in our school. Later, we learned that this girl was being given in marriage to a military man about twice her age. Because the father was the judge in the law court of Bedeno, there would be a big wedding. All of us prominent people of the village would most certainly be invited. And we were.

The feast that night was in a big tent. Assefa and I attended. Our wives were too tired or had children to put to bed or other excuses like in the biblical story. There was food and feasting, beer and wine in abundance, and music and dancing. The notables of the town were all there. Some of them made speeches. The governor of Burka joined the governor of Bedeno to grace this special ceremony with their eminent presences.

As the night wore on, the sensible people, having eaten and drunken to satisfaction, expressed their gratitude to the father of the feast and quietly took their leave. Assefa and I, the doctor and the missionary, apparently did not fit that category. We stayed on to witness the orgy to its giddy end. Well, almost, anyway!

The governor of Bedeno couldn't hold his liquor as well as the younger governor of Burka, or perhaps it was that he couldn't control the hand that moves the spirits to the mouth as well as his younger counterpart. Anyway, the governor of Burka was serving as emcee at this late hour. While people were making speeches, the drunken governor of Bedeno staggered to the microphone and began a long-disjointed speech that led nowhere and seemingly had no point, punch line, nor conclusion. Finally, the governor of Burka intervened, said something witty that made everybody laugh, and the governor of Bedeno had to sit down.

But as he sat, it finally sunk into his sodden brain that he had just been insulted by the younger governor. He became very indignant and went out.

Assefa and I decided that 10:00 p.m. was late enough, and this was becoming a mad house. We followed the governor of Bedeno out and began to get into our vehicle. The governor asked us to take him up the hill to his house. He said that he wanted to go and get his gun and shoot the governor of Burka who had insulted him so grievously in front of all the dignitaries of Bedeno!

Assefa's sharp wit and wisdom went to work at once. He welcomed the governor into the car, then proceeded to explain to him that he had got it all wrong, that the governor of Burka hadn't insulted him at all. He had only needed to make an announcement and had no intention of interfering with or cutting off his speech.

Suddenly the light came on in this man's sedated brain. He had misunderstood his good friend. It was all a small misunderstanding. Yet, he had almost gone home and brought his gun to kill his friend! Deep remorse and relief flooded his drenched soul. He got out of the vehicle and said, "If that is the case, I don't want to go home yet. I must go back in and enjoy the party!" He returned and embraced the younger man at the entrance calling him, "My dear brother!" They went back in together.

The next day, witnesses who left the party much later, said both governors were left sleeping on the table, two good friends completely wasted.

In traditional Amhara culture, as in most African cultures, it was extremely important that a father and mother protect the virginity of their daughter. They must protect her, keep her home at night, keep tabs on her every move during the day, make sure that she reaches her wedding day with the symbol of her virginity intact.

For their sons, there was another standard. For them, "boys will be boys" meant that boys and men will be sexually active. Discrete sexual activity is only natural, normal, and will happen. Self-control, abstinence, or celibacy before marriage would be asking too much.

An important part of the wedding ceremony was the moment when the groom took the bride to the bed chamber along with his groomsman, or in some cases a married woman of the bride's choosing. Her parents especially and all the guests waited anxiously for the groomsman or bridesmaid to bring out the evidence of the virginity of the bride, a white cloth with a nice spot of blood on it, evidence that the girl had safely reached her wedding day with her hymen still intact. When the parents received the evidence, there would be general rejoicing. If there was no blood, it would be a terrible disgrace to the whole family.

Sometimes, if the bride had previously lost her virginity to the one who was now becoming her husband, a chicken could be slaughtered, or a small cut made in his arm to extract the necessary blood to keep the family's honor intact. If it had been lost to someone else, but the man still loved his new bride, he might forgive her and do the same as a cover-up for her and her family's sake. If he was angry and disappointed, he could make a big scene and even annul the marriage at that point.

There was much gossip around town both before and after this wedding. It seemed that there were few, if any, in the town who admired or even liked this judge, but many feared him. He was an outsider to the community, an ex-military man. He was relatively young, had at least a grade eight equivalent education, was very conservative, even feudal in his thinking, and above all corrupt.

It was common knowledge that young men in the town were boasting how they had stolen the young girl's virginity long before the wedding. Now on the wedding night, when no evidence of virginity was brought to the father and mother in the customary manner, the honorable judge put on a dramatic demonstration of outrage that he had been betrayed by his own daughter and humiliated before the whole town. He would kill himself! Of course, the elders surrounding him had no trouble in staging a calming-him-down ritual and dissuading him from such violent action.

As for the newlyweds, the husband, being a modern man of the military, was wise in the ways of the modern world and wasn't so shocked. He loved his new bride and as far as we last heard, they are "living happily ever after."

The Judge

As for the judge, his "ever after" wasn't so happy. His innumerable perversions of justice earned him the animosity and finally the open opposition of the more honorable members of society.

One, especially, Ato Berhe, a successful merchant and a man of integrity, openly opposed the judge and tried to organize his eviction from our peaceful and law-abiding town. This step, of course, was going too far, and the honorable judge was not amused. His future was at stake, and the damage to his honor was more than he could bear. He had been a military man before he was promoted to the office of judge. Now, in a crisis, he reverted to more primitive instincts. He sent a warning to Berhe that he would shoot him. Then he took his high-powered army rifle and went about one kilometer down the road past the Mission and lay in wait for Berhe's lorry.

That the judge was lying in wait to assassinate the town's most successful merchant became the most exciting news story of the day.

Now, I had planned a trip down that road to visit some farmers before I heard this fantastic "tale." I couldn't believe that the corrupt judge could stoop that low, so I did not believe the rumor for a minute. When my time came, I set off in the Toyota with my crew in the direction of the supposed ambush.

As we were peacefully driving along, suddenly we heard a mighty explosion and the whine of a rifle bullet overhead above the engine's steady roar. In confusion, I took my foot off the accelerator for a second, looked around, but couldn't see a thing, so put my foot back down. Then there was a second terrible crack of the big gun. This time I thought it wise to stop. This guy, wherever he is, better be taken seriously.

Then I spotted him about 200 meters ahead on the edge of the road squatting in a military firing position with his rifle trained directly at us. We thought it wise to turn off the engine and await his Honor's pleasure. He sent a runner to us with the order to turn back. No one was going to pass that road, period! Needless to say, we quickly decided that today was not the right day to visit that farmer's group after all.

Some hours later, two police officers came and wanted me to make a written statement about the incident. I refused. I did not want to make any accusations or get involved in legal cases, but they insisted that I must help them out. They said this is a serious case, and they want to press charges and have the man removed from our town.

I said, "I know how you do it. You will just remove him from this town and transfer him to another town. You won't prosecute him anyway, so I don't want to get involved."

They insisted, "No! No! This is a serious case. The man will be removed from being a judge and will be punished!"

Finally, I yielded to their persistence and told them my perception of what had happened. They thanked me very much and left.

We heard later that the judge was transferred to another town where he worked as a judge for a year or two until he shot and killed someone in anger, and in turn, was arrested and executed by the new government. "Those who take the sword, will perish by the sword!"

CHAPTER 18

Missionary Travels and Travails

Ambulance Service

It seemed like doing ambulance service, taxi service, and sometimes even hearse service was some of the expected duties of the missionary that were never included in the "job description." Sometimes these duties were pressed upon us by social pressure, sometimes by human compassion, sometimes simply the love of God, sometimes by diplomatic pressure, and sometimes by force of law.

For example, when a man was brought to the clinic with his intestines hanging out through a stab wound that he incurred in a brawl, it took no logical reasoning to get me to agree to take him out to the hospital. I made that trip in a record-breaking, bone-jarring, and Toyota-testing four and one-half hours; waited long enough to see him strapped to the operating table, then returned the same day. Unfortunately, we later heard that the man died on the operating table due to loss of blood. How discouraging to learn that our earnest efforts were too little too late.

Hearse Duty

Another time the police "forced" me to chauffeur a stinking corpse all the way to the Harar Hospital to see a coroner, or perhaps it would be more precise to say, to be seen by a coroner. It was a long, smelly story:

Mohammed Ishmael was the proud owner of an ancient 1946 Chevrolet one-ton flatbed truck with which he did a general kind of delivery service for the whole community. In fact, sometimes it was so overloaded that one might have suspected that the whole community was being served at the same time. Mohammed had just refurbished this antique for perhaps the fourth time. This time it was a bright canary yellow with black fenders and black hardwood stave box. Beautiful!

He hired a certain Somali, Ahmed Mohammed, to drive this shimmering, shaking antique. Ahmed was a mad man when he was high on "chat," which was almost always. He showed little respect for man or beast or machine when in that, for him, normal state of mind.

It so happened that on this particular fateful Saturday, Mohammed's truck was taking a full load of Bedeno citizens, mostly traders and their wares, to the weekly market at Furda, fourteen kilometers away. The happy people, excited about the prospect of a profitable day, felt justified in paying the small fee to board this overloaded workhorse for a fast ride to market to secure the best places to display their merchandise, or to beat the crowd to the best bargains.

There wasn't room for all the eager paying passengers and their wares piled on the back of the truck. Three of them were standing on each of the running boards.

Somehow as this heavy-laden machine lurched back and forth, hurrying over the rough road, a man slipped off the running board and fell to the ground where the rear wheel rolled over him. He was dead!

They stopped the truck on the spot and carried the dead man to a shady place beside the road. Assefa had been on the truck anticipating a busy day at his Saturday clinic in the Furda market. Now he ran back to Bedeno to report to the police. The rest of the passengers waited. A few hours later, the police came to me, asking to be taken to the scene of the accident.

After the police completed their investigations, we loaded up the corpse and brought it back to the police station. Sometime later, the police returned with the truck, its owner, its driver, and all of its passengers, and put them all in jail. Since Assefa had walked home, he was the only one they did not lock in. The truck and the driver remained in prison for three months. The passengers were luckier. They were allowed to return to their houses before dark after they had all recorded their statements as witnesses.

Now the victim was a Muslim and according to their tradition, should have been buried before nightfall. But this was a "police case"! There was a procedure to follow.

On Sunday morning the police came to see me. The body could not be buried until the coroner's report was filed. As the nearest coroner lived and worked in Harar City, and since I was the only one with a vehicle in the village, it was quite obvious that I would have to be so kind as to escort the body to the coroner as it was just as obvious that the coroner would not be coming to meet his client at Bedeno in the foreseeable future. I saw the logic of it at once but was not so sure that my calling included the function of hearse driver. I would have to try to get out of this compelling request.

I carefully and respectfully explained to the police that my duties as a missionary were limited to serving the living, and that I had no obligations to the dead. Did not Jesus say somewhere, "Let the dead bury the dead"? I assured them that if it was a matter of saving an injured or sick person, I was ready to drive to the hospital at a moment's notice, be it day or night, rain or shine; I would do all in my power to save that life.

But when a person is dead, I have no further services to render; let the family bury him. Everybody knows that the man is dead, and there is no question as to how he died, so why trouble me? Just bury him! If they were not satisfied to do that, then it is their duty as police to see that the law is satisfied. Don't load that burden on me! I completely refused, and the police eventually went away.

Deep down inside, I knew it was not that they accepted defeat at my irrefutable logic and stubborn determination, but they needed to refine their strategy.

Sure enough, an hour later one police officer returned with the father of the dead and a few other respected family elders. In true African conciliatory fashion, the elder began with a speech saying that I was completely right and that the whole community deeply appreciated the many times I served them in times of deep trouble, and many lives were saved, etcetera, etcetera.

But then he went ahead to assure me that the law was the law, and it was not the police that were suffering in this case, nor the dead, but the family of the dead that were in an impossible bind. The family was in deep distress over the loss of their loved one, but they accepted that in true Muslim fashion as "the will of God." They only wanted to bury the body as soon as possible according to their custom. The longer the delay, the more horrible their suffering. So, not for the sake of the police or the government, but for the sake of the living, our friends and neighbors, would I please change my mind and help them in this time of sorrow as only I had the means to do?

Of course, when the request was put that way, I had no further argument. I would go willingly.

It was midafternoon by the time the body was loaded into the back of the Landcruiser. Having been dead in that warm climate for over thirty hours already, it was having a distinct odor that increased with each hot kilometer we traveled. We drove with all the windows open, and at least my head was out the window most of the way. Five or six of the closest relatives sat right on the hard floor at the back with the corpse, having cloths wrapped around their noses. The sun had already set when we finally arrived at the hospital mortuary that Sunday evening.

Business Travels

So much of my time was taken up with trips out to "civilization." I usually went alone. If the trip involved going as far as Addis, it usually took from one week to ten days. Sometimes I would take one of our daughters along for company and to afford them a special time alone with Dad. Occasionally the whole family would go.

On one such trip, we left Bedeno early on Wednesday, March 14, 1973. It was Vera's first outing in more than three months. We arrived at Deder at noon, where we had to decide on some business matters with Henry Gamber concerning the development project. The next day we continued our journey, in the Landcruiser, on to the Awash Game Park where we pitched our tent for the night.

In the morning we drove around the park looking for wild animals. We were disappointed to find only deer, one wild cat, and a few wild pigs. It was very hot and dusty, so we soon headed out of the park up towards Nazareth.

We did some shopping and refreshed ourselves at Dr. Leo Yoder's house before we went on to Debre Zeit. There we attended a weekend missionary conference that was being held at the SIM Guest House on the Babugaya crater lake. The missionary family at that time included about eighty persons, counting many children.

Following the conference, on Monday we drove to Lake Langano and camped there till Thursday. From there we back tracked to Addis where we spent another week repairing the vehicle, attending board meetings, making purchases, and doing other business.

On Thursday we drove back to Dire Dawa, having two flat tires on the way. On Friday, seventeen days after departing, we returned to Bedeno, bringing in Mr. & Mrs. John Harnish from Millersville, PA. John was a deacon in Grace's home church. They wanted to visit Grace for a couple of days. Then I escorted them back to Dire Dawa on Sunday, did some business there the next morning and returned Monday night.

One weekend I took a load of students to Deder for a sports day and related drama event. Our return journey was in the dark, starting late at 7:00 p.m. Sunday. It had rained, and the road was at its notorious worst. The Toyota got stuck in a deep hole. We struggled in the dark for one and one-half hours. Finally, we had to put chains on the front wheels to climb out. It was 2:30 a.m. when I crawled into bed.

I had to crawl back out at 5:30 to get the family loaded into the Toyota for a rush trip to Dire Dawa and Addis. I had received a message that I was supposed to meet with Dr. von Zahn, an official from our principal donor, Bread for the World, in Addis that Monday.

Back in Bedeno, while I was in Deder, Vera knew that trip was coming up, but she thought she had a leisurely Sunday to prepare for it.

Her children were excitedly making breakfast when Zemedkun, the "chicken boy," suddenly burst into her tranquility. A mongoose type animal had gotten into the chicken house at night, and a major massacre had taken place. As it turned out, eleven hens were dead, and another twelve were almost dead!

Vera called Grace, and they both went to work cleaning the dead and dying chickens. They worked all day and by 11:00 p.m., they each had six quarts of chicken meat canned and several packages of meat in the freezer.

Vera turned the lights off at 12:00 p.m. I arrived home at 2:30 a.m. Of course, I had to be clued in on the strange observance of her "tranquil" sabbath. An amazing resilient lady, Vera had still somehow managed to be prepared to go with me on the trip to Dire Dawa that next morning.

While she and the girls were vacationing in Dire Dawa, I was able to catch the 2:15 p.m. plane to Addis. I met the venerable Doctor von Zahn from Brot fur de Welt and gave him my progress report and returned by train the next day.

Visitors

Hospitality is a very important virtue in African culture. An African proverb says, "Guests are a blessing!"

Again, Easter holidays brought a flood of visitors. Robert and Alta Garber came, bringing Lois Landis and Anna Miller. Lois had worked at the Bedeno clinic eight years previously and was eager to re-visit it, and Anna was a nurse working at the Nazareth Hospital.

Next, Sam Miller and Ken Nafziger, teachers at the Nazareth Bible Academy, drove in on their motorcycles. Ken was one of the youngest missionaries and was still, among many other things, a "motorcycle freak." We had a lot of fun with them, fixing and servicing our motorcycle and testing its climbing ability on the steep hill behind the Mission.

In June we had more visitors, a teacher from Good Shepherd School with her tourist sister from Gulfport, Mississippi and Martha Hartzler and Mestawet from Deder Hospital. Later Dr. Martens brought his family with the Mel Thomas family, old friends from Addis. It seemed like the notorious road, instead of being a barrier to visitors to our remote station, was an attraction. Everybody wanted to have a "Bedeno road experience".

One day in August, I met a Swedish man driving his empty pickup to Bedeno alone. He took two of my passengers and some of my bags of fertilizer to make his load heavier and mine a bit lighter. We invited him to spend the night with us. He was working for a meat canning factory in Dire Dawa and was on his way to check out the cattle situation in the Burka area. He had some very interesting stories to tell that made our evening go a little faster. At age fifty, he was a seasoned big game hunter. He wished that I was a hunter too, then

255

we could go together on a hunting expedition in the vast wilderness in the region beyond Burka.

I would have loved to go with him to explore that mysterious land of the thorn bush and the Somali nomad and the camel. Surely there would be wildlife there too. But I was not a hunter. I did not want to hunt. I did not even believe it right to hunt for sport. I did not have a gun, and I did not think foreigners should have guns, especially since officially, it was illegal to hunt. Besides, that part of the Ogaden was notorious for having armed bandits or "shiftas," and our presence there might provoke a showdown in which I had no interest in being a part. Obviously, I wasn't the best candidate to accompany this semi-wild adventurer.

He left for Burka in the morning, did his survey, and was back in time for lunch, and returned to Dire Dawa in the afternoon. We never saw or heard of him again.

The Gambers brought their daughter, Marian, and a son, Timothy. Marian was a student at EMC in Virginia and had come "home" for vacation. The Gamber children had grown up in Bedeno, so they had a lot of people to see and special hideouts to re-visit. The car also brought Dr. Martens' brother and his wife, who were visiting the region and a Peace Corps couple who were teaching in the government school in Deder.

It so happened that these guests came just in time to help us celebrate our ninth wedding anniversary. Vera had baked a small four-tier cake and decorated it. Assefa and Grace joined us for the celebration and took pictures.

Besides substantial savings on razor blades, shaving cream, and shaving time every morning, my full, bushy beard earned me respect and dignity beyond my years in the community. I liked it. I was often addressed as "Father" by men twice my age. However, I shaved it off to celebrate our anniversary which pleased my wife immensely, but almost caused a riot among my smaller fans. They blamed their mother for this major disaster. Poor little Kristina had never seen me without a full face of bristly dark hair. She just looked and looked at me in the most puzzled manner. The laughing voice and twinkling eyes were that of her daddy, but the face was that of a stranger!

Church

In this Muslim context the very word "Christian" was identified with a culture imposed by the oppressive imperialist state of which the Orthodox Church was an integral part; a ruling culture which imposed feudalism and tolerated its attendant evils such as injustice, corruption, adultery and prostitution, drunkenness, and arrogant ethnic domination. We had to call ourselves by some other name. The people simply distinguished us from the "Christians" by calling us "Mission." We accepted that we were not "Christians" but "Mission."

Perhaps we were known mostly for what we did not do? We did not keep the Orthodox fasts and innumerable holy days, nor did we frequent the bars and taverns or drink alcoholic beverages. We did not practice nor promote prostitution nor adultery. We did not have a special kind of meat to eat.

While there were shops that sold only "Muslim meat" and others that sold only "Christian meat," there were no shops that dealt in a novelty item called "Mission meat."

We were known as profane people who did not mind whether the animal was killed with its face pointing towards Jerusalem, by a knife properly blessed by a sanctified priest at the hand of one who synchronized his deadly deed with the words, "In the name of the Father, the Son, and the Holy Spirit!," or whether it was killed with its face pointing towards Mecca, by a knife properly blessed by a qualified sheikh at the hand of one who synchronized his deadly deed with the words, "In the name of Allah, the Almighty, the All-knowing, the All-merciful!" Meat was meat, and when we needed it, we bought it in whatever shop that sold it. Our religion was "not a matter of eating and drinking, but of righteousness, peace and joy in the Holy Spirit!"

Putting modesty aside, I think it is fair to say that we were known for what we did do, more than by what we did not do. We were known as a church that cares about people as our programs in health, education, and development bore witness. We were known as a church that helped the less fortunate, regardless of tribe or race or creed. That is why so many sought our help in their moment of distress. We were known as people of integrity. That is why so few who wanted favors ever dared to bring a "gift" to soften the way.

They knew we stood for honesty and fairness and openness, while we could be moved by human compassion and by the love of Christ within us.

The community also knew us as the people who worship God in the mission school classroom every Sunday morning. We were distinctly separate from the Orthodox Church, and we were even more set apart from those who associated with the Mosque.

We were a third way, an alien religion, and hence something to be automatically rejected. Yes, we were attractive in the good lives we lived and the good deeds we did and the services we rendered to the community, but we were a foreign religion, and hence dangerous and bad and utterly unsuitable for Ethiopia! Parents would warn their children with words something like:

> *"It is okay to accept their medicine or to study in their school. They have a lot of things that can be of benefit to you, but don't let them persuade you to accept their religion! You were born Orthodox (or Muslim), and you are Orthodox (or Muslim) and must remain Orthodox (or Muslim)! To change your religion is to deny your family, your community, and your God! You would be a disgrace, a traitor to your parents and to your people, an outcast, rejected and no longer a child in our family nor a member in our community!"*

At the end of May 1973, we had a three-day spiritual conference at our school. Our mission director, Mr. Nathan Hege came with two Ethiopian preachers, Ato Gebre Selassie and another man. The Bedeno church members were very few which I likened to "the Twelve Apostles before Pentecost." They consisted of the four teachers, two development workers, one evangelist, Assefa and Grace, Vera and me, and a few interested students and community people. Most of the students attended the conference, and when we showed a "cinema" on Saturday night, a movie projected onto the white outside end wall of the school, the whole community turned out.

After the Sunday morning service, before the visitors returned to their homes, the members had a feast followed by a communion service, the first in six years.

In August we held a Bible School for the children and youth. I taught a class on Christian marriage for the youth who had returned from their various high schools scattered in the various cities of the empire.

Ahmed Adam, one of our teachers, was a very loyal Muslim from a strong Muslim family in Deder. He had heard the Christian gospel often but resisted its appeal. He wasn't feeling very well for several weeks in February 1974. He was taking a course of penicillin shots at the clinic. One day when they gave him his shot, he reacted with penicillin shock.

As he told the story afterwards, he said that when he was given the shot, he heard the sound of a bee buzzing behind his head. As he turned to see the bee, it stung him, and he died. He said he saw demons coming towards him, one demon touched him, and he burst into flames all over. Then beyond the flames he saw Jesus. He cried out to Jesus, "Save me!" Then he came back to life again.

The dresser was treating him with an antidote to counteract the reaction. Ahmed literally went down a Muslim and rose an ardent Christian! Since that moment he shared his testimony with everyone who would listen, whether Muslim or Christian. He came asking for baptism, saying he wanted to become an evangelist. Some months later, after some basic teaching, he and Mohammed Musa, also from Deder, were baptized in our living room. He was a steadfast Christian.

Ketema Belete joined our team as an evangelist in July 1974. He was deeply spiritual and in earnest about his task. Things began to happen in our community. People began to surrender their lives to Jesus as Savior and Lord. Thirty demons were cast out of one troubled girl on a Sunday afternoon. She became one of the most radiant happy Christians in the community.

Then several students returned home from the Bible Academy completely converted to Christ and filled with the Holy Spirit. Their lives were completely changed: their behavior, attitudes, speech, interests, morals, the things they spent their time doing. They added a lot of enthusiasm and interest to church life.

Bedeno Church conference - 1975

Family Separation

For the last two months in the summer of 1973, Vera was very busy. She sewed name tags on every sock and on each piece of clothing that Cindy and Karen owned. She patched dresses, altered them for growth, and sewed many new dresses. She figured out everything they might possibly need in the next nine months of school and had it all ready and packed to go.

Likewise, the girls excitedly planned all the things they needed to take along to make boarding as much like home as possible. All their barbie dolls and barbie clothes were a must. Other toys were selected more critically.

Then, all too soon, August 25th, the long-dreaded day, came for us to begin the journey to take our two oldest children to boarding school in Addis Ababa. Karen was still five years old, but she was a bright young girl and had easily passed a school readiness test, so she would be entering first grade. Cindy was ready to start third grade. They were looking forward to this day as much as we were dreading it.

On Monday morning, the 27th, we registered them at the Good Shepherd School in Addis Ababa and settled them into the boarding facility. We left them there and spent the next two days doing business in the city.

On Thursday we drove 250 kilometers west to Bako in Wollega Province where we visited two new workers, Solomon Kebede and Abebe Aseged, whom we had sent to take a six-month course for agricultural extension agents at the Agricultural Training Center run by the Mekane Yesus Church (Lutheran). Solomon and Abebe were very happy to see us.

After staying overnight at the Lutheran Mission, we returned to Addis on Friday.

We took Cindy and Karen out of boarding for a final weekend together. Their week had been interesting. They roomed together with two other girls. But Karen kept saying she changed her mind and wanted to go home with us. She was the only first grader in the dorm. This was allowed only because she had an older sister with her.

When we were ready to leave Addis on Tuesday, we stopped to say "Goodbye." For the first time, Karen broke down and cried. She wanted to go home with us. However, when it came time to leave, she tried to be brave. It was painful to leave our not-yet six-year-old in that frame of mind.

Hepatitis

There was to be a long weekend in which Good Shepherd students were having four days off near the end of September. We decided that we would combine a business trip to Addis with a camping trip with our children to Sodere over that weekend.

A week before that trip, I started feeling sick, like getting the flu. I kept on working, getting things done that needed to be done before we could go. The "flu" did not let up.

I was feeling quite sick Monday morning when the time came for us to leave. There was no one else to drive, so I forced myself. Vera had never driven the clumsy Landcruiser. The six-hour trip to Dire Dawa was shear agony. When we reached the tarmac, I asked Vera to drive the rest of the way. I felt I was finished. When you have to you can. Vera did it. When we arrived at the guest house, I went straight to bed for the rest of the day. By morning I felt a little stronger, so we boarded the train and traveled to Addis.

Then on Wednesday we got our camping things organized, took the girls out of school, and drove to Sodere. On the way we stopped at the hospital in Nazareth. It was quitting time, and we met the doctor on his way out for a holiday trip. He did not want his weekend spoiled. He heard me explain my symptoms and said, "It could be hepatitis or any number of other ailments, but if you can keep on going, just go on and enjoy your camping trip at Sodere. If you are still not well by Monday, come back."

We went on to Sodere and set up the tent after dark. That small effort made me feel totally exhausted. That night I vomited. The next day the girls enjoyed a good swim. I tried too, but just stayed in a few minutes and crawled back out and went and laid down in the tent. That evening I felt so miserable that we decided to go back to Nazareth. We took down the tent, packed our things in the car, and drove to Nazareth and spent the night with friends at the Bible Academy.

The next day, Monday, I was admitted into the hospital. They gave me a private room in the new part of the hospital. It was comfortable and nice, except I did not really appreciate the cockroaches all that much, crawling on my face and across my bare belly under the covers at night. And I did not appreciate the smell of the cockroaches in the private bathroom either.

By this time, my eyes were showing yellow. When I was having complete rest, I started to feel better. I actually enjoyed my next fourteen days in the hospital. It felt so good just to rest and forget about all my obligations. I had time to think and pray like I had not done for a long time. I read several interesting books that I hadn't had time to read for the last couple of years. I must have been quite exhausted and burned out, even without the hepatitis infection.

Vera and Sheryl and Kristina moved in with Dr. Brubaker's family so they could visit me more easily. They had a five-year-old daughter, Amy, with whom Sheryl enjoyed playing.

The Haile Mariam Mammo Memorial Hospital had just undergone a major upgrading of its facilities. They had just built four new units: a pediatrics-maternity ward, a delivery-operating unit, a clinic-emergency and laboratory unit, and a ward. The old cotton factory was still being used for about half the patients. This hospital had made a tremendous contribution to the health services of Ethiopia. At that time, one out of five practicing dressers in the whole nation had been trained there.

I had earlier been privileged to attend the inauguration of the new units. It was a special occasion at which the aged Emperor Haile Selassie had agreed to officiate. That was the last time I was to see him up close. I noticed how wrinkled and old he had become. He was past eighty years of age. He trembled as he walked. His attending officials guided him through each phase of the ceremony.

I realized then that what was rumored was true. The emperor was not in control anymore. He was already reduced by age to little more than a figurehead, for powerful interests behind the scenes were the ones who really called the shots. The once powerful "Lion of the tribe of Judah" was now little more than an obedient "puppy" being led by a string. Events in the months ahead would prove how true that was.

I was discharged from the hospital in time to return to Addis and celebrate Karen's sixth birthday. It was a real surprise for our girls. Vera even brought a cake, and we had arranged to stay with them overnight in the dorm. They were thrilled at that. Cindy was finding the adjustment to dorm life the hardest. At night she would dream of her friends at Bedeno or her relatives in the United States or Canada; then during the day she would think about them and not concentrate on her schoolwork. Karen seemed to be doing well in her class.

A Christmas Vacation

It was in mid-December when we were in Addis Ababa again. We had a long list of business items to attend to and some personal shopping to do. There were licenses to renew, an eye doctor appointment to make and keep, interviews with several people, a board meeting to attend, supplies to purchase for our agricultural supply center, a list of things to purchase for individuals back at Bedeno, groceries to purchase for ourselves and for several others, Christmas gifts to buy, auto repairs to be made, and spare parts to take back, and so on.

Sometimes I had troubling questions about the endless list of business and busyness that occupied most of our waking hours and sapped most of our energy. If all this is "mission work," then what is the difference between what we are doing here and what we would be doing back home in Canada? When do we ever get time to do the teaching, preaching, and evangelism that missionaries are supposedly supposed to do?

For one thing, I suspect St. Paul did not use much energy and time to care for four kids, or resources to put them into a private missionary children's boarding school. Nor was he expected to go about "Christmas shopping" for them. However, although the Good Book does not tell us, he must have spent some time carrying a basket around the market negotiating the price of onions, and building a fire to prepare his food, and sitting in the candlelight mending his clothes. Also, I do suppose that he had to shop for canvas and thread and needles occasionally to keep his tent manufacturing business running smoothly. Surely, he must have "wasted" some hours negotiating prices or contracts with his customers?

But this trip was extra special, and we were abnormally excited. Our girls were getting out of school on the 21st for the one-month Christmas break. They were very happy to see us again and very eager to get out of "jail" and be gone on a little camping trip with their parents and sisters. But first we had to tour their classrooms and see all the work they did and watch the "Christmas program" in which they each had a part.

These past four months had been their first time to be away from home and family. It had been a rather traumatic time of experiencing homesickness, loneliness, maybe a sense of abandonment, a time of adjustment to strange people and a regimented institutional life. However, the old adage, "No pain, no gain!" is true. For our girls, this had also been a time of tremendous growth and expansion of horizons socially, culturally, emotionally, intellectually, and spiritually. Now they could retreat to the familiar, rest and recoup, and process what they learned and integrate it with who they were and what they had experienced before.

We had come prepared with all the paraphernalia for a camping and swimming trip to Sodere. Cindy and Karen learned to swim. Sheryl and Kristina entertained themselves paddling around in their little tubes. After spending three delightful days enjoying each other, the monkeys, the water, and the sun, we moved on to visit one night at Nazareth. Cindy and Karen were eager to move on to Bedeno and "home" the next day.

It was already Dec. 29th, and the *ferrengi* Christmas had passed by the time we reached home, but we were planning to celebrate it with the Ethiopians on January 7th. Where else in the world can one have two "Christmases" each year? And two New Years? And two Easters? Vera involved the girls in the making of the special Christmas goodies and in decorating the house.

We had cut a small cypress tree on the way as we crossed a mountain and took it home. The girls decorated it with the one string of lights we had and made other decorations out of crepe paper, string and popcorn, and tinfoil. Gifts wrapped in old newspapers (to save money and our forests) and decorated with colorful ribbons appeared out of nowhere to find their places under the tree.

Then visitors came, five from the Bible Academy in Nazareth: Herb and Sharon Kraybill, Ken and Phoebe Nafziger, and Vivian Beachy. They brought along Dottie Sensenig, a nurse serving at Deder Hospital. We had a great two days showing them around and visiting.

The day after they left, it was Christmas. Everybody was excited and tried extra hard to be nice to everybody else. The gifts lying under the tree beckoned with an urgency never felt before. But first, we all had to sit quietly together while the oldest girl read the Christmas story from the Bible. Then we sang some Christmas songs.

Finally, the signal was given, and the girls took it upon themselves to be a "Santa Claus" committee. The oldest who could read the name on the package passed it on to an eager little sister for delivery. To maximize the magic of the moment and to extend the suspense for as long as possible, it was mutually agreed that one gift be given out at a time and that all eyes would focus on that parcel until it was opened, and its contents revealed before the next package would be delivered.

The girls were ecstatic over their gifts. There were two barbie dolls for Cindy and Karen and a regular doll for Sheryl from their Grandma and Grandpa Yoder, and new clothes for all their dolls lovingly crafted by their mother. There was a good watch for Cindy from her grandma as well, and a toy truck for Kristina. They all enjoyed the chocolate candy sent all the way from Pennsylvania from their Grandmother Yoder.

Later, Assefa and Grace and two other people joined us for a real Christmas dinner.

All too soon the month was finished, and it was time for little scholars to return to their studies. This time we took them back by train.

CHAPTER 19

The Famine

When Rains Fail to Fall

In Bedeno the "little rains" come in February and soften up the soil so the farmers can plow and plant their barley and sorghum and maize. The barley is harvested in June, and beans or teff are planted when the "big rains" come in July.

In 1973, the small rains failed to come. Grass became scarce and cattle became thin. Deer came to our garden at night in search of food. Farmers began worrying about what their families would eat the next season. Sorghum and maize needed the benefit of both the little and the big rains to reach maturity. Without the little rains, there would be no sorghum or maize.

Then in mid-April some good rains fell, and farmers rushed out to plow and plant their crops, knowing that there was a good chance of failure should the big rains fail to be extended. The crops grew nicely on our highland mountain.

However, things were not so good in the river valleys and in the vast lowlands sloping down to the Ogaden from the Garamuleta mountain range. The rain that fell there was not enough to get a crop growing.

The drought was worse in other parts of the nation. Nazareth had almost no rain and the cattle in the Awash Valley began dying. Hundreds of people gathered along the highway begging the motorists to stop and give them water to drink. A charitable organization arranged for a water trucking service to help these people survive. We heard that in the northern Wello Province there was not enough rain to grow a crop in three years. So many cattle died there that the vultures and hyenas could not keep up with their sanitation responsibilities.

Now people were following their cattle in death. The UN, NGOs, and various church agencies wanted to help with relief, but the imperial government refused to admit there was a problem.

Imperial pride dictated that Ethiopia must not be embarrassed in the eyes of the world. Officially there could not be any famine in Imperial Ethiopia. It would be better to sacrifice a few hundred thousand no-account remote peasants than to humbly admit there was a problem and to ask for emergency assistance on their behalf. It would be better, that is, as long as those starving were not government officials or their close relatives.

To give the aging emperor the benefit of the doubt, perhaps the severity of the situation was not revealed to him by his sycophant officials?

In Bedeno the situation was much less severe. By August, the big rains were continuing on well.

The drought of 1973 continued throughout the big rainy season in most of Ethiopia, especially in the lowlands. This meant that famine conditions would reach a crisis early in 1974. This does not mean that there was no rain, but that the rains were late and less than enough to bring a crop through to a normal harvest. In most places, including Bedeno, the yields were below normal. In many places, especially the low-lying areas such as between Burka and Genemie and in the river valleys, there was a complete crop failure.

Born and reared in poverty and want, accustomed to suffering and hardship, tough, resilient, proud, Ethiopians are survivors. But in large sections of Ethiopia where the drought had already persisted for one to three years, this added year marked the end of all normal survival. There was absolutely nothing left that resembled food in these areas. Livestock had long since died and been eaten. Seeds were eaten. All edible leaves, bark, and roots were consumed.

People who were still strong enough were walking away from this disaster, carrying their babies and weak children with them. They were migrating to the centers in desperate and often vain hope of finding food and water. Those already too weak to walk stayed at home and died. Many who began to walk never arrived, having died on the way.

It was this scene of human tragedy in Wello Province that was finally splashed on the T.V. screens in every living room of the first world that finally stirred the minds and hearts of the "haves" to respond in an unprecedented outpouring of generosity and good will.

Representatives of aid agencies and compassionate governments from all over the world rushed to Ethiopia to see for themselves and to plan what they could do to save the starving millions.

Millions of ordinary people in the first world sent in their contributions, and the aid agencies boomed, and new ones multiplied. Expatriates with any Ethiopian experience received attractive job offers.

Offices and hotels were being rented in Addis Ababa at high prices. Living space for expatriate staff was in high demand.

Food shipments flooded into the ports, congesting the normal flow of merchandise. Trucks had to be imported to move the food grains from the ports to the interior where the roads that existed were mostly seasonal rough trails.

Donors made visits to local churches and church agency offices, offering large grants of cash if they would alter their regular programs of often essential services and get involved in famine relief and rehabilitation activities.

We at remote Bedeno were hardly aware of this madness developing on the larger scene. We went about doing our harvesting and measuring the results of our research and getting our livestock projects set up. We were aware that there had been essentially no harvest in the lowlands. We knew food would be getting scarce as most people did not have a surplus to carry them on to the second year. But these people are survivors. They are extremely resilient and tough. We were aware that they were selling assets to buy maize in the Bedeno market.

A caravan of camels came up to the spring above our house one day. It was just as well that they take a good long drink of clean cool water before returning to the Somali desert with a load of Bedeno maize. But we were not at first aware that we all were running out of food resources fast.

269

When Springs Stop Flowing

It was in the scarcity of water that we first became involved in their sufferings. In January of 1974, reports came to us of extreme shortages of drinking water in the Burka area. We went to investigate.

The spring at Burka normally produces 300 liters of clean water per minute throughout the dry season. This strong stream flows many kilometers down into the desert supplying water for thousands of Somali cattle and camels along the way before it slowly sinks into the parched earth. It also serves as the only dry season supply of water for the large Oromo population and their livestock for many miles around.

We found that this flowing stream had dried up and the spring had become a shallow pool at the bottom of a five meters deep hole. About 9,000 people and their thousands of animals were depending on this hole to get the precious life-sustaining water. Police were used to regulate the traffic. The humans and the animals were to be watered separately.

Thirsty masses crowd the Burka water spring.

When it was the human's turn, hundreds of people rushed down into the water at the same time to fill their gourds and buckets and jerrycans while a horde of others pushed in from behind. The humans, standing shoulder to shoulder thigh-deep in the water, scooped the muddy life-sustaining solution into their containers, while their feet stirred the thick mixture of black mud and decaying organic particles up from the bottom. Those with full containers then passed them up over the heads of the anxious pushers to companions further back in the crowd in exchange for their empty containers which they promptly filled.

When they and their friends were satisfied, then began the desperate fight to open a way back up through the crushing throng, up the slippery slope carrying the last heavy container on their shoulder or head above the sea of pressing humanity. The struggle was incredible. The stench of sweating bodies and decaying organic matter; the cacophonous sound of a thousand excited or desperate voices calling and screaming back and forth or laughing and gossiping; and the sight of this seething mass of struggling humanity converging at this water hole was an experience that is as indescribable and unbelievable as it is unforgettable!

When the people had their share, it was the animal's turn. Now the scene changed and became just as orderly as the former was chaotic. The animals were not allowed into the hole at all. They had to remain outside the fence about fifty meters away. The men formed a double bucket brigade, a sort of human pump with two rows of about twenty men each, properly spaced between the source of water down in the hole and the upper level of the stream bed. Each line worked independently of the other line. They had as many deep basins as there were men in the two lines.

The scene was amazing to behold. The men sang a chant while they worked to keep time. The man at the bottom scooped a basin full of water and swung it up literally throwing it to the next man on the human ladder who caught it having thrown his empty basin down in exchange. The man catching the basin full of water gracefully swung it up releasing it in midair to the next person in time to catch his empty basin in turn. The last person emptied the pan into the stream bed, dammed up as a temporary watering trough, and promptly returned it down the line. The line worked clock-like with perfect timing, ten full basins passing up one right after the other and ten empty basins passing down the same line at the same time all synchronized with the song. When one link in this human chain slipped, the system temporarily broke, some got wet, and everybody laughed.

When they worked together this way, a steady stream of water flowed out of the compound to the mud drinking troughs where the cattle and camels and sheep and goats got their fill. It was an impressive exercise in community cooperation. One is left to wonder why the former scene could not have been as well organized.

Oromo men using the "bucket brigade" method of extracting water from the spring to water their livestock.

We were amazed at the spring's capacity. Even at this time of intense drought, this "pumping" action could not drain it completely. The local governor and the elders requested us to find a way to clean this spring and make it more sanitary and accessible. There were the remains of at least two major tree trunks that had fallen into it. And there was the accumulated sludge from all the filth and debris, especially leaves and other organic matter that had fallen into it through the years.

Following our visit to Burka, we retraced our steps, visiting the Gerbie water hole on the way. This time we found the pond had dried and a fifteen-meter-deep hole had been dug to reach the spring.

Here again, we found an amazing example of people working together. The crowds were not as big as at Burka, and neither was the water as plentiful. The hole's upper half was funnel shaped, and the lower half was more or less four meters across and straight down. There were a few crude poles across at different levels to assist in getting up or down.

People made their way up or down on a narrow clay ledge just big enough for a foothold here and there. They formed a human chain balancing on these narrow footholds supporting themselves by leaning against the mud wall, while those at the bottom were scooping up the water with buckets and gourds and passing it straight up the human chain, each passing it up to the one above. The ones at the top either emptied the water into a clay trough for the livestock and returned the container back down the chain or set the full container aside for the owner to take home later when all were satisfied.

This seemed like a terribly dangerous way to extract water from a hole. Each time a bucket passed, small amounts of water splashed out and made the footholds wet and extremely slippery. If anyone should slip and fall from above, he or she would be sure to dislodge others from their precarious perches on the way down. And what would happen to those on the bottom?

The people's response to our query assured us that such a thing did indeed occur now and then. They told us of several occasions that it happened. Some were injured, and some even died. One time a cow got too close and fell in, killing three people in the process. The cow, in turn, had to be slaughtered and extracted piece by manageable piece.

The people informed us that this water hole was sitting on the land of a certain *"Balambaras"* (an aristocratic title given to a prominent member of the landed gentry) who claimed connections with the emperor. They informed us that when this particular "gentleman," an absentee landlord living in Harar City, came out every year to collect the usual land rents and "gifts" of honey, chickens, and goats from his tenants, he also collected "water rights" fees from the unfortunate peasants who drank of the silty brown fluid along with its parasites and filth. They really doubted whether this man would approve of us tampering with "his" water gold mine.

Upon returning home, I began designing plans to improve these two vital water sources so that people could be assured of safe clean water. With these in hand, I submitted a funding proposal to the Christian Famine Relief and Rehabilitation Committee when we reached Addis Ababa.

My proposal was accepted, and I was given 17,100 birr almost at once.

With funding in place, it was urgent that I begin implementing the plan at once before the rainy season brought back the full flow of the springs. I already was over-extending my capacity, working all day and half the night. But there was no time to entertain thoughts of self-pity, or self-preservation.

I did not spend a lot of time worrying about what we would do about this supposedly hostile *"Balambaras"* either. If he caused a problem, I would take the case to the governor, and if necessary, I would fight it to the Supreme Court. I couldn't feel any sympathy for him or his "rights." How could a human being stoop so low as to suck the last drop of "blood" out of his starving peasants by making them pay for the dirty muck they drank, especially considering that they did all the work of digging out the hole and extracting the filthy life-sustaining liquid? Charging a modest fee for "his" water would have been different had he invested something to supply clean sanitary water for them.

I immediately went shopping in Addis Ababa to buy some of the supplies and tools there that were not available in Dire Dawa. In Dire Dawa I bought cement, re-bar, plastic pipe, boards for cement forms, and galvanized iron culverts to be used for curbing for the well. I hired a truck to deliver all this material to the two sites plus a load of crushed rock and a load of sand.

Some days later we went to Burka with our crew equipped with axes, crowbars, a chain, and a portable gasoline powered pump. The first day, after several hours of hard labor, the local strong young men removed all the tree trunks, two huge tree stumps, plus great gobs of muck out of the Burka hole.

Then we began constructing a water holding tank. We also started excavating to build a large livestock watering trough.

But we had overlooked the basic principle of community development. We had failed to involve the people in our planning. The Amhara governor and the town elders understood, but the Oromo leaders were not properly informed.

A rumor began to circulate among them that there was a conspiracy between the Mission and the Amhara's of the town to seize all the water rights for the town people and deprive the rural people of their spring altogether, or to sell it to them for hard cash. It was a preposterous rumor, but completely believable in light of past experiences with their feudal masters.

Discontent mounted and the Muslims refused to supply manual labor. When we heard that a prominent Sheikh was fasting and praying that God would intervene and cause our plans to fail, we became aware of the size of the opposition that was rising against us. We had no interest in working against the wishes of the people, much less encountering the wrath of their Celestial Ally.

Obviously, God heard their prayers, for about that time the little rains started, and the springs soon were flowing again. We stopped our work for the time being. We had no idea when another dry season as severe as this one would make the implementation of the plan possible. We also heard that the *"Balambaras"* was very upset about the rumors he heard about our intentions over "his" water at the Gerbie spring.

When No Food is Left

Around the end of February, officials from the Ministry of Agriculture and the United Nations came to our Project with a request. They asked me, being the missionary in the area and being in charge of a development project aimed at the betterment of the community, if I would consider supervising famine relief in the area on their behalf? They said that the local governors had been reporting that the food resources in the community were now exhausted, and some cases of starvation were reported.

The UN already had a supply of food grain in Dire-Dawa and would send some out to start a food for work program in the area immediately. They would provide funds and give me authority to implement the program. I would have to hire a team to work with me, rent storage space, organize food for work projects, and see that proper records were kept, and regular reporting was done. The three governors of Bedeno, Genemie, and Burka were ordered to cooperate with me fully in organizing the people, providing security.

Well, I was busy enough, but I could not say "No!" What good is a development program if the people are dying? With the animals in place, the development workers partly trained, and the water project temporarily suspended, I could see myself taking on this responsibility for a few months. If the rains persisted, the feeding program would be over in four to six months. I felt I had no choice but to submit to this request.

A few weeks later, in early March, as we were facing the challenges of famine relief work, water development, and the starting of the little rains with its new crop season, we had special visitors from Tofield, Alberta, Canada. At last, we had someone come from my own part of the world. Harold and Viola Boettger were in Ethiopia visiting their son and daughter-in-law, Dr. Dennis and Lucille Boettger, who were working in Deder Hospital. They all were our visitors for two days. I took them to Burka to show them the water situation. They took pictures of the amazing scene I described earlier. Later, Dr. Boettger entered one of his pictures in a photo contest and won first prize!

When Petroleum Stops Coming

The energy crisis that gripped the world in 1974 reached its long tentacles all the way to remote Bedeno. First diesel fuel ran out. Then there was a strike so new fuel could not reach Dire Dawa. By the time new supplies reached Dire Dawa, the road suffered an unusually generous dose of rain for two weeks and the truck could not get through to Bedeno. So, we could not run our generator. We started to use the kerosene pressure lamp, but it soon used up our supply of kerosene. Then we discovered that there is no kerosene in town either. So, we were down to lanterns and candles. A lot of people had no light at all. Students could not study for exams.

Then when it came to seeding time, we discovered that the price of commercial fertilizers had tripled. A keystone in our extension approach to the peasants had been the introduction of fertilizers that were cheap and cost effective and very much needed to increase the supply of food in the country.

Our first-year tests and demonstrations were very effective, and many farmers were convinced to use fertilizers the following year. Now we were extremely embarrassed to have to explain that the prices had gone up drastically. The Ministry of Agriculture arranged with us to supply fertilizers on credit to the farmers through our program. But even this did not counter the negative effects of the international oil crisis on our development efforts.

Up to this point, we had not been thinking in terms of "sustainable agriculture" or "appropriate technology." Those weren't current concerns in the field of development in those days. The going practice at that time was to increase production capacity through introducing all the scientific wonders of the industrialized nations, for example, chemicals such as fertilizers, herbicides, fungicides, acaricides, drugs, and exotic breeds of livestock with all the attending inputs that were needed to keep them alive, new species of plant material that might create a "green revolution," and modern labor-saving machinery that would save time and expand production.

But the shock of the oil crisis and the resulting escalation of prices opened my eyes to the fallacy or danger of dependance on all such outside inputs. If there was any hope for peasant agriculture, it had to be found within the framework of existing local sustainable resources. We would have to revise our philosophy of development and our approach drastically.

When the World Shows It Cares

Things never seem to work out according to plan. "Food for work" was to start in Burka first. We waited for the first truckload of grain. Finally, a little army truck brought a small load. The driver worked like a union man, or maybe a government employee. It took him five days to make a round trip which a normal person could have easily done in two days. It took him one day to reach Bedeno, another to reach Burka, a third day back to Bedeno, a fourth day to reach Dire Dawa, and a fifth day to rest and reload. Of course, he collected per

277

diem for each day he spent on the road. At this rate, the people would continue to starve.

By the time we started the "food for work" program, the people at Burka were seriously losing weight. They had little energy to do meaningful work. At the beginning of the day, we had any who came to sign in with their signature or thumb print. Then we set them to digging ponds or repairing the road. Some who came were too weak to work and were told to sit in the shade until the three kilograms of maize was distributed to each worker at the end of the day. With four or five hundred people waiting to be "paid" each day, work had to stop early in the afternoon if the distribution exercise was to be completed before dark.

With more experience, the program became better organized and more efficient. Eventually, three teams were implementing food for work programs at Burka, Genemie, and Bedeno. They repaired roads, built fences around school grounds, dug wells, dug ponds, and began to build a new road to the Ramis River valley but never got beyond three kilometers away from Bedeno. They learned how to break rocks taller than a man using fire and water. The largest group we fed in one day was 1,400 people. I gained a much deeper appreciation of the logistics involved in Jesus feeding 5,000.

The little army trucks were giving us a headache. A few would come with their small loads, then for several weeks there would be none. The people were getting hungrier all the time. The rains were interfering with the road. The road from Bedeno to Burka was impassable when wet, so the army trucks started to dump their loads in Bedeno. But we had no means to haul the maize to Burka.

Tsegaye Dubale came up with a creative solution. He organized a donkey brigade. Each donkey owner would get some "food for work" pay for each donkey he could bring to carry a sack of maize from Bedeno to Burka. The system worked quite well, except for a group of Somalis who brought camels instead and just kept going on past Burka and disappeared into the wilderness with their sacks of maize. They weren't about to "work" for their food!

By June, our work had become very frustrating. The people at Burka and Genemie were starving, and we were not able to get enough food to them because the government couldn't find truckers who were willing to bring it. The road was awful. It rained about every day, and the road was sheer mud in some places and eroded beyond semblance of a road in other places.

One day I went from Bedeno to Burka with a truck load of grain. The distance was only forty kilometers, but it was four days later before we returned. We started out when the sun was shining, and the road was passable. But when we had almost reached our destination, we were caught in a heavy downpour that turned the road into grease. The heavy lorry could not go ahead. I walked the rest of the way and spent the night in our storeroom with our workers.

On the second day, the hot sun shone enough to dry the road by noon. The lorry was able to move ahead and managed to reach Burka. While the grain was being unloaded, rain fell again. The truck could not move until noon the next day. I stayed behind to tend some business, planning to drive the motorcycle home later. The truck started back only to be caught in another rainstorm fourteen kilometers down the road. At my end, the road was still dry, and I came along with the motorcycle quite nicely until I neared the place where the rain had fallen.

Suddenly, I could no longer steer the cycle and the wheels clogged up with sticky clay. I had to push it up to the place where the lorry was stuck. I joined the driver and crew for a camp supper of spaghetti and canned meatballs and slept with them in the truck.

By morning I was getting anxious to get home. There was no way that the motorcycle could be driven home before noon, and how can one be sure that it would not rain again before the road got dry enough for that? A merchant and I decided to try it on foot. We loaded the bike on the back of the lorry and, foolishly, without waiting for breakfast and without carrying any drinking water with us, set out on foot.

It wasn't long before we realized our mistake in not having breakfast. We soon ran out of energy. The sticky mud clung to our boots, yet our feet spun out on the slippery goo each time we took a step. I gained a deeper respect for the barefoot Oromo women, lightly laughing and chatting as they marched gracefully past us, carrying their heavy loads to the distant Bedeno market, leaving us struggling "superior" men behind, panting, and sweating our way slowly up the slippery incline.

By 10:00 a.m. I was having an energy crisis of my own. There

CARL E. HANSEN

was completely no energy left. We had covered fourteen kilometers, but there were ten more to go and all of them were uphill. The sun was just beginning to get hot. I did not know how I could possibly do the rest of the journey. I was starting to understand why some of the hungry people just couldn't do "food for work."

Then we chanced upon a "filling station," a "fast food joint" right beside the road! Some enterprising women knew there would be struggling pilgrims coming to the market without breakfast energy to push them on. Just for people like us, they had spread out their delicacies on a cloth beside the way. Their special of the day was pieces of cold boiled sweet potato and cups of milk.

The milk was poured from a gourd and served in a dirty tin cup encrusted with weeks' worth of dried sour milk. The milk itself had the strong taste of smoke that was commonly used in cleaning the gourds.

We each quickly gulped down three or four cups of the sour, smoke-flavored milk and munched on half of a sweet potato. We felt our strength return in some measure at least, and courageously faced the last ten kilometers.

We arrived at home in Bedeno at 12:00 noon with a few blisters on our feet and some sore muscles in our legs, but after spending four days away, it was great to be home.

At the same time, the hot sun had done its work and dried the road. As we reached home, we heard the sound of the truck in the distance. It was coming, bringing our motorcycle. I'm still not sure we gained anything worthwhile besides experience and sore muscles in return for our impatience and perseverance.

Another time, I was driving the Landcruiser, returning from a supervisory trip to Burka. It was getting towards evening, and my associate and I were tired and hungry after a long day of work. It had been raining again, and the road was wet. We were about ten kilometers out from Burka when we got hopelessly stuck in a large bottomless puddle. No matter how hard we struggled, spinning in reverse and forward, we only got in deeper until the vehicle was high centered.

Half a dozen peasants came out from their homes and tried to help us. But they lacked experience; some pushed, and some pulled at the same time, and others just watched and gave advice in their

280

Oromo language. As darkness set in, one by one they abandoned their futile efforts and disappeared in the direction of their homes nearby.

We were left alone to go through the lengthy process of jacking up the car and building a road with sticks and branches under the wheels. While we were doing this, we had turned off the engine "to save gas," but we were using the lights to help us see what we were doing.

When we were ready to give one more try, the starter would not turn over the engine. The lights had drained the battery. Here we were sitting in the dark, in our inert Toyota, sitting in the midst of a pond of water and mud, alone on this desolate road, accompanied only by frogs, with no possibility of extricating ourselves in the foreseeable future, and no possibility of calling the "AAA" people for assistance. And we were hungry and tired. There was no choice but to bed down on the short seats and try to sleep and wait for the morning.

Sleep did not come easily. I found myself feeling sorry for myself. Why did these peasants just abandon us and go to the comfort of their homes? Why did they not try to push a little harder? Did they not feel any sense of hospitality? After all, we were the ones burning ourselves out giving every effort to keep them from starving. We were here in the mud because of them. They could at least have stayed and helped push us out of the mud, or at least, showed some sympathy. If they did not have any food to offer us, at least they could have offered us the comfort of shelter for the night. Why are we going through all this struggle just for them? Why not just let them starve?

Eventually tiredness overcame my negative self-pity, and fitful sleeping on the narrow car seats gave way to a rising sun the next morning. Of course, the rising sun did not bring any "breakfast in bed" and it did not charge the car battery either. But it did bring a new day with renewed courage and hope to face the challenge of how we were going to extricate our vehicle from its muddy imprisonment.

God must have heard our imploration, for before we set out on foot on the thirty-kilometer walk to Bedeno for help, on that desolate forsaken muddy road, what should show up but another vehicle! A *ferinj*, a stranger to these parts, was on his way to Burka for business. With the help of his battery, we were able to jump start our vehicle and drive out of the mudhole and on home to a warm embrace of a worrying wife and a late breakfast.

My letter home carried something of our feelings of frustration:

> We were feeding about 900 people a day in a "food for work" program at Burka. But then an additional 2000 people came in from the countryside and sat in the town begging for food. The police tried to send them away, saying that we have no food for everyone. But they refused to leave. "We will die right here!" they said. So now we are trying to feed everybody, but the grain doesn't come. So, the people starve. Some have already died and many more are dying. The people blame us. We blame the government. It is frustrating and sad.

The hunger was increasing, and the maize was not coming fast enough. I finally went to Dire Dawa and complained. How can we run a "food for work" program without a regular supply of maize? There was a huge pile of maize stacked at the depot in Dire Dawa. The problem was the lack of trucks. The government just did not have enough trucks, and the ones they had had spent too much time on the road.

Finally, I asked the man in charge, "If I would find the trucks, would you be willing to pay commercial rates for the transport?" He agreed. So, I went out to the marketplace where the truck owners do their business and lined up seven big ten-ton lorries to haul maize to Bedeno and Burka that very afternoon. The officer was quite surprised. Sometimes officials can't get off their comfortable chairs and find their way around the block where the answers to their problems are waiting.

I felt quite proud of myself when all the citizens of Bedeno stood gaping with their mouths hanging open as a convoy of seven lorries roared into their sleepy little town the next day. We had to quickly rent all the empty houses and shops in the town to store the perishable cargo. Then "food for work" began in earnest.

A part of our famine relief program was "food for work." The other part was "seed on credit." Desperate hunger had driven most farm families to eat their precious seed. Now it was seeding time, and the rains were abundant, but there was not enough seed for most of the farmers. To meet this need, thanks to the Ministry of Agriculture, several truckloads of seed came to be given to the "neediest" farmers in selected "neediest" areas only. The highlands were automatically excluded from this program because their crops had been reasonable the previous year. A survey was done to determine which areas would be included.

Without my knowledge, the elders at Genemie prepared their list of "neediest" to include all the Amhara farmers and officials, including the governor's wife, on their hill which was a highland area and had had fair crops. Through the youthfulness and weakness of our agent stationed there, they all got their "seed on credit." When I heard of it, I was furious, but it was too late to undo the distribution.

Then the elders of Bedeno tried to do the same, but I adamantly refused. They threatened to have me evicted from the community. I just dared them to try it and ignored the threat. Other head men from different communities came offering bribes to my team members to have their areas included. I refused.

One Oromo leader came several times begging to have his area included. My workers saw him in the market collecting money from the people he represented for a bribe. Soon he was offering a gift to our agent. He was refused. Finally, he came back to me. When I opened the door, he fell at my feet and tried to kiss my feet in supplication, traditionally a final measure. I lost my cool and grabbed the distinguished gentleman by the shoulders and physically threw his turbaned eminence backwards out of the house and told him to be gone. He was shocked! And so were my loyal team members. I sometimes wondered, what would Jesus do in my situation?

I was ashamed of my undiplomatic and culturally insensitive manner of reacting to these supplications, but I was under a lot of pressure and ready to blow up at even a small pretext. Sometimes when we humans are under too much stress, we are blinded to the possibility of more creative peaceful win/win solutions.

In the midst of my struggle with the dispositions and the demands of the town elders while the people were starving, the governor of Bedeno decided to go on his annual leave. I needed his cooperation to manage these petty demands from the community elders. He was gone for five weeks when I needed him the most. In frustration,

I wrote a letter of complaint to the Minister of Agriculture about the governor's absence and the governor of Genemie's greed.

A few days later, the governors were both very upset with me. "How could you write such a letter? How could you do this to me? It is going to ruin my career!" Frankly, I wasn't very concerned about their careers anymore. I figured for the good of humanity, their careers should both be terminated anyway.

By this time, the revolution had begun, and all officials were concerned about polishing up their past records and covering the tarnishes found there in hopes of preserving their careers. It was a good time to be on the side of justice, fairness, honesty, integrity, transparency, and accountability!

With the coming of the rains, weeds and grass sprung to life. In a matter of a few weeks, edible species could be picked and boiled as food. By July, the life and death crisis had largely passed, thanks mostly to the lowly little "leaf cabbage," a wild member of the cole family that sprung up voluntarily everywhere. Soon after that, the barley and beans were ready for harvest. Despite their many hardships and sufferings, most of the people survived. Only some of the elderly and babies succumbed to the diseases that always accompany malnutrition and starvation.

By mid-August, we were still building roads with "food for work" with about 2,000 people. We were getting food grain from the U.S.A., Europe, and China, and even a few loads of wheat from Canada. It made me feel proud to think that maybe that bag with the maple leaf on it just could contain wheat from my brother's farm in Alberta!

These wonderful rains that spoiled our roads and stuck our vehicles and made our relief efforts such a nightmare had one very significant redeeming quality. They did far more than thousands of us could have done to stop the famine; they made the crops grow very nicely. By November, the harvest was in full swing, and we were winding down our "food for work" program.

We only had 200 men working on a new road from Bedeno to Ramis. We had finished three kilometers of a twelve-kilometer road. The road passed through some very difficult terrain. The men broke up some limestone boulders as big as a car using only hammers, picks, a crowbar, and fire and water or lemon juice. Compared with what the hungry hoards did at the beginning of our efforts, I was impressed with what organized labor can do. But now the famine was over, and the road would remain unfinished, at least until the next famine.

"Food for Work" building a road near Bedeno.

The End of Famine at Last

Harvest season is always a special time of year. After months of clouds and rain and mud, there is no weather comparable to harvest weather. The sky is so blue and clear. The air is fresh and cool and clean. One can see distant features he hasn't seen for eight months. The mud has dried, and travel becomes much easier. The earth is carpeted with a thick blanket of full-grown vegetation that is rapidly turning golden or brown. The animals and birds are happy because this is the time of abundance when all can eat their fill. Humans are happy because the time of hunger is past. Babies and mothers alike play and romp again; children dance and sing and put on weight again; fathers arrange wedding celebrations for their or their neighbor's sons and daughters, and grandfathers tell stories again.

After a lengthy famine, there is no pleasure in work comparable to the pleasure of harvesting. The toil is tedious and back-bending while cutting each blade of crop with a short sickle, back-breaking while carrying the bundles of ripe grain home to the safety of the threshing floor, sweat-drenching while flailing out the grain from the straw in the stifling heat of a windless noon, dust-encrusting as prickly chaff and stray particles irritate eyes and throat and sinuses and clog every pore, and skin-scorching while laboring under the searing glare of a cloudless sun.

Yet there is no satisfaction that compares to bringing home to one's wife and little ones the trophies of one's labor, the evidence of one's manhood, the symbols of restored dignity and self-worth— enough sacks of the precious grain to fill their tummies, buy their clothes, pay their school fees, supply medicines, pay the rent, and stave off starvation through the next cycle of hunger soon coming.

CHAPTER 20

The Revolution

I t was a long time in coming. As the emperor aged together with his "ancient regime," everybody knew that it was only a matter of time; change must come. But what kind of change? Who will bring it about? How? When? What will be the effects? These were the questions no one was supposed to ask, yet the questions that filled everybody's mind and many a low-voiced "subversive" conversation were the cause of endless speculation.

These questions were not limited to the minds of people in Ethiopia. Back in 1969, I met a rather strange middle-aged American woman at the guest house who called herself an "evangelist." This friend of Sarah Rush, whose name I've forgotten, claimed that while she was at home in America, God spoke to her and gave her a message to carry to Haile Selassie. So, she was here asking for an audience with His Imperial Majesty which she eventually obtained, and the message was successfully delivered.

The "message" that God wanted the "Lion of the Tribe of Judah" to know was that he would live out his days and die in peace, but after his departure there would be a time of terrible bloodshed in Ethiopia. I am sure the old man found the first part of that communique at least somewhat comforting. I found the latter part very disconcerting. I had my doubts. They say that to assess the authenticity of a prophet, you wait to see if his/her prediction comes true or not. Considering the subject's advancing age, we would not have to wait long.

For many years already, the courageous and restless students dared to raise these questions openly and to demand changes with immediate effect. Police and soldiers brutally suppressed them. But the next year they would raise their voices again. Only gradually, the general population dared to whisper an echo of the students' sentiments.

Discontent was on the rise. Demands for change were in the air. But all was silent and calm and in control at the Royal Residence. Brazen young foreign correspondents, interviewing His Majesty, asked him if, in view of his long reign and advancing age, he wasn't considering retiring soon? He answered them with his characteristic charm and dignity with a trace of indulgence that "Ethiopian emperors don't retire!" Ethiopia's fate was sealed.

In his youth, Beyene Chichiabelu had been one of the earliest Ethiopians to work with the Mennonite missionaries as a teacher in the School for the Blind and as a leader in the infant Meserete Kristos Church. He had gone to the USA for further education and returned with a PhD from Cornell University and was assigned to work in the Department of Agriculture. Back when I went to consult with him, as I formulated a plan to engage in development activities, he was serving as Deputy Minister of Livestock. He welcomed me and showed real enthusiasm in support of our plans and gave me helpful suggestions.

Beyene had a strong personality and was totally fearless in expressing his opinions. In our discussion, he began sharing his deep frustrations with the corrupt and inept hierarchy under which he had to work. As he shared examples, he became agitated and shouted in his big booming voice that echoed out the open office door and down the hallway: "WHAT THIS COUNTRY NEEDS IS REVOLUTION! BLOODY REVOLUTION!"

I was a bit taken aback by his boldness. This was a government building. What if some disgruntled or jealous subordinate reported him? What if the Secret Service was listening in? Beyene did not care. As a foreigner and a guest in the country, I could not give such voice to propose such a radical remedy, although I agreed with his sentiments, minus the word "BLOODY."

By this time, I was quite aware of the impossibility of doing really effective rural development work with the peasants without meaningful land reform. And with the feudal lords in power, no land reform was on the horizon. I used to pray for "revolution," a complete upset of the then current power structure that would free the peasants from the great injustices they were forced to endure, a "liberation of the captives." But I did not pray for the change to be "bloody."

In January of 1974, the students once again organized their annual protests and strike activities. Teachers pay had been cut, so they also went on strike. This time the emperor responded by cancelling the pay cut. Then the taxi drivers and bus owners went on strike to protest the sharp increase in the price of fuel. So, the government lowered the price of gasoline by a few cents. They raised the pay of the army twice in one week. It seemed the resolve of the ancient regime was waffling a bit.

On Wednesday, February 27, we set out from Bedeno to attend our annual missionary retreat which was to be held at Debre Zeit over the weekend. I took the night train from Dire Dawa so that I could do some business in Addis on Thursday. Vera and daughters stayed with Grace in Dire Dawa overnight. They all planned to follow on the train the next morning. Without any explanation, the night train stopped in Awash station at three a.m. and sat for seven hours. No explanation was given. Finally, it started up and continued on, arriving in Nazareth on Thursday afternoon. It refused to go on to Addis. Still no explanation.

So, I got out and took a bus. No one told us what was going on. By this time, I sensed that something was unusual. On the way to Addis there were an unusual number of military check-stops. When we arrived in Addis, we heard that the government of Prime Minister Aklilu Habte Wold, who had been in power since 1961, had resigned. Everything was tightly controlled by the military. I couldn't do any business that day.

My family couldn't come because the trains weren't running. Friday morning, Vera called me and asked if she should come. I advised her to stay in Dire Dawa. The retreat was cancelled, and we did not know what would happen next. I took Cindy and Karen out of boarding school to stay with me at Mel Thomas's house. During the day, a new prime minister was announced, and the soldiers moved off the streets. That evening, I called Vera and encouraged her to come as things seemed to be calm and stable. She came on the Saturday bus just to be with the children.

Later, we learned that on that morning, the Radio Voice of the Gospel, as was the custom, opened its morning broadcast with a devotional reading of a passage of scripture. The portion chosen for that particular day was taken from the book of James, chapter 5, verses 1 to 6 which, in the NIV, reads:

> "Now listen, you rich people, weep and wail because of the misery that is coming upon you. Your wealth has rotted, and moths have eaten your clothes. Your gold and silver are corroded. Their corrosion will testify against you and eat your flesh like fire. You have horded wealth in the last days. Look! The wages you failed to pay the workers who mowed your fields are crying out against you. The cries of the harvesters have reached the ears of the Lord Almighty. You have lived on earth in luxury and self-indulgence. You have fattened yourselves for the day of slaughter. You have condemned and murdered innocent men, who were not opposing you."

We marveled more when we learned that the reader was none other than Ato Million Belete, General Director of the Ethiopian Bible Society and a respected father in our fledgling Meserete Kristos denomination, and that the reading was pre-recorded several months in advance. That it should be broadcast on the very day of the beginning of the revolution! A mere coincidence? No! How prophetic!

Later, we learned that a group of junior officers in the army's Second Division had revolted and had arrested their generals and taken control. They had seized the city of Asmara and demanded an increase in their wages and a voice in government decisions and policies. They demanded that the present government resign, and that the emperor appoint a new prime minister and cabinet based on talent, skill, experience, and youthful progressive outlook instead of on aristocratic pedigree.

The king complied by appointing a new prime minister, the younger Lej Endalkatchew Makonnen, an Oxford graduate, who in turn chose a new cabinet that looked a lot better than the old one but was still too closely tied to aristocracy.

The officers accepted the choice for the time being and went back to their barracks. They would give the new government a few months to revise the constitution and start some desperately needed reforms.

We took the Wednesday train back to Dire Dawa. Rumors were running wild. People warned us not to travel to Bedeno on Thursday because the Labor Union was calling for a big demonstration, and we might get our car stoned! We got up at 3:30 and set out for Bedeno while all the "troublemakers" were still asleep. We arrived safely at 9:00 a.m. Later we heard that over 500 cars were stoned in Addis that day.

Rumors quickly spread to the remotest corners of the empire, and that included the community around Bedeno. A local Muslim peasant was eager to share his views with me. I was impressed. With a great deal of emotion and conviction, he exclaimed, "If there is a God above, then there must come a radical change in the way things are!" In his theological world view, there was no question intended in that "If." God is just, and change must come! I could see that, even though the Muslim population seemed to be rather fatalistic, attributing their oppressed position in the social hierarchy to the "will of Allah," their complacency had its limits, and those limits had been reached. The situation was over ripe for change.

A month later some significant changes could be felt. Censorship of the press and radio had largely been lifted. For the first time in recent history, the Ethiopian newspapers were interesting to read. People were beginning to hope for a better future.

People were waking up to their rights to have some say in the affairs of their nation. The elementary school students of Bedeno organized a protest against the exorbitant prices some merchants were charging on scarce goods. They marched downtown and demanded that the governor force merchants to lower prices, then went back to school. The merchants got together and gave the governor a 500-birr bribe to let them keep the prices up.

Next day, the students returned en mass, threatened to destroy the governor's office and to break his head too if he did not get with it! So, the governor was forced to obey. He ordered a new price list to be posted that the students drew up.

Farmers heard about this action and readily supported the students. Students infiltrated shops to monitor the prices at which goods were being sold. Several defiant merchants were called to court and fined for exceeding the price list. The police supported the students too. Injustices no longer need to go unchallenged. At last, the oppressed people were getting a taste of power. And it was very sweet (and scary)!

In the Empire as a whole, by Easter most of the government schools were closed for the rest of the year. Postal workers went on strike every now and then. There was general dissatisfaction with the new cabinet. It was felt that it was still tied too much to the aristocracy and wasn't serious enough about needed reforms that would inevitably hurt their interests. They were still offspring of the former regime, men of privilege who were not about to sacrifice their privileges for the benefit of the masses. Corruption continued.

The people were getting impatient. Already two coup attempts have been thwarted. They wanted to see something more done to bring justice and equality for the suffering millions. The new government could not do enough quickly enough to satisfy the people and keep the peace. More and more people accepted the opinion that the eighty-one-year-old emperor himself must go. But up to that time, there still had been no bloodshed. It was a popular and peaceful and "bloodless revolution."

Finally, in late April, the military acted against the members of the old government, arresting all the former ministers along with some of its top generals and officials. They were to be investigated for alleged abuse of power and crimes against humanity and duly punished.

Somehow, with the famine relief efforts and the revolution happening simultaneously, a certain amount of chaos was inevitable. The effects of the worldwide energy crisis did not help make matters any easier either. Under normal circumstances it was difficult to get any item of business done the first time one tried. Now it has become impossible. The inevitable bureaucracy and paperwork connected with government and United Nations involvement in famine relief was intimidating enough. Now every organized body seemed to think this was the right time to strike and demonstrate its newfound autonomy. The Ethiopian economy started to show signs of stress.

For example, with the terrible famine stalking the land, all trucks were needed to haul emergency supplies and food from the ports inland to the famine areas. This meant that other imported goods moved very sporadically and slowly to the cities, so the cities were chronically short of essential goods. Of course, it was the ideal time for the dock workers to go on strike. This made the movement of essential goods and relief supplies even more complicated. It was more than mildly frustrating to travel all the way from Bedeno to Addis Ababa to get a much-needed item only to hear that it is "out of stock" or that "It will come next week!" You clearly remember they said the same thing every time you came over the last four months.

Late in July, the junior officers announced themselves openly as the "Armed Forces Coordinating Committee" or simply the "Derg," or "Dergue" which means "Doers." They adopted the fascist motto "Ethiopia Tikdem," or "Ethiopia First." They demanded the dismissal of the prime minister and cabinet and appointed a new prime minister themselves. Endalkatchew was arrested and replaced with Mikael Imru, the liberal-minded son of the emperor's relative and war hero, Ras Imru. People were happy with this change and optimistic.

By mid-August, the new cabinet was working on a new constitution that would reduce the emperor to a figurehead and make the prime minister subject to parliament. They were working on a land reform bill as well. The Derg was getting more active and vocal. The rhetoric on the radio was getting fierier and more revolutionary. They were systematically arresting the most corrupt and notorious power figures of the "ancient regime" one by one.

This was truly a "creeping revolution." The Derg worked very quietly, almost reluctantly and timidly at first, then gradually they gained a sense of direction and came out with bolder more radical changes.

By the end of August, they had stripped Haile Selassie of all his real power and much of his property. They nationalized all his palaces. They made him a virtual prisoner in his own Jubilee Palace. They were conducting investigations into him and his former colleagues. They announced that the emperor had over the years taken more than two billion Ethiopian birr out of the country to invest in other countries and to hide in Swiss banks. Whether this was true or not, we had no way of knowing. But that was enough to finance the complete imperial government budget for at least four years at the current levels. They alleged that he was doing this while traveling abroad on begging missions among the rich countries seeking aid.

They alleged that while Haile Selassie was busy enriching himself and his friends and begging for military and economic aid, he deliberately tried to hide the existence of a serious famine in the north that had been quietly going on for almost four years. During that time, an estimated 100,000 people died of hunger.

Finally, a BBC correspondent managed to document on film the horrible spectacle of death going on in Wello Province and splashed it on all the T.V. sets of the rich nations and on the front pages of the major newspapers of the world. Even when this tragedy was exposed, Haile Selassie and his government had angrily blasted BBC for slandering Ethiopia. They tried their best to discount the story, to continue hiding the tragedy. Now the new government was accusing the old cabinet of mass genocide.

Just before school opened in September, the Derg announced plans to close the University and grades eleven and twelve of all high schools for one year so they could send the 40,000 students and their teachers out into the countryside in a National Service Campaign called "Zemetcha." Its purpose was to conscientize the masses against the old regime, its king, and the feudal system, to make them aware of their political rights, to teach literacy, hygiene, and democracy, and to indoctrinate the masses in the principles of socialism and the meaning of "Ethiopia Tikdem."

Then on September 11, 1974, the Derg presented a special documentary on T.V. which they encouraged everybody to watch. I happened to be in Addis at the time and saw this documentary. It was cleverly put together from different newsreels with running commentary for propaganda purposes.

It showed scenes of the emperor at great state banquets with his ministers and diplomatic guests seated before vast tables spread with the finest delicacies and loaded with rare wines and imported liquors. These clips were interspersed with scenes of his starving subjects waiting in line for a bowl of famine rations. It showed pictures of His Majesty gleefully playing with his pet dogs, giving them choice slabs of meat, then pictures of starving mothers holding their dying children.

It showed detailed pictures of the $7,000 tombstone the emperor erected for his pet dog, Lulu; then it showed a mass grave dug for the burial of his loyal subjects who died of starvation in Wello. All the while the running commentary provided a wealth of facts and figures to show the contrast between His Royal Highness's lifestyle and utter detachment from the sufferings of his people. It kept interjecting the question: "Is this really the kind of man you want to rule over our nation?"

The documentary went on for a full two hours, and by the time it was over, most of the people were deeply angry. The next day Emperor Haile Selassie I was quietly deposed. There was no objection. I saw the little green Volkswagen cross Meskel Square, carting the emperor from his Jubilee Palace on his way to the prison at the Fourth Division Army headquarters. Following the slow-moving procession, people were dancing in the streets. It was a very pathetic ending to a sometimes-glorious fifty-year reign.

His government was sacked, and a "Provisional Military Government" headed by General Aman Andom, the "Lion of the Desert," a popular hero of the Ogaden war, took its place. Ethiopia officially ceased to be an "empire," and the word "imperial" was blacked out on official documents.

General Aman Andom was very popular with the people. He visited the rebels in Asmara, trying to persuade them to settle their differences peaceably and join in the successful revolution to build a new united socialist Ethiopia of which Eritrea would be an important part. In light of the fact that the Eritrean Liberation Front (ELF) and the Eritrean People's Liberation Front (EPLF) were both fighting to liberate their people from the exploitative relationship with Haile Selassie's feudal system and were both espousing socialism as the road to a more just and prosperous future, it only seemed logical that they should now find common ground to make peace with the new Provisional Military Government of the now socialist Republic of Ethiopia.

The Eritrean response gave some hope of there being light at the end of the tunnel in the long dark struggle between them and the rest of Ethiopia.

But somehow this action by General Aman Andom and the stance he took did not please some members of the "Derg." After his return from Asmara, they accused him of treason, surrounded his house with a contingent of troops armed with artillery pieces and demanded his surrender. According to the reports, the general realized that he was overpowered by ruthless elements in the "Derg," so decided to die fighting rather than surrender. He was eliminated in the ensuing gun battle, and his house was demolished by the artillery.

Having gained control of the Derg, those ruthless elements went ahead that same day and executed fifty-nine key prisoners including former ministers, two former prime ministers, several generals, and other top officials of Haile Selassie's government and buried them in a mass grave.

We were visiting Assefa and Grace that night, November 24th, 1974, when they announced this event on the radio. They began by reading off slowly and clearly a list beginning with the name of General Aman Andom followed by the names of each of the former dignitaries concluding with the blood-curdling words, "were all killed!"

These words triggered chills of horror down our spines and fear in each heart, as they sent shock waves across the nation and around the world. Up to now we were uneasy but proud that at least our "civilized" revolution was "bloodless." But now that the veins had been cut in the most ruthless manner, what was to prevent the flow of blood from continuing unabated? Power that comes out of the barrel of a gun has no respect for human dignity nor the sacredness of human blood.

The announcement continued, ordering that no one should weep for them or ask for their bodies or hold any memorial services for them. They were exploiters and enemies of the people, and not worthy of the taxpayer's food they were eating in prison!

This event marked the turning point in the revolution. The Derg had lost its innocence. It was the end of the "bloodless revolution" and the beginning of the "red terror." The Eritrean rebels lost their interest in doing any business with the bloody butchers of their beloved General Andom. From now on there would be only war, war, and more war until Eritrea either sacrificed its last drop of blood or stood victorious and free from the tyrant's domination.

From now on, Colonel Mengistu Haile Mariam was making his weight felt as he ascended steadily to the pinnacles of power within the Derg. He literally rose to power over the dead bodies of his buddies in the Derg. One by one they fell from favor and were eliminated. He was known to have pulled out his revolver in a committee meeting and shot a member who dared to disagree with him right on the spot at the committee table! Obviously, he ran a very well-disciplined committee after that! Though he could hardly pass for an educated man, this brash young officer possessed an inborn political cleverness and diabolical ruthlessness.

During these times of political unrest and tension the Provisional Military Government imposed a dusk to dawn curfew. No one was to travel anywhere without special government permission and escort. Anyone caught on the highway or street could be shot on sight. But Bedeno wasn't really in the new "Republic" of Ethiopia. Life went on by its own rules.

One evening in November, just as we were finishing supper, some people came bringing a badly injured man who had fallen out of a tree. Could I please rush him to the hospital in Harar at once? Well, this seemed to be a genuine case, a real emergency, so I responded instinctively in the usual manner, feeling obliged.

As we passed the invisible boundary somewhere in the dark that separated the remote hinterlands from "civilization," it dawned on us in the car that we had heard a rumor somewhere that a nationwide curfew was in effect. What shall we do? What might happen to us if we are caught? We pressed on to find out.

At 2:00 a.m. we were entering the sleeping city's limits when a row of soldiers with guns at the ready took their positions across the road in front of us. There was no way we could overrun them or outrun their bullets or turn around. So, we stopped. The soldiers scolded us very severely, demanded to see our I.D.s and demanded to know where we thought we were going. We pointed to the injured man in the back and gave our excuse. They warned us that we had committed a very dangerous and serious offence. Then they escorted us to the hospital and ordered all of us to stay with the vehicle in the hospital compound until dawn. We were glad to oblige.

I had applied to the *Zemetcha* organizers to have four students placed with our development program as their place of national service. My request was approved. We must pay them living allowances, but no salary. They must wear the Zemetcha uniform. We were happy to have Belayneh Kassaye, Gebre Meskel, and Mohammed Musa join our team at Bedeno, while Wondimu Gashow assisted Mr. Gamber at Deder. Later, when the goats came, Mohammed Musa was transferred to his hometown, Deder, to be trained as an expert in dairy goat management.

On January 1, 1975, the Provisional Military Government

announced the nationalization of all banks, finance companies, and insurance companies as we entered into the new era of "Ethiopian socialism." This was in line with a series of nationalizations that started with the emperor's property and then the businesses and properties of certain other rich, powerful people associated with his reign. Italians, Armenians, and others of foreign origins, whether they were Ethiopian-born or citizens or otherwise, were early victims to this policy. We noticed that this action was very popular with the masses.

But it was very brutal to some of the honest, industrious businesspeople. I listened to the fears of one Armenian businessman. He told me that one day last week his friend had been the owner of a small flour mill business which he had built up over the last forty years to a net worth of about three million birr. The next morning, he was penniless. Police had come on the premises during the night and seized everything including bank accounts in the name of the government on behalf of "justice for the exploited masses." Since it was a private business, he had not kept his personal money separate from his business money. Now he came begging his friend for a birr to buy cigarettes. He had no idea what he or his family would do to survive.

The new government also secularized the state. Under the old regime, the Muslims had to keep the Christian holidays while their own holidays were ignored on the national level. They had to celebrate them as best they could. From now on the Orthodox and the Muslim were to be treated equally. They abolished many of the old religious holidays and established thirteen national holidays, of which three were Muslim, five were Christian, and the rest secular.

The Provisional Military Government was determined to turn the old feudal empire into a modern socialist state. In March, they declared the long-awaited land reform. All land now belonged to the state. All landlordism was abolished. "Land to the tiller" was the slogan. The peasants were all entitled to keep and use the same land they were using before. They would no longer have to pay rent, only taxes. No one could farm more than twenty-five acres. All large farms, commercial farms, and plantations were nationalized, along with the tractors and machinery. They would become state farms.

The government also began to institute price controls to block the exploitation of the poor by the merchant class. Seven merchants were arrested and executed for "hoarding." This drastic action provided a powerful incentive to the other hoarding merchants to release their goods to the public.

They were also changing the civil administration throughout the country. Old fashioned, semi-literate, and corrupt officials, like our governor, were being sacked and replaced with young, educated officials.

The mood of the people was still optimistic and expectant and happy. No one could have dreamed two years before that so many radical changes could have been introduced so easily and with so little bloodshed.

However, there hung over the nation the specter of war. The civil war in Eritrea was intensifying since the murder of General Aman Andom and the massacre of the sixty. There were rumors of armed insurrection and banditry in the Ogaden from the Republic of Somalia. There was talk of a dissident group fighting in Wollega Province in the west.

People fully expected the announcement of land reform to trigger serious armed resistance in many parts of the land. The landed aristocracy numbered something like a half million, most of them staunch conservative feudalists with armed services training and experience. Most of them owned guns and many of them would rather die than surrender an inch of land to one of their peasants.

CHAPTER 21

Retreat From Bokay Teffe

A to Damti had worked on our project at Bokay Teffe by himself for two years. With a few oxen and some day laborers, he had cut out a little farm in the wilderness of about twenty acres. But it was no use. With almost no rain during the past year, he got nothing. We had to make some changes.

We had no intentions of permanently abandoning the estate. We were not retreating in defeat. We were just making a temporary tactical adjustment backwards so that we could regroup, change our strategy, and advance again. Perhaps we would come back and set up a cattle ranch if we could find funds to invest in some cows. This was our thinking before the revolution. In the meantime, we had moved Damti to our Burka project where he found the circumstances more comfortable and pleasing.

However, Ato Damti was worried about the machinery and equipment we had left at Bokay. Some Somalis might steal the steel of the improved moldboard plows to manufacture weapons. We must make a trip back there to retrieve all the valuables that were left behind.

So, on a Thursday in late March 1974, Ato Damti and I climbed into the Toyota and set our faces steadfastly towards our 1000-acre estate 326 kilometers away at Bokay Teffe.

As a sign of ill omen, rain began to fall upon us as soon as we left home, and it rained on us all the way to Bedessa. This should have been adequate warning to even the simplest of minds not to try the Bokay road. But being mere mortals with an excellent built-in capacity to make foolish decisions, we resolutely continued towards our personal "paradise" somewhere near the "end of the earth." That last ninety kilometers took us five hours, all of it in pouring rain. It was amazing that we did not get stuck. Water splashed the sides of the trail, scoured the floorboards under our feet, and sprayed up over the windshield, mingling with the pouring rain that kept the wipers occupied the whole way. It was still raining when we arrived at our camp at 8:00 p.m.

So far so good. Now we would sleep in the hut, get up in the morning and load our things and drive back at least to Deder by Friday night, and Saturday morning we would reach home at Bedeno, or so we thought. We forgot to add, "the Lord willing, and the creek don't rise" to our plans for the next day.

It continued to rain all night, but when we got up in the morning, the sun was shining. We had a little breakfast, then loaded our car with four moldboard plows, two sections of harrows, and one oxcart on the roof, plus some seed grain and other things inside. At exactly 9:00 a.m., we started heading towards Bedeno.

But, unknown to us, the outpouring of grace had run out with the cessation of the outpouring of the rain! Now we had to come to terms with the sticky realities of our situation. We had hardly gotten onto the trail when we experienced difficulty with the mud. Such sticky mud! Up to this time, apart from high-centering, I had never seen a road where our friend, Mr. Toyota, couldn't go. With four-wheel drive, low gear, chains on the front wheels, and lots of power, I figured, if there is a bottom to the mud, it could go anywhere.

But this mud was different. Without the lubricating effect of yesterday's rainwater, today the clay had the most tenacious adhesive quality imaginable! The rear wheel wells plugged up so tight with mud between the tires and the fenders that finally the wheels couldn't even turn. The mud was acting like a giant brake. I had to shift down to the lowest gear. Even then gradually the friction of the mud stalled the engine. I had my roots in the famous grey-blue gumbo soils of Alberta, but I had never seen anything quite like this.

We had to get out the jack, lift the body of the car from the running gear so that there was space to dig out the sticky goo from each of the rear wheel wells. That wasn't easy as all we had to work with was a tire iron, a narrow round short iron bar with which we could scoop out a narrow strip of mud one width of the bar at a time. Then the mud stuck to the bar so it had to be wiped off onto

301

something else more stationary before one could reach back up past the tire into the wheel well for another narrow bar-shaped gob of goo.

It took considerable time and much exertion of effort to clean both wheel wells and put away the jack. Then we could drive one or two kilometers before the bunged-up wheel well-brakes would shut down the engine again. Then we would have to repeat the whole process, get out the jack again, lift the rear end, clean the wheel wells, put the jack away, get in and drive as far as it would go, and repeat again and again.

By 4:00 p.m. we had gone fifty-one kms. Then I noticed that the main hub bolts on the front wheel were breaking off. In fact, there was only one bolt remaining where there used to be six. All the power of the front wheel drive passes through these bolts to turn the wheels. So, we were beat. We could not use the front wheel drive mechanism anymore, and it was still too muddy to go anywhere in two-wheel drive.

Again, it started to rain. We ate our last two pieces of bread. It had been a tough day. Though it was only past six p.m., we got out our sleeping bags. Damti stretched his short frame out on the rear seat while I scrunched my seventy-one-and-a-half-inch frame into the sixty-inch space between the front door posts with my legs bent against the steering wheel. We would go to sleep and decide what to do in the morning.

It was so peaceful and quiet out there all alone in the tar-black night. The heavy sodden blanket above snuffed out any hint of glowing luminaries in the infinite spaces beyond. No trace of human habitation could be seen anywhere, and no sound of engine or beast or wind marred the magic of our total isolation. Only the steady relentless persistent splatter of zillions of tiny droplets against the resilient exterior of our Toyota cocoon mingled with and became a part of the deafening silence of the night. In the morning, the rain stopped.

By 7:00 a.m., Ato Damti was on his way, walking towards the next village to look for food. The village was supposed to be about sixteen kilometers away. The sticky mud slowed down his pace considerably, so it took him more than four hours to reach the place. The plan was for him to bring back enough food to keep him for three or four days. His humble presence, supposedly, would guard the car against any possible ill intentions of the roving bands of nomads whose impeccable reputation in the field of banditry was well known. Upon his return, I would walk the forty kilometers to Bedessa, phone or go to Addis Ababa, get a new hub and bolts, and return to fix the machine.

While Damti went for the food, I stayed to watch the car. I saw this was a rare free time to pray and meditate. There was nothing to distract me and nothing else to do. My prayer times had been irregular, brief, to the point, and infrequent. How can one possibly be a good missionary, yet be too busy to pray? How could I know if I was on course if I did not check regularly with my "Commander"? Why was contact with "Headquarters" so hard to maintain? If I was really that busy, then wasn't I too busy? Weren't my priorities a little eccentric? Could I really expect to succeed if I went ahead of the "Boss"? Why am I stranded out here in this rain saturated "Sinai" desert? Had I really heard a call from God to get involved with this Bokay Teffe mess in the first place? Did God really send me here on this trip during this particular rainy spell? Whose voice have I been listening to? Am I following Jesus, or do I have a problem with an inflated eccentric ego or personal ambition?

It was a time to be honest and evaluative and repentant before God out there alone in his wet "desert," trapped in his mud. It is amazing sometimes the lengths God goes to or the methods he uses to get our wandering attention. It was a precious time, a retreat worth all the stress and agony and the time and money it cost to get there.

After a couple hours of that, the sun was shining, and it was getting hot. I decided I could use my time to do some general maintenance on the car like tightening up loose bolts on the fenders and replacing missing ones. So, I got out the can of assorted bolts and screws and my tools and set to work.

After doing that for about a half-hour, I decided to give the offending hub a closer look. The bolts had broken off in the hub and the threads were damaged. But then I noticed there were a few extra empty holes in the hub, and that I could screw in four bolts that would hold the hub temporarily at least. While I worked, the sun was also at work drying up the road. When I finished and put the tools away, it was 12:00 noon. I started up the machine and went flying down the road towards the village.

Damti had just left the village laden with four-days' supply of boiled eggs, "enjera," and "wat" when I met him. He couldn't have been more surprised if I had been raised from the dead! Anyway, we ate greedily and then drove on to the village. Here, I sold the cart to a local farmer who begged me for it. The load was too heavy anyway. We had eaten well, and we would be back in "civilization" before dark, so we gave the extra food back to the villagers. While we were off-loading the oxcart, it started pouring rain again.

We waited in the man's house and visited for about one hour until the rain stopped. He said he had been arguing with Damti before I came. Damti had explained to him that we had broken down and how I had said that I couldn't fix the car and would have to get spare parts from Addis. The man had replied that he did not believe that. "If he is a *ferinj* he can fix it, because *ferinjoch* can fix anything!" He had worked with the Italians during the war and spoke with conviction born of experience. Soon after that, they heard our vehicle roaring in the distance. The man continued his argument: "See, did I not tell you *ferinjoch* can fix anything!"

Damti still wasn't convinced when he set out on his way back with the food. It had to be that there was another vehicle in the area somewhere. Well, he lost the argument, but gained a ride. Sometimes it is okay to be proved wrong!

The rains put a crimp back into my driving style, but the area of the tar-like mud was behind us. We made slow but steady progress until around 6:00 p.m. when we found ourselves stranded in the center of a large "lake" where there should have been a road. The wheels had sunk into a bottomless pit, and we were high centered again. It was pouring rain and total darkness set in. What could we do but spend another night on the same narrow sixty-inch seats that we luxuriated on over the previous night, another night in the rain, another night—this time in a frog pond surrounded with mud and mosquitoes, and worst of all, another night without supper!

It was Sunday morning when we woke up, and the sun was just rising over a clear horizon. The rain was gone, and the bird choir took over from the singing frogs who were by now exhausted from their all-night marathon performance. Could we possibly get to Deder in time for church? We skipped our Sunday morning ritual of brushing teeth, shaving, showering, and dressing in fresh attire. In our eagerness to get home, we even skipped breakfast! We sat up, took off our shoes and socks, rolled up our pant legs, and stepped out into the cool water to investigate possible ways to extricate our machine from the wet bottomless habitat of the frogs.

We surveyed the available resources at our disposal. There were no stones to build a road under our sunken ship. But there was a field of harvested sorghum stocks nearby. Ato Damti suggested using the stocks to build the needed road. I had serious reservations. Whoever heard of a "sorghum stock road"? They would just disintegrate or sink out of sight. But there was nothing else to fill the deep ruts we were in, so I finally consented to give it an honest try.

We found a piece of log to set the jack on so that it would not sink out of sight. With the jack, we lifted the front of the vehicle until both wheels were above the water. Then we carried in all the sorghum stocks that we could stuff in the ruts under the wheels. Then we let the jack down slowly and watched the vehicle sink lower and lower, squishing the air and the water out of the stocks and pushing them into the mud, almost as deep as before. So, we jacked it up again and packed in some more of the spongy stocks. This time it did not sink so low.

Finally, we lifted the back up in the same way and placed stocks under the rear wheels. After doing that several times, we started the engine and tried. It moved ahead about one car length. Then we had to repeat the performance. After two hours of intense and hopeful labor, the Toyota drove out onto solid ground. We were glad to leave the frogs and mosquitoes behind. I could see that we were going to be late for church.

By this time, the Toyota was having an energy crisis of its own. On the trip into Bokay, it had traveled 230 kilometers on one tank of fuel. But with the heavy labor of the journey out, it had consumed the second tank in only eighty kilometers. The gauge showed "empty" by the time we left the frog pond. With one eye on the gauge and the other on the road ahead and both ears tuned to the inevitable first sputter and cough of the engine, we pushed on hoping against hope that we could make it to the highway at least. Each kilometer traveled meant one less kilometer to walk with the empty jerrycan.

Finally, it happened at 9:00 a.m., less than a quarter of a kilometer from the main road. The engine sputtered, shook, jerked ahead a few times, sputtered some more and just died as the body rolled to a halt. I grabbed our jerrycan and walked to the highway where I caught a bus to the nearest gas station which happened to be sixty-five kilometers away at Asebe Teferi. By the time I returned it was already 3:00 p.m.

We poured the gasoline into the tank and got moving again towards Bedessa. But Damti had not eaten a bite for twenty-five hours, so there had to be a stop at a restaurant. It was 8:00 p.m. when we drove into the Deder Mission Station. Yes, we had missed church!

By this time, the news had spread that we were missing, and our mission people welcomed our reappearance. A warm shower and a soft bed felt good after four days on the road. We would go on home to Bedeno the next morning.

When morning came Vera phoned (Yes, occasionally the Bedeno phone line worked), trying to hear if anyone knew of my whereabouts? She found me. I assured her that I had not forgotten her yet and still loved her and that we would be home "before evening."

Afterwards I found that one of my improvised bolts was broken. I knew the other three would not stand the rigors of the Bedeno road, so we changed our minds and went to Dire Dawa. I phoned Addis Ababa and ordered a new hub and bolts to be sent out on the airplane.

By 3:30 p.m., Tuesday, we started out on the final leg of our trip back to Bedeno. All this time it was raining an inch or two every day. The road was absolutely soaked at its worst. It was a struggle all the way. We got stuck several times but arrived home at 12:30 past midnight, Wednesday morning. I was never so happy to be home. Six days for a two-day journey. I had seen enough rain and mud to last a long time.

But when we woke up that morning, a message was passed to us: Several Bible Academy teachers, our good friends, would be waiting for me to pick them up at Watter that day. One teacher's father had passed away near Bedeno, and they were coming for the funeral. Of course, one cannot say "no" to a friend in such circumstances, so I spent a seventh day on the rain-drenched road arriving home after dark.

The very next morning there was a knock on our door. Would we please take a sick man to the Harar Hospital? Fortunately for us, and unfortunately for the sick man, we discovered that the brake line had ruptured as the car came in the night before. To go on these mountain trails in soaking rain without brakes? Absolutely impossible! I was glad for a good excuse to say "no." We had to order a new line from Addis. Until it arrived, the vehicle would be going nowhere.

But there are exceptions to every rule. On another occasion, just as we had set out from Bedeno on a trip to Dire Dawa, all the brake fluid leaked out, and the vehicle was completely without brakes. We had no brake fluid with us nor at home. What could we do now?

I was not the kind of person who changed his mind easily once I decided upon a thing. And on this particular day, I was in no mood to compromise or change my plans. I would do the "impossible," or at least die trying if I must. We would reach our destination. If there were no brakes, I would drive that rig over the mountains and gullies of the Bedeno road without brakes!

By this time, I knew the road like the back of my hand, and I knew the Toyota like it was an extension of my own body. I took that trip slow on the down slopes being very careful to gear down into the lowest gears so that there would be no "runaway."

We made the trip with no problem. When we reached "civilization" we met another vehicle. I stopped it, and the driver gave me a can of brake fluid that enabled us to safely negotiate the main highway with its twenty-kilometer steep winding descent into Dire Dawa.

CHAPTER 22

Unfinished Business

A Family Vacation

I was very exhausted by the famine frustrations, so when Cindy and Karen finished school in June, we decided to celebrate our reunion by taking a ten-day family vacation camping at Lake Langano. This was our favorite vacation spot. The children loved to play in the water and build sandcastles on the beach. They entertained themselves there every day while Vera and I sat in the shade and read books or wrote letters.

The Ed Erickson family were camping nearby. Their daughter, Laurie, was one of Cindy and Karen's roommates this past year in school. So, it was nice to have a friend to share this vacation with.

By this time our baby, Kristina, was becoming quite active. At two years old, she had a good command of the Queen's English, could count by herself up to fourteen, weighed twenty-eight pounds, and stood thirty-four inches tall. She was a very healthy and happy child. Give her some water to splash in and some sand to dig in and she would entertain herself all day.

Upon arriving home after being absent for two weeks, as was the custom, all the workers and many community people, especially children, came to welcome us and to satisfy their curiosity as to what strange new contraptions or merchandise the *ferinj* may have brought home this time.

The workers told us that the dog was not acting normally. They said he did not eat and snapped at workers whom he normally did not snap at. I looked at him and petted him. He did seem troubled, but not seriously.

Then, we opened the back doors to unload the Toyota. The curious gathered close to see what there was to see. One shepherd boy was eating some bread while gawking like everybody else. Suddenly the dog snapped at the hand holding the bread, biting the half of the thumb right off and sinking its teeth deep into the palm of the hand! The terrified boy climbed right up on top of the guard to save his life. But the thumb was gone!

We suspected the dog must have had rabies, but there was no way of knowing without endangering others, so we decided he must be put to death at once. He was the best watchdog we ever had. He was totally brave, even driving off two huge hyenas one night. But now he had bit off a community member's thumb and could not go unpunished!

With a heavy heart, like an unwilling murderer, I was forced to put him to death. I felt like the worst "Judas!" Once again, the children lost a valuable pet, and we lost a true friend.

But worst of all, a small neighbor boy had lost his thumb and stood in danger of losing his life, if indeed the dog had rabies. We had to special order anti-rabies vaccine from Dire Dawa to treat him. He recovered okay.

Another neighbor boy of fourteen years of age wasn't so lucky. He was bitten by a mad dog too, but his parents took him to the holy medicine man for treatment instead. Some weeks later he was brought to our clinic showing all the symptoms of rabies. At that stage there is nothing modern medicine can do. He died a horrible, agonizing death some four days later.

Bringing Daniel Home

Being great with child, Grace had gone (not by donkey this time!) to the Deder Mission Hospital to await further events. In the fullness of time, on August 5th, she brought forth her firstborn son and wrapped him in proper nappies and laid him in a bassinet.

As the news spread far and wide, it even reached Bedeno. And there was in that town a certain dresser working hard in his clinic. Immediately upon hearing the glad tidings, the busy Assefa left the patients he was tending, and departed with haste and found the mother with the little child just as it was told to him. And they rejoiced together greatly over their child, and they called him "Daniel Assefa Haile"!

After some weeks of resting, healing, and adjusting to motherhood, Grace was eager to bring the young child home to Bedeno. The honor and the duty of transporting the happy family fell to us. Necessity demanded that we bring them to Dire Dawa to take care of some vital business before continuing on home.

It was 7:00 a.m. on a Saturday morning when we left Dire Dawa, fully loaded with six adults, two children, and the precious baby Daniel, plus all the luggage that the back of the Landcruiser would hold and the roof rack piled high with valuable cargo. From Dire Dawa, we slowly twisted our way twenty kilometers up the mountainside and reached the highland plateau.

It was a beautiful morning with a cloudless sky, a favorable omen for one not initiated in the weather patterns of these parts. But for us, this was still the rainy season, and we well understood that a clear sunny sky in the morning was a dependable sign of a heavy rainstorm by late afternoon. But the day was young, so we were quite confident that we could make it home before the "deluge" overtook us.

We were peacefully cruising along in a carefree jovial mood, winding our way at a good speed on the smooth asphalt road that curved around the various gullies and ridges that make the side of a mountain.

As we were in the deep swing of one of those curves, suddenly the left rear wheel broke right off, and the heavy load banged down on the pavement and we skidded sideways to a stop a few feet from the edge of the road where the mountainside fell away in a steep drop towards the distant desert thousands of feet below.

We were very grateful to be alive as we got out of the vehicle to survey the damage. Had it been the right wheel on the outside of the curve, we would have gone over the edge for certain.

But, by God's grace, it was just a broken rear axle. On that particular model of Landcruiser, the wheel was bolted directly to the axle. When the axle snapped, the wheel would come right off.

Now we needed a new axle and needed to repair the brake pad assembly which was crushed in the skid. Obviously, there were going to be some major adjustments in the day's itinerary.

We flagged down a bus and sent the women and children back

down the mountain to the Mission in Dire Dawa. Then we got out our tools, took off the remnants, and surveyed the damage. Finally, leaving Assefa to guard the goods, I also boarded a bus and returned to Dire Dawa.

We were exceedingly grateful to discover a spare set of axles and brake parts hidden among the collection of treasures that filled Mr. Garber's garage. The women and children remained at the Mission while Robert and I went back up to the remains of the Toyota, equipped with his expertise and his set of tools.

Hours later we had it together again. Robert returned to Dire Dawa and sent the women and children back up the hill by taxi to rejoin us on our journey.

It was 5:00 p.m. when we resumed our journey. Our spirits weren't quite so buoyant as they had been ten hours earlier. And our bodies were not as full of energy either. It would have been wise to stay overnight and leave the next morning, but we all were eager to bring Daniel home and voted to go ahead. By the time we reached Watter, the small town that marked the half-way point and the end of the good road, it was 6:00 p.m. The sky over Garamuleta was dark and menacing.

We hadn't gone far up the long slope when the first raindrops began to fall. Soon we stopped and put the chains on the front wheels. The rain was coming down in sheets and Assefa and I were soaked by the time we dashed back inside.

We did not advance more than about fifty meters when we suddenly found ourselves sitting crosswise on the slippery road with a deep gully in front of us, a soft plowed field behind us, the rear wheels sunk down to the axle under us, a torrent of water gushing down the ruts beneath us, rain falling in sheets above us, and darkness descending around us, and hunger and exhaustion stirred up within us! There was nothing we could do now to help ourselves out of this mess. We might just as well eat and sleep right where we were and hope for the best in the morning.

And that is exactly what we did. Well, I will not over emphasize the "eat" part, nor the "sleep" part for that matter either.

Grace did pass around a few edibles she scavenged from her grocery box, hardly what you would call a banquet. Sleeping was something else. With six adults and two children plus a baby squeezed in a six-passenger vehicle, there isn't a lot of stretching out that is going to happen. I was wet and cold. But exhaustion brought about some sleep, and the night soon passed.

We welcomed the first streaks of Sunday morning in a most desecratory manner by building a road under the car. Two hours of jacking up the vehicle, carrying stones from the field, placing them under the wheels, and repeating.

When we finally drove over the next ridge, our hearts sank to the bottom of our empty abdomens. There confronting us, where the road should have been, was a vast lake of water and muck! We sat there and surveyed the shimmering scene and debated. We knew well that our Toyota was mighty, but it was not almighty. It was not amphibious. And there was no ferry anywhere on this mountain.

We sadly turned around and returned towards Watter. There was another road, twenty-one kilometers longer, that went around the eastern side of Garamuleta Mountain and joined the Grawa road. We were told that the trucks often used it during the rains. We had never been on it before, but this was a tempting time to try it. We knew what the alternative was.

So, after buying some "enjera b'wat" from the local restaurant in Watter to appease our complaining empty bellies, we set out on this "better" road. Whether this "long scenic route" was really "better" or not can be debated at length. What we do know is that we only got stuck seven times!

The sun was sinking low when we finally crawled into Bedeno "bloody but unbowed" on our last ounce of fuel that unforgettable Sunday evening when we brought Daniel home.

Baby Daniel did not complain at all about the thirty-four hours we took to bring him to his new home. As for the rest of us, had we been Oromo women, we could have brought him there in a third of that time on foot. Such is the advantage of humankind's expensive machines!

Four days later it was deemed necessary that I go out to Watter again to bring back a group of evangelists and singers for a conference we were about to have at Bedeno. It took twelve-and-one-half hours, but I returned the same day with the guests.

Of course, this necessitated the returning of the guests a few days later. And as though tradition could not be broken, it rained again just as I reached Watter. This time the car broke on the way back, but I was able to fix it enough to drive home.

It was already dark when we came upon a tree that had fallen across the path. We had no axe or saw to cut it into manageable bits. My companion was kind of shocked when I drove up to one end of the tree, got out and threw a chain around it and fastened it to the bumper, then backed the vehicle pulling the tree out of the way so we could pass.

The Devil Takes a Beating at Bedeno

The two preachers were both young Ethiopian Pentecostals. One was a university graduate who worked as the Assistant Director of Dire Dawa High School. The other, Ato Teklu, was a full-time evangelist. Three of our town's worst boys, high school students, were remarkably converted and filled with the Holy Spirit. Several of the "better" boys and girls were also converted or rededicated their lives to serve the Lord. Altogether, there were about ten people converted, and many others deepened their commitments. All of them were also filled with the Holy Spirit and spoke in tongues! The Bedeno Church was quickly becoming a "pentecostal" church.

Our evangelist, Ketema, was also of that experience. We had become the "outsiders" in our own church, but we praised God for the new life and power and hope we saw in these new believers.

One of our clinic workers was very unhappy. She was convinced to turn to Jesus. Then she wanted the evangelist to come with a group of others to pray for her mother who was an invalid. She had been taking treatments for rheumatism for four years.

When they began praying for her, they found that she was possessed of demons. The demons said, "We are the ones who made her crippled!" They said that they did it when she was walking to church four years ago. They made her fall, and she couldn't walk since. The evangelist and his friends cast out 130 demons, and she was liberated. When they were all gone and she had come to her senses, she did not know what had happened. They told her to get up and walk. She did! She was fine!

For many, many, years, Ato Nicola's wife, Zenebework, as was customary among many Orthodox women in that area, had kept a fetish or idol, an object that represents a demon to which she sacrificed a chicken every year so the demon would not bring bad luck. All five of her children, who were educated in the mission school and in the Bible Academy, were dynamic Christians. Now she called all her neighbors together so she could declare to them that from now on she was going to trust and depend on Jesus Christ alone for her protection. Then she threw the idol down and destroyed it. She became a strong follower of Christ.

The neighbor women were all horrified. They all had the same kind of thing in their houses upon which they depended. One of them finally said, "I'll be watching you. If nothing bad happens to you, I will throw mine out too." These women were all members of the Ethiopian Orthodox community. They were all in bondage to Satan through these superstitions.

Such unusual activities supplied fodder for the gossip in the town. Word went around, "The Mission was dead, but now it has become Pentecostal!" Of course, to their way of thinking to become "Pente" was the most dreadful kind of heresy to fall into. One night they started throwing rocks at our downtown reading room to warn us of their hostility towards this new departure from the accepted norm, the faith of their fathers.

Home Schooling Revisited

In some ways our girls benefited a lot by attending the Good Shepherd School in Addis. The instruction was of superb quality, and the atmosphere was excellent. Even boarding was a learning experience that taught them a lot about living with others. But we as parents did not feel good about sending our little ones so far from home. Their tears of parting, and their begging to be allowed to stay at home really spoke deeply to us.

Was it really God's will that parents should separate themselves from their small children at such a tender age? Did not God intend that a child should have the right to the security of a home, to the protection and love and discipline and example of his/her parents until he/she reaches maturity? The first twelve years of primary parenting go so quickly, we reasoned, and if we put them under the care of others during that time, our opportunity to be good parents will be lost forever. Can we really afford to rob our little ones of their God-given rights? Would it not be fairer to sacrifice some of the quality of the finest education that a large school can give for the emotional and spiritual benefits of family togetherness during those tender years?

By September of 1974, we had decided and made all arrangements to keep Cindy and Karen home for the next school year. We had ordered the correspondence materials in good time, we thought, though they hadn't arrived yet. We hired Belayneh Kassaye, a top student from the current graduating class of the Bible Academy, to be a full-time teacher of our three children. We cleaned up a tattered little room at the back of the Primary School and put in three desks and chairs made especially for these privileged students. Our Mission agreed to the experiment. After all, it represented a 50% saving to them.

Our little school was to open in the last week of September. But the revolution that was going on in the bigger world outside was not to spare Bedeno. It even reached its long tentacles of power and interfered with our little three-student mini-school. Belayneh was drafted to join the *Zemetcha*, the National Service campaign. As a fresh graduate and potential university student, he had to leave his job and report for duty in Addis Ababa. So, we had to search for another teacher for our children.

We acquired the services of Kebede Tsige, another fresh graduate of the Bible Academy, to accept the challenge of educating our young ones. The books had not arrived yet, but he used other materials to start. Sheryl also began by learning the ABC's and numbers. The books finally came in mid-October.

The girls decided they did not like Kebede, mostly because they had come to love Belayneh and were disappointed in his early removal from their classroom. They made a determined decision to dislike Kebede, and there wasn't anything he could do to change that. They were relieved when Kebede was also drafted into the *Zemetcha* at Christmas time.

At that point, we gave up on hiring a teacher for our girls. Obviously, it was a good idea, but now was not its time. Vera had to stand in for the rest of the term, the very thing that, based on past experience, she had resolved to never attempt again.

Cindy, Karen, Sheryl, and Kristina with Yishareg - 1974

Unsung Heroes

Assefa and Grace were great colleagues and an integral part of our team, though they were making their own living running the clinic on a private self-supporting basis. Assefa was station manager, responsible for the school, clinic, and the development activities as far as the station was concerned. For this he received no pay and little thanks.

He was also active in church activities. He was recognized in the community as the spokesperson for the Church and Mission. Little happened at the Mission without his involvement or approval. He and Grace even put out their own money to buy a plot in town for the eventual building of a church meeting house. However, events did not allow that to take place.

Assefa and Grace both worked very hard in their medical service to the community. They always tried to keep good supplies of the best medicines on hand and tried to treat each patient with honesty and integrity. It was common practice of many practitioners to dilute medications or substitute cheaper formulas to increase profits. Not so at the Mission Clinic at Bedeno! They were always careful to have someone on duty every day. Many a night they or one of them were called out to attend to some emergency that couldn't wait until morning. They were always willing to go.

For example, one dark night, a desperate stranger came to Assefa's door begging him to come with him to attend his wife who had been in labor for many days in their home down in the valley.

Assefa took his black medical bag and a torch and went with the stranger on foot, out into the darkness and danger of the cold night. For three hours he followed him down into a distant valley to a humble hut where the young woman lay in the dark.

He found she had been in labor for ten days already and was about to die. So, there amid the filth and dirt in this dark mud hut, equipped only with his flashlight and the few contents in his black bag, Assefa proceeded to do what he had seen the doctors do in a modern operating theater. With his surgical knife, he reached up into the womb and cut the dead rotting fetus into small manageable pieces and extracted them one by one.

After he had removed the stinking afterbirth, placed a handful of strong antibiotics in the empty womb, and gave the woman some medications, Assefa said to the on-looking family, "The rest is up to God!" He packed his bag and walked back up the escarpment, arriving home in time for breakfast and a full day of work in the clinic.

About a week later, both the man and the woman stopped in just to thank Assefa for what he had done. The woman was fine. He had saved her life.

There was an underlying current of opposition to Assefa's and Grace's work emanating from the operator of the "illegal" clinic in town. In many subtle ways, Solomon sought to undermine their reputation and their business. With this constant underlying current of resistance, their business did not earn an acceptable level of income. They chose not to fight back.

Assefa tried hard to bypass the opposition by going out to the people, traveling great distances, holding clinics on market days in

Burka, Furda, and in the Ramis Valley. Sometimes he went by mule, by bicycle, and even on foot. It was hard work, and the rewards were only marginal. For three years, they struggled, but business did not get better, and the hostility was still felt.

This negativity wore them down, making them susceptible to other opportunities. In October 1974, Assefa and Grace were offered jobs with the Leprosy Control Center at Bisidimo. The salary was attractive, and the living and working conditions were so much better. They were tired of the criticism and the opposition, tired of being lied about, tired of the traveling, and tired of the struggle just to make ends meet. They decided to accept the offer and made plans to leave Bedeno in January of 1975.

Due to this nagging hostility, we had been experiencing with the other "illegal" clinic in town, the division it caused in the community, and the mood of the Meserete Kristos Church to cut back on services, especially where there was duplication, it was decided to close the Bedeno Mission Clinic for the time being at least. We would be alone. We would miss their partnership very much.

Alpine Goats for Abyssinia

In October 1973, we received word that our application to Heifer Projects International for one hundred dairy goats was approved. The Swiss Mennonite Organization (SMO) and Mennonite Central Committee (MCC) had agreed in principle to give us the goats free of charge if we could raise the transport costs from Switzerland to Deder. That was a big problem for us. At $2.00 per pound for airfreight, it wasn't exactly cheap, even if it was a gift.

The Heifer Project game plan was to give the poor "a gift that keeps on giving." The goats were to be distributed free, one to one farmer in exchange for the first female offspring which in turn was to be given to another farmer on the same basis. A good Swiss dairy goat was reputed to be able to give as much milk as four local Zebu cows.

We responded to the SMO that we had no budget to transport the goats. Could they find a willing donor to help us with that problem?

A year passed, and in our busyness, we almost forgot about their intention.

Then one day in October of 1974, we received word from SMO that they were going to reduce the number of goats they would send due to the escalating cost of purchase of good purebred stock. They informed us that "Brot fur Die Welt" had agreed to pay for the air freight. They wanted to know if we were ready to receive forty-six dairy goats that would arrive in six weeks or so? And did we have the proper permit from the Ministry of Agriculture to import them?

That news and that question about government permission sent me on a fast trip to Addis Ababa. When I brought a letter of request to the right government office, I got a big surprise.

The official reacted with amazement, "Forty-six Swiss dairy goats! Do you know what you are doing?" He directed a torrent of excited questions at me: Did we have a place prepared to receive these goats? Did we have an adequate food supply? Did we have a veterinarian on hand to monitor their health every day as they made the adjustment to a new climate with all its local parasites and diseases? Did I have on hand all the possible vaccines and medicines and acaricides that would be needed?

I was dumbfounded. I had no experience with goat keeping whatsoever. I grew up with the myth that goats never got sick. Goats could eat anything: garbage, flowers in the garden, clothes off the line, although I had some doubts about them eating the proverbial "tin cans." Goats just got born, ate whatever there was to eat, grew up, gave birth, gave lots of milk, were mischievous, climbed everything except trees, chased dogs and coyotes away from the sheep, and so on. I had never imagined a sick goat, nor a malnourished goat.

Now this intelligent officer, in the presence of two other experts, was directing all these sensible questions at me, the "*ferinj*" expert, the director of Meserete Kristos Church's development program. I was shocked and embarrassed to reveal my total naivete.

I finally regained my composure and decided to follow the old adage: "Honesty is the best policy." There is no use to pretend, to put on false airs, to attempt to cover with conceit and arrogance one's ignorance. So, I simply, humbly admitted my lack of knowledge of and lack of experience with goats. I explained that our good intention was to give one female dairy goat to each selected poor farmer who did not have even one cow to provide milk for his family. In return that farmer would give back to the Project the first female offspring to be passed on to another needy farmer. It would be a gift that keeps on giving.

I further explained that now the donor has forty-six goats ready to ship to us from Switzerland, coming in six weeks, if we can get the import permit. I admitted that by their questions, I see that importing dairy goats is not quite that simple.

The officials informed me that it was a free country, and we were a private organization, and we could do that if we liked, but he assured me that it was most likely that every one of the goats would die within a few months. Memories of my struggle with dying sheep flashed in my mind, making me even more humble.

The official went on and informed me that up to that day, to the best of his knowledge, there were no exotic dairy goats in Ethiopia, and that the Ministry of Agriculture was currently planning to bring in three or four dairy goats for research purposes, but not forty-six! He also revealed that they were planning to bring in semen to do cross breeding experiments. He was completely flabbergasted at the thought that we would boldly bring that number at one time.

By this time, I was very humble and willing to be taught. The officials talked among themselves. Then they said they could give us a permit to import the goats if we insisted, and we could do as we planned, but they would be willing to offer us help in keeping the goats alive through their EPID program with the aid of SIDA (Swedish International Development Assistance). If we were agreeable to collaborate with them.

They offered to supply a Swedish veterinary officer for six months and a budget to buy the feed and medicines that would be needed. This officer would also train our extension workers in their maintenance and eventual distribution. They did not think we would be able to distribute any of the forty-six goats for at least a year or until they could be acclimatized. It would take a lot of feed to keep them healthy through that period. Also, each of the thirty-six females that would be on the plane would be pregnant. So, there would be a lot of goats by the end of the year, if they did not die.

Our contribution to this project, besides supplying the goats, would be to prepare a proper sanitary facility to house them, to supply the necessary personnel to care for them, and to provide the required extension agents to train each potential recipient in their care before he would be given his goat and to supervise him afterward. By now I was very agreeable to enter into an agreement with these people.

Our earlier plan had been to split the goats between Deder and Bedeno, but now we decided to keep all the goats at Deder for that first year.

With this agreement approved, my first task was to rush to Deder and get started in preparing the barn for goat keeping. It was mandatory that the goats be housed at first on slated floors for health reasons. They would not be allowed to graze or roam about.

As the time drew near, a Swedish man, Mr. Lasse Everitt, moved to Deder and put the finishing touches on the facilities, brought the medicines, and stockpiled the feed.

The goats finally arrived on January 18, 1975. They came by a special charter flight directly from Switzerland to Dire Dawa, from the piercing cold of the wintry Alps to the searing heat of the equatorial desert in scarcely eight hours. Now that requires some adjustment, even for a rugged Alpine mountain goat! We had two trucks waiting at the airport when they arrived to whisk them off, almost before they could "thaw," to their new home in the highlands of Deder.

Even so their adjustment was traumatic enough. Lasse was on hand to check all forty-six goat temperatures even before they disembarked the plane and found two of them already stressed with a fever. He injected them with antibiotics before they boarded the truck. The next several days, he was busy day and night checking temperatures and injecting the sick as the purebred Toggenburg and Sannen goats slowly made the crucial adjustment to the alien climate and flora and fauna of their adopted Abyssinian home. Two *Zemetcha* students, Mohammed Musa and Wondimu Gashow, were assigned to assist him.

After the immediate danger of initial adjustment waned, Mr. Everitt began training his crew in the science of modern goat-keeping along with zero grazing and fodder crop cultivation, and basic extension practices. They organized and prepared the farmers to receive their goats. Each farmer would join an association that would then produce cheese.

321

A Time to Celebrate

Dr. Peter and Arlene Block arrived from Nazareth a few days after Christmas with their family of four lively children. They took the now famous mule trail from Deder. After they left, we had our family celebration on Ethiopian Christmas day.

One day in February, we had to take some people to Harar, so we decided to bring our family along and pay Assefa and Grace a visit. Bisidimo was a large leprosy control center about twenty kilometers east of Harar City. At that time, it was being financed and managed by a German Catholic group. The center had a modern hospital and a farm where the patients worked and learned skills. It was an irrigated oasis in the desert and boasted a modern dairy herd of Friesians. It also had an extension program that oversaw all leprosy work in the Harar Province.

While Grace worked in the clinic, Assefa was employed as an inspector of clinics in the general area. He traveled a lot checking on the workers in those clinics that were supposed to be supplying pills to all the leprosy patients. Lepers could take their pills at home without joining leper colonies around hospitals like they used to do in the early days. If they were faithful in taking the medicine, the patient could be sure of being cured, but the supply of pills had to be constantly available.

At Bisidimo, Assefa and Grace welcomed us very warmly. Daniel had grown so much. Assefa and Grace were both very happy with their new jobs and general living conditions in Bisidimo. They were relieved to be free of the many hassles they experienced at Bedeno. We had a great time catching up on the latest developments in each other's lives. Common experiences had bonded us together. We were true friends. After spending a night with them, we returned to Bedeno the next day.

Grace and Assefa Haile with Daniel outside
their home in Bisidimo - 1975

CHAPTER 23

Journey's End

B y October, we were well into the fourth and final year of our contract. It was time for the Mission, Church, and us to plan ahead and make some decisions about our future involvement. A delegation from the Addis office paid us a visit. They were Nevin and Blanch Horst, Asrat Gebre, Tesfatsion Dalellew, Everett and Phyllis Ressler, and Dr. P.T. Yoder. Some of them came to inspect the development project, others to visit in the community, and others to discuss with us the options that lay before us.

From our point of view, I loved my work passionately, I enjoyed living in Bedeno, and had all kinds of visions for a long bright future for our involvement there. Vera had a very different perspective. She suffered asthma for about eight months out of the year. She was basically occupied with our four small children and the related homemaking and domestic concerns. She did not really enjoy working in the community. She was getting to resent deeply the amount of time I was away from home on project business, often for ten days or two weeks at a time. Her life there was not at all socially stimulating or emotionally satisfying.

Then there was the matter of our children's education that disturbed both of us very much. We both felt that we just couldn't abandon our children to the care of a boarding school for nine months out of every year for the remainder of their childhoods.

From the Mission and the Church's point of view, there were several options. We were entitled to a five-month home leave. First, we could go home at the end of March 1975, and return at the beginning of September and continue with our work as before. We could keep on with home schooling, or we could put our children into boarding school.

The second option was to return in September and make Dire Dawa our "home." It would be good for Vera's health and put us closer to the boarding school by half the distance. I would supervise the development programs in Deder and Bedeno from there. This would entail a lot of driving and being away from home, but I was doing that anyway.

The third choice was to terminate our services with the EMM at the end of our leave and go home. Our visitors gave us one week to decide. They went to their comfortable homes and left us with this pivotal decision. Our counselors were few.

Vera and I decided we would accept the second option. I had a lot of questions as to how I would do development in Bedeno by living in Dire Dawa. But we were willing to give it a try. EMM was to find another missionary couple to take our place at Bedeno.

But our restlessness persisted. By early December, we were still doubting the finality of our decision. Putting our little girls into boarding school was the main problem. Children were made to be in families, and families were meant to be together. The thought of separation just tore us apart inside.

There were other considerations as well. The effects of the stress I faced with the famine relief program added on top of all the other involvements, was taking its toll on me. Unknown to myself, burnout was affecting my attitude and my ability to think objectively.

Further, in making his annual tours, EMM's Field Secretary missed visiting our work at Bedeno because "the road is too bad and travel there would take too much time." This was disappointing and made us feel a tinge of bitterness towards the Board leadership. We were condemned to practically live on that "bad" road, and yet this important world traveler couldn't take a few hours out of his busy schedule to come and witness what we were doing and how we were living, not even once in three years! We saw how we and our development work ranked on the bottom of the totem pole in comparison to him and his work. We needed a little bit of sympathy, a word of encouragement, some modest praise. But we did not get it.

I reasoned that it was not good to have a program wrapped around one person and had asked the Mission Board to send another couple to fill in while we were away and to make it a team effort after we returned. The couple never came.

Further I reasoned, the future of the foreigner in revolutionary Ethiopia was uncertain. If the revolution fulfilled its promises, it would not take long before we would no longer be needed. The government would soon be setting up its own development program in our area. Maybe our presence there was not as important as we had thought.

I also saw that the Church was developing good leadership and did not feel that we were needed in the Church.

We agonized long and hard over this decision. When the Field Secretary made his annual visit in January, we were called out to Deder to discuss the matter with him. But returned with no more clarity. We prayed a lot. We just were not satisfied with our decision to come back after furlough. It did not seem right.

But somehow it did not seem right to quit either in light of the needs of the people. The Project had only begun, and the goals were not yet met. There was so much work to be done, especially work that I enjoyed doing anyway, and there was still no prospect of anyone taking our place.

It seemed God was nudging us steadily to let go and trust Him, but my skin was terribly thick, and I wasn't getting His signals very clearly. We felt alone. There was no one with whom we could counsel.

Finally, in mid-February, we brought the suspense to an end by making a clear decision and informing EMM that we would be ending our services with them and that we would be leaving sometime in May. For me, it was one of the most heart-wrenching decisions that I ever made. We had no idea what we would do next or where we would settle.

I finally felt at peace. Let God lead on. Let Him who knows the future control the future. Ours was only to trust Him and step out in faith. Deep down inside I had the quiet feeling that I would be called to pastoral work. I need not worry or panic nor search for the place. It would become clear in the "fullness of time."

Final Exit

Once we had made our decision in February to end our services to Ethiopia, we became anxious to wind up our affairs and leave. We were very tired and exhausted. We just wanted it all to be over.

To leave the country by May 2nd meant that we had to leave Bedeno by April 20, or only two months from the time we made our decision. Mr. Gamber would continue to manage the Deder project, Belayneh would manage the Bedeno project, and Dr. Yoder had already taken over as Development Coordinator for the whole enterprise.

Leaving was hectic. People came every day of the last week; some to beg for a token of remembrance, some to get something free, some to buy something we were selling, and some to express their sadness that we were leaving. So many came that we could hardly work. Finally, we just let them watch as we continued our work. This seemed to be a custom acceptable to Ethiopians.

On the day we left, people started coming at 6:45 a.m. Ato Nicola was the first to come. He did not want us to slip away without saying goodbye. During that morning he came three times, as there were a lot of demands from his business. He was sad, waited, like a mourner when a good friend dies. People crowded into our house, filling its narrow passageways. We could hardly move.

Finally, by about 1:30 in the afternoon, our goods were all packed and our good-byes were all said. It was time to leave. We started up our heavily burdened old Toyota and, forcibly tearing our hearts away from the many unions forged by our three years among the good people of Bedeno, we headed down the lane for the last time, leaving our empty "home" and the yard full of friends and an important part of our lives behind.

Then the tears came. For the first time in my adult life, I cried! Yes, I broke up completely as we turned our back on three years of intense living with its deep relationships, remarkable achievements, shameful failures, and unfinished dreams, and simply drove away.

It was heart-wrenching to leave Bedeno; but it was a distinct pleasure to drive that final run over the too familiar Bedeno road, leaving behind forever its bone rattling rocks and ruts, its sticky mud holes and slippery gullies, its familiar twists and turns, its narrow-slanted rain-soaked cliff ledges, and its steep low-gear inclines. Our cup of suffering on that road was now complete!

We spent that Saturday evening and Sunday resting and visiting Assefa and Grace and little Daniel at Bisidimo. On Monday, we got exit visas stamped in our passports at Dire Dawa and the next day drove to Nazareth.

That weekend we spent at the annual missionary retreat at the Bishoftu SIM Guest House. There we went swimming in the deep crater lake. Our children enjoyed the playground and the water with all their friends. We enjoyed the ministry of Dr. Norman Kraus from Goshen College who was our guest speaker. Already healing began to take place as we relaxed in the realization that a heavy burden had just rolled off our shoulders.

After the retreat we had a few days to buy our tickets, exchange money, clear our three barrels of books and souvenirs through customs, and say "goodbye" to our friends.

We flew out of Addis Ababa on Friday, May 2nd, 1975. Our itinerary would take us to three-day stops in Cairo and Athens, a night in the airport hotel in Paris, and a week in Amsterdam where we would rent a car and drive north to Denmark and back to Amsterdam.

EPILOGUE

Looking back on our "Ethiopian experience" from the perspective of forty-seven years later, it is possible to make some observations and evaluations. First, we can say that Ethiopia has changed our lives as a family in a much more profound way than we ever impacted Ethiopia.

Our children's world view and life course were set in the context of Ethiopia. They were never quite the same as the other kids among whom they settled in Canada. As "third culture kids" ("TCK's), they saw everything from a different point of view. Cindy decided from the age of ten that she was going to be a missionary. She never deviated. Though she never went to serve in Ethiopia, she served with her husband, John Kreider, and family as missionaries in Cusco, Peru for fifteen years. And today, their four children take part in direct Christian ministry related careers.

All four of our daughters have been staunch fans and defenders of Africans, African Americans, and indeed everything African. Karen, Sheryl, and Kristina each married African Americans. They all seek out cross-cultural settings. They all are actively involved in careers that serve, supplying healing and hope to the less privileged part of suffering humanity, particularly in the areas of education, nursing, and rehabilitating social work through counseling.

Vera and I, with our four daughters, settled into a quiet pastorate with the Salem Mennonite Church in Tofield, a small town in rural Alberta surrounded by peaceful, loving, progressive Mennonite people. There we raised and educated our children.

Yet, somehow, after what we had been through in Ethiopia, it seemed so placid, so predictable, so easy, almost like going into premature retirement. We felt wanted and appreciated, but we never felt needed. The crises and the challenges all seemed so small and easy. The call of Africa burned in our bones.

During our nine years of "exile" in Alberta, we tried several times to make ourselves available for re-assignment to Ethiopia.

But Ethiopia was pre-occupied with implementing its revolutionary experiment in Marxist socialism while fighting a war against Somalia in the east, a civil war against Eritrea in the north, and a "red terror" campaign against dissidents at home. It was not the right time to place western missionaries with families there.

We returned to Africa in 1985 with the two youngest teenage children. This time we were assigned to collaborate with a community development project at Ogwedhi, a quiet rural community in southwestern Kenya. Yet Ethiopia still was the point of reference, the standard by which we measured and evaluated all things.

As for the results of our work in Ethiopia, only God can evaluate that. Many of our former Bible Academy students went abroad for higher education only to find themselves stranded, prevented by the social, economic, and political upheavals from returning home. Others joined the "brain drain," the steady flow of refugees fleeing from war, famine, or persecution, or seeking freedom from religious and political or economic oppression.

Those who remained suffered through the hard times rendering outstanding service to their country, their churches, and their families. Many of them endured torture and imprisonment for their faith and their integrity. The tough survived and gave outstanding leadership through their productive years.

After our departure from the Wobera Garamuleta Rural Development Project, our replacement never came. One agriculturist and his family did arrive in Ethiopia to take our place but was diverted to a more accessible assignment by the administrators. The program slowly declined, lacking leadership.

Upon hearing this news as I settled into a comfortable life in Canada, I struggled with a lot of guilt. I had retreated while the work had hardly begun. The great ambition and optimism I had felt at the beginning had not been translated into reality in three years. The Gospel had not been preached to the adult Oromo population. An adult church among them had not emerged. I had not been a good missionary.

I had betrayed the rising expectations of the people of our project area. I had deserted the team and disappointed the Church. Our listening to God had been intercepted and distorted by personal priorities, desires, and exhaustion. I felt like a coward, a traitor. I quit too soon. I was a failure!

I struggled with my doubts and guilt until 1977 when news reached us that the whole of Harar Province was engulfed in an all-out war with Somalia. Many of our friends and neighbors were killed by the invaders or their collaborators at Bedeno. All missions and church projects ceased to function in the area.

Indeed, the story was the same all over Ethiopia. Almost all missionaries had to withdraw from the rural areas, and most of them from the cities. There was no room for God and his Bible in Marxist Ethiopia, and little room for anyone from the "Christian" or "capitalist" west or their sympathizers.

It was then that we began to realize just how faithful God had been in leading us with his keen foresight. We had heard him more clearly than we had realized. Had we returned as originally planned, our time would have been wasted, our intentions frustrated, and our efforts blocked by the roll of events much bigger than ourselves. God was faithful and his leading perfect!

Whether anything good and lasting remains as a result of our immense efforts at development, we don't know. We leave it to God to decide. We do hear that the Bedeno community continues to suffer from periodic droughts and famine, that massive poverty continues even worse than before, that it has been a hotbed of tribal animosity that resulted in horrible assassinations and a major massacre, that a new road has been built joining the community to the markets of Harar and Dire Dawa, at least when it is not subject to attack by subversive elements.

The most exciting story of all is the amazing growth of the Church in all of this. It is a story of the sovereign work of God. Though the growth of the Church was close to our hearts, we certainly had little to do with it. The indigenous little "pente" revival that sprang up among the students in the schools all over the empire and was vigorously beaten down by the imperial government in league with the Orthodox Church, found its way into the Meserete Kristos Church as well as into many of the other evangelical churches. Its impact on the Meserete Kristos Church was profound. The little body that scarcely numbered 600 weak vacillating "members" that we found scattered in five "congregations" in 1967 had grown to 1,700 enthusiastic committed members that overflowed our buildings in 1975 at the time we left Ethiopia.

As Marxism consolidated its grip on the nation, it presented a clear challenge to the Christian churches. The believers' response became a mighty spiritual movement which attracted multitudes until the government saw it as a threat in the all-out struggle for the minds and hearts of the young people.

Whereas in 1972 one had to include the babies to count fifty people in the 400-seat Bole Chapel in Addis Ababa, by 1982, on a given Sunday, more than 3,200 devoted worshipers, most of them young people, could be counted flocking there to sing and pray to the God who did not officially exist. There they eagerly drank in every word of the long sermons and carefully took notes. And without outside compulsion, they diligently studied the ancient scripture texts, preferring them to the logical dogmas of "modern scientific socialism." Obviously, the youth preferred the "opium of the people" to the grim realities of the Marxist utopia!

The ideological cadres in the government correctly saw that the "myth of God" was not going to "vanish from the earth" very quickly with this kind of "reactionary" activity. For the wellbeing and happiness of the "broad masses," they would have to intervene.

On January 25th, 1982, the government nationalized the Bole Chapel, primary school, Menno Bookstore, Meserete Kristos Church office complex, and guest house along with furnishings and church vehicles. A few days later, bank accounts were frozen, and seven leaders were detained "for questioning," and the congregations' buildings throughout Shoa and Harar Provinces were also nationalized. The government ordered the Meserete Kristos Church to cease all religious activity. Officially it no longer existed.

The Bible Academy, by this time, had grown to accommodate 360 students and had become the number one high school in the nation in terms of quality academic output. The Marxist government allowed it to complete the academic year and then took it over and turned the compound into a provincial teacher training college.

The Christians had expected the possibility of something like this happening and had made contingency plans. They moved into a secret underground house-church mode. In Nazareth where one church was closed, fifty house-churches opened. Stripped of her meeting houses, offices, vehicles, bank accounts, publishing house, bookstore, schools, and service institutions; deprived of her top leaders whose detention "for questioning" stretched out for four and one-half years; denied her right to assemble for mutual encouragement, teaching, or planning; and harassed by the constant vigilance of zealous party cadres eager to detect even the slightest sign of counter-revolutionary "religious activity," the Meserete Kristos Church disciplined itself, adapted to the conditions, grew mightily and prospered.

Ten years after it had officially ceased to exist, when religious freedom was restored in 1991, the Church that went underground in 1982 with 5,000 members on its list re-surfaced with 35,000 highly disciplined committed Christians eager to share and live their faith in the disillusioned world of the collapsed workers "utopia." So attractive was the presence of the suffering Christ within them that by the end of the year their roster had swelled to over 50,000 committed members. Today that growth continues and 783,804 persons fellowship in 1,462 congregations and 992 church planting centers scattered in all the administrative regions of Ethiopia!

Twenty years and eight months following our departure from Ethiopia, Vera and I landed in Addis Ababa on January 5, 1996, to begin an assignment in response to the invitation of the Meserete Kristos Church to assist them in establishing a relevant leadership training institution.

Somehow the assignment seems strangely similar to the assignment that first drew us to Ethiopia back in 1967: "to train leaders for the churches of Ethiopia." It is as though we have come full circle. "Why?" "Why us?" We can only submit. This is another of the remarkable mysteries of God's running of his universe! We are delighted to have a small part to play in it. If the "past is but prologue to the future," then what will this second odyssey in Ethiopia bring forth? We can only stand in awe and worship!

> *He who goes out weeping,*
> *carrying seed to sow,*
> *will return with songs of joy,*
> *carrying sheaves with him!*
> -- Psalms 126:6 NIV

Other Books by the Author

This is the third book in his *The Odyssey of a Family* series in which the author tells the story of his family. In *Pilgrims Searching for a Home*, he recounts the life story of his grandparents who escaped the horrors of the Bolshevik revolution in Russia with their family, only to settle in Western Canada in time to face the hardships, disappointments, and trauma of the Great Depression and the "dirty thirties."

In his second book, *Shaping of a Servant*, the author begins by telling the story of his pioneer parents, their cross-cultural marriage, and continues in an autobiographical form, remembering his growing years in their family of seven children in rural Canada. He notes and evaluates the circumstances and events that God used to shape him and prepare him for a life of service. It is the story of the formation of a young man growing in self-awareness, struggling with a sense of divine call. It leads to a romance in which he finds his significant other. Together they form a team, finding direction and committing themselves to lives of service in God's kingdom.

All three books are available from **westbowpress.com/ bookstore.**

Printed in the United States
by Baker & Taylor Publisher Services